Representing Time

To commemorate the centenary of J. E. McTaggart's
'The unreality of time' (1908)

Representing Time: An Essay on Temporality as Modality

K. M. JASZCZOLT

OXFORD

UNIVERSITY PRESS

OXFORD

UNIVERSITY PRESS

Great Clarendon Street, Oxford OX2 6DP

Oxford University Press is a department of the University of Oxford.
It furthers the University's objective of excellence in research, scholarship,
and education by publishing worldwide in

Oxford New York

Auckland Cape Town Dar es Salaam Hong Kong Karachi
Kuala Lumpur Madrid Melbourne Mexico City Nairobi
New Delhi Shanghai Taipei Toronto

With offices in

Argentina Austria Brazil Chile Czech Republic France Greece
Guatemala Hungary Italy Japan Poland Portugal Singapore
South Korea Switzerland Thailand Turkey Ukraine Vietnam

Oxford is a registered trade mark of Oxford University Press
in the UK and in certain other countries

Published in the United States
by Oxford University Press Inc., New York

© K. M. Jaszczolt 2009

The moral rights of the author have been asserted
Database right Oxford University Press (maker)

First published 2009

British Library Cataloguing in Publication Data
Data available

Library of Congress Cataloging in Publication Data
Data available

Typeset by SPI Publisher Services, Pondicherry, India
Printed in Great Britain
on acid-free paper by
the MPG Books Group

ISBN 978–0–19–921443–3 (Hbk.)
      978–0–19–921444–0 (Pbk.)

1 3 5 7 9 10 8 6 4 2

Contents

Preface

In 2000 I still thought that propositional attitude constructions and in particular the semantics of belief attributions would occupy me for the rest of my working life. I owe my thinking about time entirely and exclusively to a Cambridge atheistic idealist John McTaggart and his mind-boggling argument that time is unreal. Published exactly one century ago (1908), his paper 'The unreality of time' still triggers passionate discussions, most of them objecting to his way of thinking about the problem and yet using his concepts. McTaggart distinguished two possible discourses about time: one in terms of the past, present, and future, and one in terms of precedence, simultaneity, and following. As he says, without the past, present, and future, there would be no change and, since time involves change, the past, present, and future are necessary concepts; precedence, simultaneity, and following will not suffice. So, he tried to assume that the latter discourse presupposes the first, in that if A precedes B, then at some moment in time A must be past and B present. But this reasoning led him to argue that the first kind of discourse is flawed because it would have to entail that every event has to have the three properties: past, present, and future and they are obviously incompatible. Of course, we can get out of the problem by stipulating that events are past, present, and future at different times rather than having these properties all at once. But then, we presuppose the very notion of time which we are trying to explain and we end up in infinite regress. Time, he concludes, is not real.

But the concept of time *is* real: we have the impression of the flow of time, we are born and die, our lives consist of a sequence of events to which we can assign temporal location. We experience time, as even McTaggart himself was forced to admit. The problem that attracted me is precisely this concept of time, as well as its linguistic expression. In order to explore it, I explored the question of the relation between 'real' time of space-time and our internal time, the concept which we use in everyday thought and parlance. I also explored the question as to whether this concept is primitive or rather founded on some more basic component or components of thoughts. After about seven years of thinking about McTaggart and about the views his paradox (or, as many would say, pseudo-paradox) generated, I came to the conclusion that the concept of time humans use and the concept of evidence humans have for different states and events in the world surrounding them are intrinsically connected. We locate events in time just as we locate them in space; in short, we locate them in space-time. We do so because we have evidence or strong beliefs that they are happening, did happen, or are likely to happen. This cognition of reality is not accidental but rather is affected by the very nature of time itself: events have the potentiality to happen and some of them did happen, are happening, or will happen, while others remain in the realm of more or less distant probabilities. They are probable symmetrically into the past and into the future: just as future is uncertain, so the past survives only as far as our memories of past events survive. In other words, both time in the world and time in the mind are modal through and through. Naturally, conveying time in language also utilizes expressions whose semantics reveals them as modal through and through.

Representation of time as modality is a broad philosophical topic which requires arguments from the metaphysics and epistemology of time before we can reach a territory more familiar for linguists, that of semantic representations. The broad framework adopted in the first two chapters of this essay would not have been achievable without the discussions I had with various knowledgeable colleagues from different disciplines. To Rachel Padman I owe instilling in me the, however fundamental, understanding of space-time as a property of the universe. She patiently answered my questions concerning the theories of relativity, space and time dimensions of contemporary mathematical models of the universe, and, most importantly perhaps, calmed down my unnecessary excitement on reading that according to one famous Nobel Prize winner the universe has many different histories all of which are equally real! All *bêtises* that remain in my divagations on relativity and multiple dimensions of the universe are entirely my own responsibility. To David Cram I am grateful for his helpful feedback on the manuscript. Frank Brisard made me aware that time as modality is not an extravagant notion in some areas of linguistics, no matter how extravagant it sounds to truth-conditional semanticists. His, and Ronald Langacker's, insightful analyses of the concept of time assume the perspective which is akin to mine, albeit using a very different framework and kind of explanation. To Jiranthara Srioutai and to the many years of our collaboration I owe my understanding of how expressing time works in a language where neither tense nor aspect markers are obligatory. In Thai, 'rain fall' stands for a wide array of propositions, from *It is raining* to *It might rain*, to no detriment of the clarity of communication. John C. Chang collected and discussed with me a wide range of examples of how time is conceptualized in Mandarin Chinese, including not only the standard 'the future is in front' and 'the past is behind us' horizontal axis but also vertical, cyclical, as well as variations on the relationship between the state of affairs and the agent. My basic understanding of the consecutive tense in Swahili

I owe to Lutz Marten and Andrew Smith. To Helen Engemann I owe thanks for her very careful reading of the draft. I also thank Anja Sysoeva, Luna Filipović Kleiner, Thomas Forster, and Aly Pitts for taking on my teaching responsibilities at the Department of Linguistics, University of Cambridge, while I was occupied with what follows. To my colleagues, Fellows of Newnham College, Cambridge, I owe an atmosphere most conducive to thinking and writing, including endless talking about time at college lunches. The fabulous antique ticking clock in my College office tried to adversely affect my theory that real time does not flow and support the common-sense intuition that for humans it does. But since its idiosyncratic measure of time reflected its own private concept of time, its attempts ended up being unsuccessful. On a more serious note, my particular gratitude goes to John Davey of Oxford University Press for his helpful assistance with practical aspects of publishing.

Finally, my good spirit while writing what follows I owe to Charles and Lidia Berthon's jokes that I am writing that time does not exist and at the same time keep saying that I have no time for anything else. This book is for you both, with love.

Cambridge, April 2008

Figures

Abbreviations and Symbols

Abbreviations

Acc	Grice's acceptability operator
ACC	acceptability operator in Default Semantics
$\text{ACC}_\Delta \vdash \Sigma$	'it is acceptable to the degree Δ that Σ is true'
CD	cognitive default
Cons	consecutive-tense marker
CPI	conscious pragmatic inference
Dem	demonstrative pronoun
dnn	dispositional necessity present
DRS	discourse representation structure
DRT	Discourse Representation Theory
e	event
enf	epistemic necessity future
enn	epistemic necessity present
enp	epistemic necessity past
epf	epistemic possibility future
epn	epistemic possibility present
epp	epistemic possibility past
F	future-time operator
fp	futurative progressive
Fut	future-time marker
Ind	indicative-mood marker
Loc	locative-case marker
n	now
p	proposition
P	past-time operator
Past	past-time marker
pf	periphrastic future
Pl	plural number
pm	primary meaning
pn	past of narration
Pple	past participle
Pres	present-time marker
Prog	progressive-aspect marker
Refl	reflexive pronoun
rf	regular future

rn	regular present
rp	regular past
SCD	social and cultural default
SCWD	social, cultural, and world-knowledge default
SDRT	Segmented Discourse Representation Theory
Sg	singular number
sm	secondary meaning
tf	'tenseless' future
WS	word meaning and sentence structure

Symbols

1, 2, 3	Person
¬	truth-functional negation
∨	truth-functional disjunction
∧, &	truth-functional conjunction
→	truth-functional implication
↔	truth-functional equivalence
∃	existential quantifier in predicate logic
∧	intensional operator
○	temporal overlap
⊆	inclusion/temporal inclusion
⊂	proper inclusion
□	necessity operator
<	temporal precedence
>	temporal succession
Σ	merger representation
→Σ	'results in a merger'
⊢	epistemic modality/Grice's alethic modality
!	deontic modality/Grice's practical modality
Δ	degree of acceptance/epistemic commitment

Single quotation marks are used for mentioning words and italics for concepts and for technical terms.

Introduction: Thinking about time and living in time

'I have no time!', 'There isn't enough time in a day!', are some of the most common expressions used in the academic world these days. Fast-growing numbers of hours that academics are required to devote to administration, teaching, and grant applications make more and more people resort to complaints about time. Perhaps it is worth asking oneself, what exactly do such expressions mean? If I don't have time, *what* is it exactly that I don't have?

Let us imagine the following scenario. There is a ski lift going up a snowy mountain and a line of skiers waiting to catch it to be lifted up on their skis. The lift is moving at a certain steady speed and most of the skiers manage to latch on and go up, but some less experienced ones miss their slot or fall off the lift before they get to the top. If the lift represents the flow of time, and skiers the events or states of affairs that can be placed in it as if on a line of the time flow, then we have one possible explanation, through a metaphorical concept, what I and my fellow academics mean by their frustrated 'I haven't got time': some events just won't take place. Just as two skiers can't normally attach to one slot in the lift (unless it is designed as double) because they would both fall off, so one person wouldn't be able to give a lecture and sit at a department meeting at the same time.

Now let us consider a different scenario. In spite of his academic preoccupations, our typical academic has found time to do his laundry. He has a rather long washing line in his garden but he also has several loads of washing to hang and therefore is hanging the washed garments next to each other, starting at one end of the line and moving towards the other, trying to use all the available space. The garments must not overlap because they wouldn't dry: it is a typical English cold summer day. If the washing line represents the time line and the garments the events or states of affairs, then we have another way of representing metaphorically what our academic means by saying 'I don't have time': the garments for which there was no space on the line had to be left out – or squeezed in, making them all dry more slowly or become crumpled, just as we try to squeeze in yet another meeting or yet another class into our timetable, badly affecting all the remaining activities of the day in the process. On this metaphor time doesn't flow, it is just a series of ordered events and states of affairs.

It is not difficult to see that the first metaphor is much more successful: people normally think of time as motion, flowing from the future into the present and from the present into the past. We anticipate states of affairs or events, then experience these or other events and states, and next retain some of them in memory. But is the flow of time *real*? Does it really happen in the world, or is it merely a way our mind comes to terms with the fact that events do not present themselves to us all at once? This question of real time and psychological, internal time is the topic of the first chapter which constitutes a philosophical preamble for a more language-oriented discussion that follows. It concludes that internal time does indeed conform to the ski lift metaphor (called in Chapter 1 more properly the A series), while real time is more like a washing line (called there the B series). Next, if we imagine looking at a washing line on which all the garments are already hanging, then we get even closer to real time: there is no change, just event-like units ordered in a sequence. This is what McTaggart (1908) calls the C series but for him this series does not pertain to time: where there is no change, there is no time. This C series is simply the B series from which we subtract the conscious agent who imposes on it psychological time and interprets the order in the sequence as earlier-than and later-than relations. Therefore, *qua* sequence itself, C can be equated with B and the discussion can be confined to the A- and B-series, as is customary in the literature. I will argue that they belong to different levels of description but are compatible, and there is even some form of supervenience of the internal (A-) time on the real (B-) time. *Supervenience* will be an important concept for this investigation and I will mean by it *dependence in the sense of constitutive characteristics*. In other words, where there is a difference in the concept of time, there will also have to be a difference in its physical equivalent (Kim 1987; McLaughlin and Bennett 2005).

Chapter 2 presents arguments in favour of the view that the concept of time as a ski lift is not basic but instead can be traced to the underlying concept of modality in the form of epistemic possibility realized as degrees of acceptance of a proposition. Both real and internal time are argued to be inherently modal, in the sense of metaphysical probability and epistemic possibility respectively. I analyse the concepts of the future, the present, and the past and assess the grounds for regarding them as modal. I also look at linguistic expressions of the future, present, and past and conclude that the explanation of time as modality applies to such temporal expressions, both grammatical and lexical, and they should be assigned a modal semantics – to be developed further in Chapters 3 and 4.

In this essay I am discussing the idea of supervenience of time on modality in two ways: as (i) supervenience of the *concept of time* on the *concept of epistemic detachment*, and (ii) as supervenience of the *concept of time* on the *properties of time-space.* I suggest that these two relations are closely connected. There is a correlation: just as the concept of time is founded on a more primitive concept of uncertainty, probability, and detachment, so it is founded on the probability and relativity of real time. Therefore, it is not just the *construal of reality* that requires modality as conceptualist semanticists have it; it is *reality* itself. Our concept of time reflects the properties of time of space-time. I argue in Chapter 2 that time is a highly malleable and undeniably modal construct in contemporary physics. Supervenience will therefore mean two things: (i) supervenience of internal time, *qua* a concept derived from real time, on modality, and (ii) supervenience of internal time on real time. In other words, both internal time and real time are supervenient on a form of modality: the first one on epistemic detachment, and the latter on probability and various possibilities concerning real, alternative histories and predictions concerning the universe. The type of supervenience, i.e. whether it is metaphysical or nomological, weak or strong, individual or global, etc. (Kim 1987; McLaughlin & Bennett 2005) will not be in focus of my attention, although the discussion in the first two chapters will shed some light on the possible classifications. This choice is justified in that the semantic representation of temporality given in Chapter 4 will result in our entertaining the possibility that the relation between the two investigated categories may be stronger than that of supervenience, namely that of identity. Supervenience will be used here only as a useful technical construct and will be applied in the wide sense in which it was originally intended.

In Chapter 3 I discuss various candidates for the unit of which the epistemic commitment is predicated, focusing on various construals of the concept of an event. The notion of an event is ultimately rejected and replaced with the construct of a post-Gricean pragmatically assembled proposition (*merged proposition*) defined as utterance meaning recovered by the Model Addressee as that intended by the Model Speaker and construed in the interaction of information coming from linguistic and non-linguistic sources. This construct (Σ', which together with the specification of the modal detachment forms a representation of the utterance Σ) conforms to the radical version of pragmatic compositionality proposed in my Default Semantics, according to which all sources of information about meaning are treated on a par.

Chapter 4 provides further support for the modal basis of temporality and offers semantic/conceptual representations of expressions with future, present, and past-time reference in the form of merger representations – structures of Default Semantics that conform to the radical pragmatic compositionality view. Modulated propositions Σ' proposed in Chapter 3 are now prefixed with a modal operator ACC (for 'rational acceptability'), indexed with the degree to which the modal statement under analysis expresses detachment from the state of affairs referred to in the utterance. Merger representations Σ are given for a wide range of temporal expressions. Subsequently, expressions are ordered on scales of epistemic commitment.

All in all, the essay offers a view on the concept of time that treats it as part of a broadly conceived structure by assessing its relations with real time – the ontology of time, as well as with the linguistic analysis of temporal expressions. Modality emerges as the *explanans* and hence the tool in all three domains: the ontological, the conceptual, and the linguistic.

The theory I am offering in this essay may strike some as rather controversial. One may say: 'Of course I have a concept of time. I get up at 6 a.m., work until 5 p.m., and all my daily routines are governed by time. It is absurd to say that time is not a basic human concept.' Naturally, humans have a concept of time. But that does not yet mean that time is the primitive building block in the conceptualization of time. For example, it is not so eccentric to claim that human concept of time is founded on the concept of space: metaphors such as 'to run out of time', 'to be ahead of time', 'put back in time', and so forth testify to the existence of the underlying concept of space realized as a time line, with an arrow pointing into the future.[1] But once we accept this spatial construal of time, there is only one step from there to realizing that even that spatial underpinning is not the ultimate concept. Time line and the point on it in which we are *now* carry the whole array of other conceptual assumptions, such as that whatever is not present at this point is detached, removed, not experienced, and *a fortiori* in some sense *less reliable* and *less certain*. The modal account of time offered here, and the evidence from how we speak about time in natural language, exploits precisely this implication of detachment – a *graded detachment*, realized as *modality*, graded along a line determined by what is encoded and grammaticalized in languages.

The essay does not aspire, however, to the status of contrastive typologies of modal systems: these are already available in various forms and would require different methods and objectives. It is rather a philosophical-semantic, as well as a linguistic-semantic, enquiry into the concept of time and its linguistic representation.

---

[1] For recent evidence see e.g. Vallesi *et al.* 2008 and Casasanto and Boroditsky 2008.

1

Real time and the concept of time

The big questions to be addressed in this chapter are the following. On the one hand, we know even from a basic understanding of physics and from popular knowledge of Einstein's theory of relativity that time is not absolute: it varies depending on the frame of reference, the velocity with which objects are moving. On the other, we have a very robust and deep-seated conviction, grounded in everyday experience, that there is something we can unequivocally call the past, the present, and the future. This incommensurability of information coming from modern physics and the concept of time by which we live our lives prompts us to ask: are these two concepts of time independent? If so, why are they independent? Are they incompatible or rather does our experienced time supervene on the 'real time'? I do not propose to give definite and final answers to these deep and perplexing problems but rather offer some partial answers, in view of what philosophers, scientists, and linguists have said about these issues in recent cutting-edge discussions. The overall aim in discussing these big questions is to set the scene for the main discussion of this essay, namely how time is to be best portrayed in semantic (and thereby, by our understanding of the term, mental) representations. For the labels for the contrasted concepts I borrowed the apt terms from Mellor (e.g. 1998) – *real time*, and Husserl (e.g. 1928) – *internal time*, used here interchangeably with *the concept of time*.

1.1 Einstein's legacy

Real time in Isaac Newton's physics was intuitively plausible and conceptually simple: time was conceptualized as a horizontal line, extended indefinitely in both directions; it was separate from space, and was the background against which events took place. Time was absolute: it was believed that time could be measured with certainty. This, essentially Aristotelian, picture was popularized in Newton's *Principia Mathematica* towards the end of the 17th century. However, even this concept of independent time gave rise to profound philosophical and religious discussions concerning infinity, creation, and

God's intervention: if the universe is governed by strict scientific laws explaining the past and predicting the future, then there is no more room for divine power. It was also questioned in physics, since around that time it was suggested that the speed of light might have something to do with the observed times of eclipses of the moons of Jupiter: the further they were from the Earth, the later they appeared to be. This marked the beginning of a series of studies that aimed at explaining the travel of light, including the infamous theory in which light was assumed to travel through a mysterious substance called ether and its constant speed was to be measured against ether. However, since the speed of light did not seem to vary whether or not measured in the direction of the Earth's motion, the constant value of the speed of light had to have a different explanation.[1] Henri Poincaré and Albert Einstein are credited with exorcising ether theory and pointing out that time may not be absolute. This brings us to the beginning of the 20th century and the special theory of relativity.

In special, and subsequently general, theory of relativity, on the other hand, time and space are intertwined. According to the special theory, the speed of light appears the same, independently of the speed with which the measuring agent/instrument moves, but the distances covered and the time the travel takes may vary from observer to observer. In short, moving clocks tick slower than a stationary clock of the observer and two events that are simultaneous to a stationary observer will not be simultaneous to a moving observer. These theses led directly to a new theory of gravitation called general relativity. As is well known by now, when a star collapses into a black hole, time 'slows down': signals sent from such a collapsing star would take longer and longer to reach the observer, until they stop when the light wave ceases to escape. Whatever is inside the so-called 'event horizon' is at the same time within the boundary of space-time from which there is no escape.[2] The universe is construed as expanding. Moreover, extending this line of reasoning, time is construed there as having a beginning: it is the time *of* the universe, measured from the big bang. The Newtonian idea of determinism also had to come to an end: Heisenberg's uncertainty principle exposed the fact that the universe cannot be measured and future events cannot be predicted. The current position and velocity of a particle cannot be accurately measured because, when one shines a quantum of light on a particle in order to perform the measurement, this quantum of light alters the position and velocity to be measured. The more accurately one tries to measure the position (by shining

---

[1] For approachable introductions see Hawking 2001, 1988, and Penrose 1989. For the current controversy concerning the status of time dimension(s) see Ambjørn *et al.* 2008.

[2] See Hawking (1988: 87–9) for a detailed scenario and discussion of the possibility of time travel.

not more than one quantum of light), the more one alters its velocity. *A fortiori*, the future position and speed of the particle cannot be predicted either. Although the finding was accommodated with the subsequent rise of quantum mechanics – a kind of physics that respects the uncertainty principle – the relativity of time and uncertainty of the future open up new foundations for modelling time and space. On the one hand, we have the general theory of relativity with its relative time, on the other, the uncertainty principle.

One of the tasks of this essay is to assess the extent to which these physical notions constitute foundations for human concepts of time as expressed in natural language. Is there causation, some form of supervenience, or dissociation? We have to pose this big question before we propose how time is represented in semantics in order to clarify the properties of the concept to be represented. While there is extensive experimental evidence in favour of relative time,[3] its empirical support need not mean that this concept is at all useful in understanding time thoughts: after all, our everyday events don't occur in the speeds approaching the speed of light. In the following section I discuss philosophical approaches to time according to which time is an internal human construct and, in Section 1.3, try to juxtapose real and internal time, taking on board some recent hypotheses in the philosophy of time.

1.2 Time consciousness

Before we proceed to the building blocks of the concept of time in Chapter 2 and to its semantics in Chapters 3 and 4, we have to analyse human thinking about time. There is no better place to start discussing the concept of time than Edmund Husserl's *Lectures on the Phenomenology of the Consciousness of Internal Time* (Husserl 1928). In Husserl's phenomenological analysis, i.e. his method of, so to speak, *getting to the things themselves*, a conscious mental act, such as believing, doubting, or remembering, is always *aimed at something*. In other words, it is *intentional*: believing that it is Tuesday today, doubting that I will finish this chapter today, remembering that I have to meet a friend this afternoon. Consciousness of time has to be understood in this context: it permeates all intentional acts. Husserl distinguishes here the apparent time of external objects and the internal time of mental acts through which the external objects become known to us.[4] He also adds a third sense of time: the *flow of consciousness* that itself *constitutes* time. It is this third notion

---

[3] See Penrose (1989: 257).

[4] His terms for external and internal are 'transcendent' and 'immanent' respectively, coming with the phenomenological baggage from which they are derived.

of time that is most important as it is the foundation of the other two senses in that it provides a foundation for the unity, what we can call the mutually dependent constitution, of the object (in his example: tone duration in music in internal time, see Husserl 1928: 84) and the flow of consciousness.

To use more modern terminology, events, states, and processes appear to us as temporal objects, as past, present, or future. Acts of perception, for example, combine the past, present, and future perspective thanks to their *intentionality*: they are *about* those events, states and processes (the so-called 'phases'). This account was later developed into three so-called 'moments of awareness': the past, present, and future, instead of being phases of an act of perception, become properties, so to speak, of consciousness itself. The past, present, and future make us aware of perceptual and other intentional acts. We are aware of such mental acts as *acts extended in time*. Perception at the present moment is now called 'primal impression'; 'memory', the past, becomes 'retention'; and 'expectation', the future, becomes 'protention'.[5] Consciousness is understood as temporal, as a 'flow'. This flow is intentional in a sense that it is about an internal (immanent) temporal object, such as hearing a phone ring, and it is also intentional in another sense, in that it is 'about itself': the past, the present, and the future make up the flow of consciouness itself:

... *two* inseparably united *intentionalities*, requiring one another like two sides of one and the same thing, are interwoven with each other in the one, unique flow of consciousness. By virtue of one of the intentionalities, immanent time becomes constituted – an objective time, a genuine time in which there is duration and the alteration of what endures. In the other intentionality, it is the *quasi*-temporal arrangement of the phases of the flow that becomes constituted – of the flow that always and necessarily possesses the flowing 'now'-point, the phase of actuality, and the series of phases that have preceded the phase of actuality or that will follow it (those that are not yet actual). This phenomenal, preimmanent temporality becomes constituted intentionally as the form of the time-constituting consciousness and in it itself. (Husserl 1928: 87–8)

In each of them, i.e. in the past, the present, and the future, in turn, we can discern impression, retention, and protention in the sense introduced above. In other words, each of them once was, is now, or will be an act of perception.[6] To sum up, Husserl proposes an absolute flow that constitutes our consciousness of time. Once this is in place, we can be conscious of acts such as believing that a dog is barking or hearing a dog bark ('immanent temporal objects') and through those acts, in turn, we become conscious of external

---

[5] For an excellent presentation see Brough's introduction to Husserl 1928.
[6] See *ibid.*, p. LII.

('transcendent') temporal objects such as the barking of the dog. On Husserl's (1928: 77) proposal, there are three levels of constitution of time: (i) objects of empirical experience in objective time; (ii) various appearances belonging to different levels, belonging to the internal, 'pre-empirical' time; and, most importantly, (iii) the absolute flow of consciousness that constitutes time.[7] We end up with a very rich concept of temporality in which the main emphasis is placed on the intricate interaction of conscious subjects with the external world: although there is time in reality, this time is not of much help in our experience of this world. It is only when we develop representations of events, states, and processes that we are able to connect with them. And *a fortiori* (for Husserl), it is only when we develop our own concept of the flow that we are able to 'impose' time on our beliefs and experiences, and through them on the events, states, and processes that we experience. To simplify, for the purpose of our semantic analysis, we learn from Husserl that time comes from within, from the concept of time, and applies to the world only indirectly. We can now come back to the question asked in Section 1.1: is this internal time in any way determined or affected by the external time of real situations happening in the world? At first sight, the answer seems to be positive because we can detect the importance of a causal link: there would not be any conscious awareness, any mental states (acts) without the prior concepts of extendedness, temporality. But then, one must observe that the direction of causation is reverse to the ordinary, common-sense one: there seems to be time in the world because there is time in the mind that experiences this world, rather than the other way round. This direction is incompatible with that proposed in modern physics. While for Stephen Hawking (1988) the direction of causation (and determinism) was from the properties of the expanding universe to the properties of human thought, in Husserl the perspective is the opposite: it is the mind that creates 'real time'. For Hawking, time is relative because it is an element of space-time; for Husserl, time is relative because it comes 'from within'. I come back to Hawking's idea of determinism in Section 1.3.

On the other hand, Husserl's concept of time is only natural when we look at it from the vantage point of human life. The person who experiences the world also experiences him/herself in time, because he/she is aware of his/her own beginning and end. We are all finite: we are born and we die, and we have

---

[7] See also Husserl 1900–01, 1939, 1950, Jaszczolt 1996 and Bell (1990: 192–3) on the *horizon* of an act of consciousness: acts of consciousness (hearing a dog bark) leave some aspects of their objects (dog's barking) undetermined and the determination can be provided by further experiences. Similarly, the object (dog's barking) has its horizon in the sum of possible experiences, and an additional external horizon in experiences of other objects present in the background.

indirect experience of these boundaries through witnessing births and deaths of others. We are aware that some experiences already happened and some lie ahead. This, in Heidegger's system of *Being and Time* (1953), is the foundation of the 'vulgar', as he calls it, concepts of the past, the present, and the future. Human life is finite and we don't conceive of the future as the infinitely extending arrow with lots of 'nows' yet to come. Neither do we become 'disconnected' from some external time: time is *our* time and, as Heidegger says,

Just as the person who exists inauthentically constantly loses time and never 'has' any, it is the distinction of the temporality of authentic existence that in resoluteness it never loses time and 'always has time'. (Heidegger 1953: 377)

Just as for Husserl, for Heidegger understanding time is a prerequisite for understanding oneself. But Heidegger gives temporality a more general dimension of the understanding of being: the boundedness ('horizon') of being and the boundedness of life in terms of birth and death.[8]

Husserl and Heidegger should be discussed here in the context of the Kantian idea of retention they subscribe to. According to these three philosophers, and Locke and Hume before them, humans have no capacity for experiencing and conceptualizing duration; time is not something we perceive but something that perceived instants sum up to. Duration is not an impression that can be discerned and separated from the experienced moments but instead the moments are just arranged in this way: all there is is moments and arrangements. For Kant, this arrangement meant *reproducing* past moments in the present experience; for Husserl, it meant *retaining* them.[9] Retention provides missing parts to the experience and is explained through this experience's intentionality: experience relies on what has just passed.[10] This concept of retention should be viewed in the wider perspective of Husserl's phenomenological conception of the past. The past consists of memories, knowledge, and experiences that are already fixed.

In contrast, William James in the 19th-century philosophy, and subsequently C. D. Broad, talk about perception of time that has *intervals* as its units, and hence units are of some duration. To quote a well known passage from James,

[T]he practically cognized present is no knife-edge, but a saddle-back, with a certain breadth of its own on which we sit perched, and from which we look in two directions

---

[8] See Young 1997 on the dissociation of the conceptualization of time in *Being and Time* from the political situation in Germany at that time.

[9] For an excellent discussion of retention vis-à-vis specious present and references see Kelly 2005.

[10] My interpretation differs slightly from Kelly's. See Kelly (2005: 232–3).

into time. The unit of composition of our perception of time is a *duration*, with a bow and a stern, as it were – a rearward and a forward-looking end. [W]e seem to feel the interval of time as a whole, with its two ends embedded in it. (James 1890: 399)[11]

The present is conceived of not as a moment but instead as an interval extending into the past and into the future. It is called *specious present* where 'specious' means 'appearing to be actually known or experienced'.[12] Specious present is a short unit during which the experience has the status of an entity, a whole, but has a characteristic feature of being extended in time, with earlier and later parts. In other words, according to the idea of specious present, humans are aware, at every moment, not only of the very present moment but also of what is immediately before and after it, as long as these past and future parts are parts of one and the same experience. This extendedness of perception is frequently criticized on intuitive grounds in that it is difficult to conceive of perception as being of something other than the *now*. What does it mean to be *perceiving* something that is yet to come? Equally, it is difficult to understand what the 'perception of duration' would mean. Specious present has even been recently reinterpreted as 'a mixture of perception, memory and anticipation' (Le Poidevin 2007: 81), *pace* Kelly's (2005) more orthodox analysis of it where it is understood as temporally extended perception. On Le Poidevin's weaker reading, specious present is even compatible with Husserl's retention and with my analysis of retention presented above.

On all these grounds, including the contentious idea of experiencing duration and the element of retention in specious present, we can submit that Husserl's idea of retention should be regarded as less objectionable than specious present. It carries with it the assumption that perception is not in the void, but instead is well situated with respect to what happens before and after the act of perception.

Next, rounding up the discussion of the concept of time, we can tentatively propose that the concept of *now* is an entirely subjective construct in that it does not supervene on any *real now* – the claim to be reviewed in due course. It is either extended or punctual (a moment), and, if extended, it can be extended through a form of 'contextualizing' retention or repeating the past moments as part of the current experience. As we shall see in Sections 1.4 and 2.3, it is precisely this internal, conceptual status of *now*, as well as its indispensability for living in time and experiencing time, that make any plausible theory of real time insufficient: there is no *real now*.

---

[11] Cram (2007: 193) comments as follows: 'The image of the vessel travelling through water is a useful one: the specious present is like a boat which (...) leaves a wake behind it in the immediate past, and which also projects a bow-wave into the immediate future.'

[12] The term 'specious present' was introduced by E. R. Clay (see James 1890: 398).

I have tried to show in this historical introduction that the consciousness of time, as understood by phenomenological philosophers such as Husserl and Heidegger, entails creating 'internal time' for the purpose of experiencing the external world and, generally, for the purpose of living and comprehending the fact that life has finite duration. As the opening sentence of Schopenhauer's seminal work *The World as Will and Representation* says,

'The world is my representation': this is a truth valid with reference to every living and knowing being, although man alone can bring it into reflective, abstract consciousness. (Schopenhauer 1819, vol. 1: 3)

Consciousness is the only thing immediately given:

[N]othing is more certain than that no one ever came out of himself in order to identify himself immediately with things different from him; but everything of which he has certain, sure, and hence immediate knowledge, lies within his consciousness. Beyond this consciousness, therefore, there can be no *immediate* certainty (. . .). (Schopenhauer 1819, vol. 2: 4)

The concept of time is precisely such a representation of something in the world, namely real time. But the properties of this concept may not come from real time of physicists' space-time. They may derive instead from the finiteness of our lives or from experiences and emotions associated with events encountered between the boundaries of birth and death. The supervenience will, indeed, be argued here to be of a delicate kind and founded on a concept which underlies both of the related entities.

I have chosen this example out of the plethora of philosophers who wrote about time, because the view that time is a construct of human consciousness, that is that time is *only* conceptual, is very appealing, although at the same time is the most difficult one to reconcile with the view that time (under a suitable definition) is real and objective – whether absolute or relative. It is necessary to emphasize that for this way of thinking about reality 'the world is our representation': it is not things themselves that are objects of our beliefs but rather representations of these things. The same goes for our concept of time: we represent time and create internal time. But there is a link between the two realms, the psychological (internal time) and the ontological (real time). Although Husserl recognizes three senses of time, it is the internal time, the flow of consciousness, that 'produces', so to speak, the time of external events. To repeat, in special relativity, there is real time, but this time is relative. Through being relative, though, it becomes 'psychological' in the sense that it belongs to the observer, albeit the natural direction of causation is seemingly opposite to that proposed by Husserl: it is from the world to the mind, from the real to the internal. 'Seemingly' because the time of real, external states of affairs is for Husserl still a category of time conscious-ness, and hence the question of real vs. internal is not really addressed there. It simply cannot be addressed within the framework of phenomenology.

To conclude, an attempt at a comparison and searching for compatibility of real time and internal time is not without foundations. We are not dealing with incommensurable paradigms of phenomenology on the one hand and physics on the other. We just have two levels of explanation whose object is time. These two levels focus on two different aspects, the ontological and the psychological, of one and the same phenomenon. We shall end on a methodological note: Fine (2005: 320), when discussing the meaning of *tense* (which we can take for the current purpose to be his label for *time*, as he talks about 'tensed facts' and 'tensed reality') says that controversies can be either *doctrinal* or *ideological*. They are doctrinal when the opponents share the understanding of the core concepts, and they are ideological when they differ in their understanding of the terms and as a result there is no mutual understanding of their respective positions. Fine argues that the dispute around the reality of time is largely ideological in that the sides have a different notion of reality, and hence different notions of real and unreal time. Our discussion so far corroborates Fine's point: volumes have been written addressing the question as to whether time is real or unreal. It seems that it is both, although the negative term 'unreal' is not the best of labels for internal time and time consciousness. 'Real' and 'unreal' are very misleading labels when juxtaposed in this way. Instead, we will from now on distinguish between the time of space-time in physics (real) and time of experience (internal). We will focus on the question of the possible compatibility of the external (real) with the internal, and in particular the internal absolute time with the external relative time. We shall, therefore, go beyond cognitive approaches to time which define time as internal only, i.e. as a human concept, or sometimes as a polysemous term pertaining to a number of separate concepts (Evans 2003, 2005).

Even at this introductory point the labels 'internal time' ('concept of time') and 'external time' ('real time') look promising. Proceeding to definitions of time in Section 1.3, and thereby elaborating on our ski lift and washing line metaphors from the Introduction, will prove them to be adequate for our purpose. In what follows, I defend the concept of time that, unlike Husserl's or Heidegger's internal time, is weakly dependent on real time. This dependence is indirect. It will be argued that both the concept of time and real time of space-time can be traced to a more basic category of modality. The concept of time relies on the underlying, more basic concept of degree of certainty or epistemic possibility, while real time relies on probabilities, the ways things have been, are, and will be. From Chapter 2 onwards I will concentrate on the concept of time and its semantic representation but the theses of the modal nature of real time and the weak supervenience of the concept of time on real time will occasionally surface in the discussion.

We can now formulate our three-pronged Thesis of Supervenience, to be defended in what follows.

Thesis of Supervenience

(a) The concept of time supervenes on a more basic concept of modal possibility, epistemic detachment.
(b) Real time supervenes on probabilities of states of affairs.
(c) The concept of time indirectly supervenes on real time, in the sense that the concept of time is founded on, and restricted to, experiences, memories, and anticipations.

Part (a) is widely accepted in a range of cognitive approaches within linguistics[13] and is independently supported by the arguments put forward in Chapter 2. Thesis (b) is supported by findings from modern physics. Real time, as a component of space-time, pertains to possibilities, possible 'histories of the world', and hence is modal in nature. Part (c) follows from (a) and (b). It will be argued that internal and external time have similar properties, and that, since internal time is the product of the way the universe is, or at least *is seen by us*, it is reasonable to claim that real time gives rise to the human concept of time. Thesis (c) is further supported in the discussion of the anthropic principle in Section 2.4, as well as in the discussion of Dummett's views on realism in that section. Once the thesis of modal supervenience is sufficiently supported, we will be able to move to semantic representation of time in Chapter 3 and to giving precise representation structures of linguistic expressions of time in Chapter 4.

1.3 The direction of time: A solution to McTaggart's paradox?

In *A Brief History of Time*, Stephen Hawking (1988: 145) distinguishes three senses of the direction of time, calling them three arrows of time. The first one is thermodynamic and corresponds to the direction of time in which disorder (enthropy) increases in the world.[14] The second one is psychological and

---

[13] I discuss this topic in Section 3.1. See also Langacker, e.g. 1987, 1991, 1999, 2001, and Brisard, e.g. 2002, 2006.
[14] Hawking (1988: 144) illustrates this law of thermodynamics with the naturalness of seeing a cup breaking up into pieces (increased disorder) but oddity of seeing pieces of a broken cup gathering together to form a whole cup (decreased disorder).

stands for the direction in which the time, as felt by human agents, passes. It is evidenced in the fact that we remember the past but cannot remember the future. The third arrow of time is cosmological and stands for the direction in which the universe is expanding (as opposed to contracting). Hawking goes on to argue that the three arrows of time have to be commensurate in order for human life to be possible: they have to point in the same direction. The psychological arrow is determined by the thermodynamic and cosmological arrows and the latter two have to point in the same direction in order for us to exist and to have the experience of time. He assumes the universe with no boundary and the thermodynamic and cosmological arrows of time that do not always point in the same direction: there are times in the history of the universe when the directions do not coincide. But, for intelligent life to exist, they have to point in the same direction: the co-directionality of the two arrows creates conditions for human life. The interesting question then becomes: 'Why does disorder increase in the same direction of time as that in which the universe expands?' (Hawking 1988: 145). The answer seems to be teleological: humans make an essential use of the properties of the expanding universe. Energy comes in the ordered form, that is mass, and disordered form, that is heat. Our bodies are so constructed that they require food (mass) and have to transform this mass into heat, in accordance with the thermodynamic law of the increased disorder of the closed system.

Having introduced this relation between the direction of real time and direction of internal time, we can now address the question as to whether real *time* and psychological *time* are similarly connected. In other words, do the considerations that pertain to the arrow of time also pertain to the concept of time? If the psychological arrow of time is determined, in the teleological sense, by the cosmological and thermodynamic arrows, how does this causation affect the internal concept of time? In pursuit of an answer we shall begin with the classical distinction between the A- and B-theories of time and respective arguments in their favour. Next, we shall address the question of ontological and explanatory priority of these two models, and finally we should be in a position to return to the main question of supervenience.

In truth-conditional semantics, temporality is analysed by extending the metalanguage of predicate logic to include tense logic. Propositions are relativized to times in that the models against which the logical form is checked for truth value should give extensions for predicates relativized to a particular time t. In other words, and using the language of one of the most influential truth-conditional approaches, Discourse Representation Theory (DRT), there is a function from times to models: a model M is 'a pair consisting of a time structure $T = <T, <>$ together with a function

M which assigns to each $t \in T$ a corresponding model M_t' (Kamp and Reyle 1993: 486), where '$<$' stands for the 'earlier-than' relation and T for a set of temporal events. This way of representing time in formal semantics originated with Arthur Prior's (1957, 1967, 1968a, b, 2003) tense logic in which four tense operators are added to standard predicate logic. The two that are of interest to us are P for the past and F for the future: Pp stands for 'it was the case that p' and Fp for 'it will be the case that p'. P and F have the status of sentential operators or one-place sentential connectives.[15] Example (1) is translated into such a metalanguage as (1'):

(1)   Mark painted a picture.
(1') $\exists x$ (Picture (x) $\wedge$ P Paint (Mark, x))[16]

Prior's logic reflected common intuitions about time and was couched in what we called the ski lift metaphor of time: in our experience time flows, we experience the past and the future, and hence there are formal equivalents for these experiences in his logic. For Prior the past, the present, and the future exist on the level of explanation for temporality.[17] He opts for a view of time that takes the speaker's perspective; what Recanati (2007a: 63) calls an *internal* view of time. Since humans experience the flow of time and the experience is located in time, this is the natural perspective to take. However, it is only one of the two main construals of time which contemporary philosophy and semantics inherited from McTaggart. The next task is to assess the position of these two construals with respect to internal and real time.

For McTaggart (1908), all time is unreal. He distinguishes two ways of construing time: as earlier-than/later-than relations between events, or as past, present, and future which are characteristic features of events:

... I shall speak of the series of positions running from the far past through the near past to the present, and then from the present to the near future and the far future, as the A series. The series of positions which runs from earlier to later I shall call the B series. The contents of a position in time are called events. (McTaggart 1908: 111)

---

[15] See also Øhrstrøm and Hasle 1995 on the history of temporal logic from the antiquity to artificial intelligence and Hamblin 1972 or Leith and Cunningham 2001 on an example of aspect and interval logic.

[16] See also Kamp and Reyle 1993, Chapter 5 and Jaszczolt 2002, Chapter 12 on the need for operators 'since' and 'until'.

[17] For a recent defence of temporal sentential operators see Recanati 2007a, esp. pp. 56–7 where he points out that tenses are quantificational *qua* being sentential operators and that deictic and anaphoric uses of tenses can be accounted for by means of contextual domain restriction. In this way he responds to Partee's (1973) objection that sentences such as 'I haven't turned off the stove' necessitate the treatment of tenses as referential variables. An alternative response to Partee was provided by Ludlow (1999: 112) who introduces a *when*-clause to the logical form.

The latter kind of relation is permanent, the first is changeable; an event that is now future will become present and then past. The A series allows for change because time is the property of events. According to the B series events are real and ordered but not tensed; time is psychological and there is no real change. In fact, even the 'earlier-than' and 'later-than' labels are dependent on time and presuppose the A series. If we were to be strict about reality here, we would need a timeless ordering of some timeless equivalents of events which McTaggart calls the C series. Prior, St Augustine before him, and more recently Quentin Smith (1993), Peter Ludlow (1999), or Øhrstrøm and Hasle (1995) are among the supporters of the A series. In particular, Prior supports the version of it called *presentism* according to which all there is is the world right *now*; events will happen or did happen but there are no existing past or future events. Or, for the purpose of formal semantic analysis, presentism says that 'every possibly true sentence includes presentness in its semantic content' (Smith 1993: v). Followers of the B series are more numerous and include Bertrand Russell, Albert Einstein, Hans Reichenbach (1948), Hugh Mellor (1998), and more recently Joshua Mozersky (2001) and Robin Le Poidevin (2007). However, as we shall see shortly, the main concern is not which of these two theories is correct but what exactly are they theories *of*. Once this question is answered, we can assess their possible compatibility.

The A series is deemed necessary because without it we would not be able to represent change. The B series does not suffice, although the earlier-than/ later-than relations are necessary for ordering events, because it presupposes the A series and thereby the existence of time. It presupposes the A series in that the A series captures the concept of change and time involves change. McTaggart goes on to demonstrate that time is unreal because the A series is its necessary characteristic, and at the same time cannot be fulfilled: an event which was future becomes present and then past, while no event can be simultaneously past, present, and future. One may try to argue that the qualification 'simultaneously' is the culprit. But when we remove the qualification 'simultaneously', we introduce the presupposition of time by the back door and the argument becomes circular. The conclusion McTaggart offers is that past, present, and future belong to our experience: we have memories of events, perceptions, and anticipations, which result in the experience of the past, present, and future respectively. In this way we have now conveniently come back to the issues of the internal consciousness of time discussed in Section 1.2. But McTaggart's conclusion need not necessarily be correct; even if A series and B series are indeed both inadequate as models for time, it does not yet follow, *pace* McTaggart, that all time is unreal. I shall first assess some post-McTaggartian arguments for the unreality of time and next move to the opposition.

Firstly, the question of the reality of time has to be distinguished from the question of the reality of time flow. Mellor (1998) argues that there is no real flow of time. Events don't change from future to present and then to past. Humans live in time and hence they interpret events as if the time flow were real. He is a B-theorist and a Kantian, for whom causation is an important dimension of our internal time. B-theory is all there is: if there was an objective *now*, then the A-theory could be anchored to it and also be real. However, as Mellor argues, there is no such objective 'present moment': the *now* of observing a supernova is not the *now* of the explosion itself. The explosion took place in the remote past. As he says, an event is considered past at a certain time when it is *earlier* than that time; it is present when it is *located at* that time; and it is future when it is *later* than that time (see Mellor 1998: 2). In short, nothing in reality is *now* or *then* (*ibid.*: 52). Next, Mellor invokes a causal order of events that we perceive and proposes that it is this causal order that gives rise to our experience of time. As a result, our beliefs are irreducibly A-type. Time flows in our experience but this internal flow of time need not supervene on the real time flow. There is no real time flow.

Quite independently, it seems that the 'arrow of time' addressed by Hawking and discussed at the beginning of this section can still be *real* in the ontological sense: memories create the past, and anticipations the future. There is no reason why we shouldn't attempt to construe the arrow of time along the lines of Mellor's causation. Furthermore, on Mellor's account, if the causal theory of time is correct, then time cannot be cyclical or branching. The present and the future do not influence the past, and the causal link, founded on the precedence and following of events in the B series, ensures the linearity.

This construal differs in a few aspects (albeit not in the main orientation) from the concept of time that I propose in the following chapters. To anticipate a little what follows, on my account (i) psychological time with time flow is 'unreal' simply *qua* being different in its properties from real time: *the concept x is not x itself*; (ii) B-theory is correct but it is correct of real time and not of time at large. Next, (iii) time can be translated into a more primitive notion of *modality* which suffices for its explanation. Both the concept of time and real time are founded on modality in the form of epistemic and metaphysical possibility respectively. Consequently, (iv) modality obviates the need for a linear structure understood as a linear sequence of events, and (v) the order of causation is equally redundant: modality is used as an *explanans* instead. I introduce the theory of time as modality (degrees of detachment from certainty) in Chapter 2.

Let us now go back to Hawking's arrow of time and put it in the context of McTaggart's A- and B-theories. We can see that Hawking's determinism and locking the psychological time to the physical time will not suffice to provide the full answer to the supervenience question. Hawking's observation belongs to, so to speak, one level higher than the question of the adequacy of A- and B-theory. The best starting point is to ask: is there real time or are there just ordered events? Assuming that 'real' means 'absolute', the physicist's answer is 'no'. Assuming that 'real' means time flow, then the answer again is 'no': there are positions in space-time instead. But if 'real' means measurable with respect to other parameters, then the answer is 'yes' and the question of supervenience of the psychological on the physical can be reopened. Probably the best way to proceed is to think, contra McTaggart, of A- and B-theories as theories of the *concept* of time and conclude that while A-theory is more adequate to represent this concept, B-theory is better at capturing the link with real time: after subtracting the moving observer and his/her internal time, we obtain a sequence of event-like objects – in other words, real time, no flow. Similarly, since for the adversaries of the perception of duration (such as advocates of specious present discussed in Section 1.2) there are only perceived moments arranged to give a subjective impression of time, for them time is unreal. But it is only unreal in the sense of flow, not of the time dimension itself. On the other hand, although Hawking's 'arrow of internal (psychological) time' is predetermined by 'the arrow of real (thermodynamic and cosmological) time', we must remember that there is no absolute real time and therefore we can count only on limited help from physical sciences to shed light on the consciousness of time.

Now, in Horwich's (1987: 15) radical interpretation of phenomenology, time is 'temporally asymmetric': while the past is built out of memories, the future is built out of instances of anticipation. In addition to the difference of direction there is also an epistemological difference: past experiences are known, while future experiences are only predicted. There is also a difference in the order of explanation: the past is used to explain (foresee) the future, and past actions help plan future actions.[18] This construal seems to rely implicitly on the arrow of time: there is a physical arrow of time that coincides with, and determines, the psychological one. We will try to shed some more light on this issue when we move to the idea of branching time and time as modality in Chapter 2. It will become obvious that there is no relevant qualitative difference between the past and the future.

---

[18] See Horwich (1987: 199–200).

Finally, we have to eliminate further terminological confusions inherited from the phenomenological tradition in philosophy. If we follow Husserl's idea of conscious flow, then time is according to him 'real' because it belongs to consciousness and consciousness *is* real. We shall not use 'real' in this phenomenological sense but rather in the sense of space-time of the universe.

In short, we have several distinctions to juggle: (a) absolute – relative; (b) instant (no duration) – interval (duration); (c) earlier/later – past/present/future; (d) objective – subjective. In this section, I have been focusing on (c) and (d). Distinction (a) was attended to in Section 1.1. Distinction (b) is the subject of Section 3.2 where I attempt to provide semantically adequate notions of event and state. In this essay I follow the essentially B-theoretic perspective on real time but I reject the question of choice between A and B theories as wrongly posed. It would only be posed correctly if it concerned the properties of internal time and this is not what McTaggart had in mind: he was concerned with *real* time *qua* change, flow, and the question of its existence. We do not need to do this because we assumed that real time must be the ontological time, the space-time of the universe. My B-theoretic perspective on real time follows naturally. If there is a question to ask about the choice between A- and B-theories, it is the question of which of them captures the psychological (internal) time, the time of human experience. In other words, is the ski lift metaphor from the Introduction (A-theory) or the washing line metaphor (B-theory) more adequate in capturing the experience of time? Here our extensive discussion of internal time consciousness was utilized as a theoretical underpinning of the answer that can be given intuitively by lay informants: we do experience the passing of time, time flow, and we either 'flow with it', to which the English construction in (3) testifies, or we stand by and observe how it 'comes to us', as in construction (4).

(3)   We are approaching the new era of globalization.

(4)   Winter has come.

The picture we obtain is far from the one intended by McTaggart: on this very (and deliberately) unfaithful reconstruction, we assume that the A series is correct of the internal, psychological time, and the B series shows how this psychological time relates to the change-free (for him: 'timeless') world. So, we used McTaggart's concepts for a different kind of discussion. To sum up, real time utilizes B series resources, while internal time utilizes A series resources (albeit not exclusively: B series resources have not been refuted in our discussion so far). But also, real time is relative, while internal time is absolute. I shall now devote more attention to the question of their compatibility, and in particular to the relation between the metaphysical (real) time and the concept of time.

The question of supervenience has been well aired in the recent philosophical literature. Sattig (2006), for example, argues in favour of logical supervenience of psychological time, called by him 'ordinary time', past, present, and future, on the physical time, which he considers as an element of four-dimensional space-time. The main task in tackling the question of supervenience is, as he says, to identify those facts of the first and those facts of the latter which are linked by this relation. He founds his analysis on the assumption that an object occupies many temporally punctual (unextended) regions of space-time and develops a theory of supervenience of the perceived *persistence* of objects on their spatiotemporal location, and the perceived *becoming* on an atemporal instantiation in unextended regions of space-time. This is a very important advancement in the philosophy of time: if supervenience is logically possible when real and internal time are understood in this most plausible way from the point of view of physics and psychology, then the onus of proof is on those who choose to deny that such supervenience takes place, especially in the light of Hawking's statement on the convergence of the arrows of time.

At the current state of the discussion about A- and B-theory it seems hardly controvertible that mental states are better viewed in terms of an A series, while metaphysical time is better defined in terms of a B series.[19] Ever since Prior (1959: 84) pointed out that a state of relief expressed in 'Thank goodness, that's over!' relies on the experience of *now* (such as that, say, an examination is over *now* rather than it is over at 12.05 p.m. when it is now 12.05 p.m.), there have been extensive debates over the A and B series but little controversy on this particular point. One way forward in delimiting the functions which A- and B-theories are best assigned is to employ the notion of *representation*. Le Poidevin (2007) points out that the representation of time does not give a direct access to the represented object itself and that it is necessary to research that relation between the world and the representation as a separate object of study. This is what I discussed earlier as the difference between *x* and the concept of *x*. The most important aspects of his stance are that real time does not flow, although our experience and memory construe internal time as a flow from the future to the present and then to the past. Yet, Le Poidevin moves from there to arguing that what we call real and internal time can be

---

[19] I use the indefinite article here in order to stress the perspective on which there are many different A series and many different B series, which is explained by the special theory of relativity. See Mellor 1998.

reconciled. Only B-theory can successfully account for representing internal time in that it accounts for episodic memory, i.e. recollections of experiences: states of affairs are recorded as constant and are kept as such; they are not changing as they do for an A-theorist. *A fortiori*, what makes a belief true is the same truth-maker as what makes the memory of it true: a state of affairs as it occurred at a certain time *t*.[20] On the other hand, A-theory would correspond to antirealism about the past: if the sentence is about a past situation and no corroboration of its truth can be found at the later moment of evaluation, the sentence lacks the truth value or is false. However, a past sentence about the same situation, issued at the time at which it took place, may still be true.[21]

The *nows* and *thens* seem to us objective, albeit egocentric. If so, then, *pace* Le Poidevin's argument, internal time itself seems best accounted for as being of the A kind. To repeat, if we assume that real time is indeed Einsteinian, the only way we can make sense of the passage of time is when we talk about its representation in the human mind. Our experience tells us that time passes from the future to the present and from the present to the past. Now, as for Mellor, for Le Poidevin an event that is present to experience triggers a causal link that determines how this event is perceived. The object perceived is the cause and the resulting state its effect. This causation works equally for the relations of precedence and succession: it is not precedence and succession in the world that matters but rather how the mind links the events. In short, there are constant events of a B-series type that trigger the phenomenological time, the experience of time flow. The mind, through establishing causation, tells us that there is a flow where in reality all there is is the fourth dimension *t* of time – just as the familiar dimensions *x*, *y*, and *z* of space.[22] On this view, duration and precedence are real; they belong to the world. The past, present, and future are world-dependent, although on the other hand they are triggered by the causal links provided by the mind. In the approach I propose in Chapter 2 I shall take it to be a sufficiently supported tenet that this supervenience of the psychological on the ontological should be assumed. I shall also take it as a sufficiently corroborated hypothesis that real time does not flow but nevertheless exists and serves as the real correlate and sufficient

---

[20] The question of what makes statements about the future and about the past true (truth-makers) is extensively argued in the literature as it constitutes an important argument in debates concerning the reality of the future and the past. Since (i) we have adopted the Einsteinian and therefore a B-theoretic perspective on real time, (ii) relegated the considerations of A-theory to internal time, and (iii) adopted the B-theoretic definitions of Prior's P and F operators in terms of earlier-than/later-than relations, the question will not be in focus of our discussion. But I address it briefly in discussing Dummett's view on the past in Section 2.4.

[21] See also Dummett 1969, 2004, 2006, and Section 2.4 below.

[22] *Pace* the multiple dimensions of space assumed in advanced mathematics.

condition for the experience of time flow: the psychological arrow of time depends on the properties of the physical world, as Hawking points out, and the psychological time makes use of the A-series resources, while it is best theorized about in terms of B-type resources, as Le Poidevin's philosophical argument demonstrates.

Independent support for the B series is present in the truth-conditional-semantic definitions of Prior's A-theoretic P and F operators. In current truth-conditional semantics, the truth conditions for P*p* and F*p* are as in (5) and (6) below:

(5) P*p* is true in M at *t* iff ∃*t'* (*t'* < *t* ∧ *p* is true in M at *t'*)
(6) F*p* is true in M at *t* iff ∃*t'* (*t* < *t'* ∧ *p* is true in M at *t'*)

where *t* stands for time instant,[23] 'iff' for 'if and only if', '∧' for the logical relation of conjunction, and '∃' for the logical operator of existential quantification ('there is a time *t'* ...'). Hence, the Priorean operators are partly removed from A-theory and are interpreted in terms of the earlier-than/later-than relations.[24] They are 'partly removed', though, rather than fully dissociated. P is analysed as time *t'* defined with respect to time *t* where the latter stands for some agreed *now*: the proposition has to be true in a model *at a given time*. Once we introduce the egocentric, and hence perspectival notion of *now*, we obtain by force an admixture of A-type resources. I come back to this question later on in this section while discussing Hans Reichenbach's influence on formal semantic theory.

All in all, we can conclude that one can be an A-theorist about psychological, internal time and at the same time a B-theorist about real time. But, to repeat, we must remember that this is not the most popular way of viewing McTaggart's opposition. Within presentism, the A-theoretic commitments are sometimes stated in stronger terms. For Quentin Smith, 'presentness inheres in events absolutely' (1993: 135) and Einstein's special theory of relativity is 'not about time but something else' (*ibid.*). However, on closer inspection, the difference between Smith's and my discourse about time seems merely terminological: while for me, just as for Le Poidevin, time is still time if there is no past, present, and future, and hence time is still time if there is no flow, for Smith time has to entail time flow and the *now*. Psychological time is for him *the only time*. It is very important to expose such terminological

---

[23] Representing time in terms of instants (moments) and intervals has given rise to extensive discussions in the literature. See, for example, Dowty 1979; Kamp and Reyle 1993.

[24] See also Mellor 1993 on tenseless facts: all facts have to have tenseless truth conditions.

incompatibilities before jumping to the defence of one or the other view and before classifying oneself as an A- or B-theorist.

Now, quite independently of the definition of time in A-theory, we should mention and briefly discuss one potential weakness of presentism. It is sometimes claimed that it has a problem with accounting for cross-temporal relations such as those in (7) or (8).

(7)   I was at the same Oxford college as Margaret Thatcher.

(8)   I am ten years younger than you were when you got married.

We have here cross-temporal comparisons that require tensed properties: being at Oxford at time t_1 or t_2, x's being ten years younger at t_1 than y was at t_2. Brogaard (2006) successfully defended presentism from this alleged weakness and aptly explained why this is not a real difficulty for a presentist: just as we can have modal relations of type (9) while being committed only to the actual world, so can we have cross-temporal relations while being committed only to *now*.

(9)   I could have built a house that is prettier than the one I actually
       built.   (from Brogaard 2006: 199)

Brogaard argues that relations can be irreducibly tensed, which is a perfectly justifiable assumption for any A-theorist for whom fundamental concepts are those of the past, present, and future.

In contrast to Smith, Parsons (2002, 2003) develops a modal version of the A-theory that is compatible with the overall B-theoretic outlook. He emphasizes the importance of A-theoretic terms for making practical judgements: it is better to have had a painful operation *yesterday* than to have to have it *tomorrow* – a variation on Prior's 'thank goodness' scenario (e.g. 'Thank goodness the root canal is over!') discussed above. Time is to be formally represented as sentential operators for the past and the future, conceived of as possibility operators: 'it was the case that p' is true iff there is a past time t at which p is true-at-t (see Parsons 2003: 4). In other words, 'it was the case that p' is true iff there is a past time t such that were it that time, p would be true (cf. Parsons 2002: 10). The change inherent in standard A-theory becomes reinterpreted as modality. The egocentric and deictic indicators of time are fundamental and irreducible. Parsons is a realist about the past and about the future, though, and at the same time a committed B-theorist. The ability to observe supernovae that took place in the remote past testifies to the reality of these events. Future is equally real: its reality is secured by the fact that causal relations must obtain and that present events have to be linked with future causes for which they are sufficient and necessary conditions. As he himself says, his theory does not make claims about the physics of time and his reinterpretation of A series is not diametrically opposite to the B-theory conception.

Physics does not need to refer to the flow of time. How do A-theorists respond to the objection that they are building a temporal psychology while the world itself is atemporal in the sense that there is no time flow? Prior was well aware of the differences between the special relativity view of time and the concept of time assumed in his temporal logic. His defence of tense logic proceeded on the lines of capturing human thinking and experience: there may not be a privileged *now* in the world and in physics, but there is a very important *now* in human lives. There may not be an answer to the question as to which event happened first because the answer depends on the relative velocity of the subject, but in real life a sequence of events simply *must* be assumed because it is a fact of human experience.

Although the discussion between A-theorists and B-theorists is sometimes couched in terms of Kuhnian paradigms and hence incommensurability of assumptions (Øhrstrøm and Hasle 1995: 243), it is evident from the above analysis that it is in fact not so. The B-conception appears as real time and the A-conception as internal, psychological time. Fierce debates over what to do with indexicality of temporal expressions, the difference between (10) and (11) below, can be perfectly well explained by means of contextual enrichment: either as an addition to the logical form which is performed through pragmatic inference (Ludlow 1999) or through a free enrichment of the proposition expressed (Recanati 2007a).

(10)   The deafening noise of the pneumatic drill will end in two minutes.
(11)   The deafening noise of the pneumatic drill will end on 9 January 2008 at 12.40 p.m.

A theory of internal time pertains to the experience of time and hence it is perfectly natural that egocentric terms such as 'now' or 'in two minutes' are present in the representations of this experience.

By the same token, we can easily find compatibility, and more reasons for predicting supervenience, between A- and B-theories. We shall reject claims such as the one made by Tallant (2007) that we can have no understanding of B-time because our mind is entirely A-theoretic. Or, to use his words, 'Our temporal phenomenology is mind-dependent and reflects no feature of reality.' (Tallant 2007: 147). While is it indeed true that we live in time and impose our experience of *now*, the flow of time we experience directly supervenes on the locations of states of events in time: it either supervenes by exploiting the concept of causation, as Mellor and Le Poidevin argue, or by exploiting the concept of modality, as Parsons suggests and I develop in what follows. Moreover, as Oaklander and White (2007) point out in their response to Tallant, it is by no means true that the temporal phenomenology is A-theoretic and entirely mind-dependent. For example, perceptions do not have to be perceptions *of a certain time* and the experience of succession need not be inherently tensed. To compare, Ludlow (1999: 96) asks: 'If the world contains only B-theory resources, then precisely how do we avoid having a B-theory psychology?' We do not 'avoid' B-time psychology, we interpret B-series resources in the egocentric, A-series manner. In fact, we need both, just as we do in semantics.[25] Enough said, until Chapter 2.

The above comment concerning A- and B-series resources in semantics requires further clarification. Let us therefore return to the question of the semantic representation of time. As I pointed out with the help of definitions of the operators P and F presented in (5) and (6) above, in spite of the fact that we experience the concepts of the past and the future, the formal representation of temporality uses a mixture of B- and A-type resources. Formal representation of time has become more B-theoretic also thanks to the influence of Hans Reichenbach (1948). For Reichenbach, the problem of time is the problem for physics. According to special relativity, and in particular Minkowski's version of it, time and space have similar properties: time exists as a dimension of reality. Reichenbach adopted from Jespersen the concept of reference point and proposed a representation of tenses by means of two relations: (i) a relation between speech time and reference time, and (ii) a relation between the event and the reference time. For example, for Present Perfect the event time (E) is placed before the speech time (S) and the reference time (R) on the time line, while the latter two are cotemporal as in Fig. 1.1 which represents the temporality of example (12).

(12)   I have read *Cloud Atlas*.

$$E \qquad\qquad S, R$$

FIGURE 1.1 Reichenbach's representation of the Present Perfect

The temporality conveyed in the sentence is the reference time R: in Present Perfect, the speaker is talking about a present state of affairs (R = S) as resulting from a past event (E). Naturally, we can also add states and processes to this representation and depict the fact that they are extended in time by allocating to them a section of the time line rather than a point. This addition will not, however, interest us at present and we will leave the discussion of duration until Chapter 3 (see Reichenbach 1948: 290; Steedman 1997: 910; and Jaszczolt 2002: 267). What will interest us here is the relation between A-series

---

[25] See also an overview in Ludlow 2006. See Farkas 2008 who argues that truth-conditional semantics is neutral with respect to the A-theory/B-theory dispute.

concepts and B-series concepts in the type of truth-conditional semantics that uses the definitions in (5) and (6). Throughout this chapter we are using DRT (Kamp and Reyle 1993) as an example of such an account. In DRT, a B-series concept of precedence ($t < t'$) is an *explanans* and we cannot fully translate the A-series psychology into the B-series reality. What is required in the representation of temporality conveyed in discourse by means of tenses, temporal adverbials, or pragmatic inference, is a combination of A- and B-series resources. In addition to, say, $t < t'$ we have $t = n$ for representing *now*, which is a psychological and egocentric concept through and through. For example, sentence (13) acquires in DRT the representation structure (DRS) as in Fig. 1.2. Condition $e \subseteq t$ stands for temporal inclusion of the event e in time t.

(13)   Mary went to London on Monday.

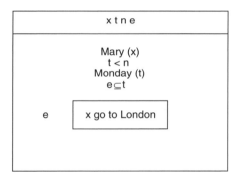

FIGURE 1.2 DRS for example (13)

I discuss DRSs in Section 4.2 while introducing my analysis in terms of merger representations of Default Semantics which are loosely modelled on the representations of DRT. For the current preliminary philosophical discussion all that matters is the fact that the past is represented in terms of temporal precedence relation $t < n$ as well as the egocentric concept of *now* (n). Without this anchoring, the past time of the event and the corresponding past tense of the sentence would not be adequately represented.

    McTaggart's paradox relies strongly on the argument that no event can be at the same time past, present, and future, while past, present, and future are more fundamental than earlier-than/later-than relations because they have to be presupposed in order to account for change. To repeat, the qualification 'at the same time' cannot be removed because removing it would presuppose time which is the *explanandum*, and hence would create circularity.[26] As a

---

[26] But see also Prior's (1967: 6) defence of the A series, also discussed in Øhlstrøm and Hasle (1995: 255).

result, for McTaggart, time is unreal. We can see now that this conclusion is too strong: it is not time that is unreal but merely the flow of time. Once we remove change as the necessary characteristic of time, the compatibility of A and B series and consequently A and B resources for semantics is vindicated.

1.4 Time and the observer: Back to the future?

We can now move to the question of the relative positions of the subject of the experience and the arrow of time. We concluded that psychological time is a flow, represented by an arrow of time. But here we encounter cross-cultural differences with respect to the positioning of the experiencer vis-à-vis this time arrow. In English, like in most other Indo-European languages, the future is predominantly conceptualized as lying *in front of* the observer; we anticipate and predict what 'lies ahead'. The past is *behind* the observer; we are advised not to 'look back' but instead 'move forward' with our plans and ambitions. But for the Maori, for example, the past seems to be conceptualized as lying in front: *ngārā mua* means in Maori 'the days in front' and is used to refer to the past. *Mua* means 'front', but also 'before', 'in advance of', 'formerly', or 'first'. On the other hand, *kei muri* means 'behind' and is used for the future. *Muri* means 'behind', 'the rear', 'the hind part', but also 'the sequel', 'the time to come', 'the future' (see Thornton 1987: 70). Similarly, it has been reported that in Aymara, a language of the Andean region of Peru, Chile, and Bolivia, past states of affairs are talked about in such a way that it is evident that the past is conceptualized as being in front of the experiencing agent. The word for 'past' derives from the lexical item *mayra*, meaning 'eye', 'sight', and 'front'. Analogously, the future seems to lie behind: the word for the future is *q'ipa*, meaning 'back' and 'behind'. Both enter into a phrase with the word *pacha*, 'time'. Evidence from gestures made by Aymara speakers supports this thesis of the conceptualization of the past as lying in front and future as lying behind: the further into the past, the further in front the speaker points. These gestures also correlate with the evidential system in Aymara in that events close to the moment of speaking are more likely to have been witnessed and the speaker can report them with higher probability.[27] So, time is linear and may flow in the same direction as that conceptualized by speakers of English, but the relative position of the time arrow and the observer are different. Moreover, Hausa, a West African language, conceptualizes the sequence of events in a way which could be interpreted as consistent with the future being at the back of the observer. For example, in Hausa,

---

[27] See Evans (2003: 194–5) for the example and further references.

Tuesday is 'before', or 'in front of' (*gaba*) Monday and analogously Monday is 'after', 'in back of' (*baya*) Tuesday. On a time arrow, Monday is indeed located 'after' Tuesday in that Monday passes from the future to the present and from the present to the past sooner than Tuesday does: it follows Tuesday in the graphic, and conceptual, representation. But should the observer face the same direction as the arrow of time, this conceptualization would be difficult to explain.[28] Also, in some ancient Indo-European languages, the concepts 'in the future' and 'behind' seem to have been referred to by the same lexical item. In Ancient Greek, the stem *opi-* meant 'behind', 'at the back', but also 'afterwards' and 'in the future' (see Davies 1983: 302). When one looks even further into Myceanean, there was a preposition *opi*, meaning 'back', 'behind', 'afterwards', 'secondarily', 'additionally' which developed into *epi* in Ancient Greek.[29] The fact that the concepts of being at the back, behind, and the concepts of futurity or following in time are lexicalized as one unit constitutes strong grounds for stipulating that the future was conceptualized in these cultures as lying behind the speaker, where the speaker faces the better known or experienced past. The argument, however, is not conclusive. Be that as it may, this fact of the variation in the orientation as regards the relative position of the observer and the future may open up a question of relativity or universality of the conceptualization of internal time. However, it will leave its A-theoretic foundations (and the flux) intact: in the concept of time, time moves and all that differs is the way languages depict the relation between internal time and the agents who live *in* this time. On one interpretation, all that this difference shows is that for some cultures the past becomes marked in their lexicon as the salient orientation, while in others it is the future. On this reading there are yet no grounds for opening up the question of linguistic relativity. Analogously, the fact that some Australian aboriginal languages have several words for sand while English has one is not yet sufficient ground for proposing different conceptualizations. On this reading of our example, the orientation of the experiencer is the only element that is here culture-specific. On the other hand, it would be difficult not to notice a parallelism with the conceptualization of space. Space can be thought of in terms of absolute points of reference (such as north, south, west, and east), relative to the speaker (left, right) or intrinsic between two objects (*x* facing *y*), as is discussed at length in Levinson 2003,

[28] For a different explanation called an *in-tandem alignment* of the observer and the events see Evans (2003: 232–3) and further references there.

[29] Davies's (1983) argument concerns the classification of Myceanean prepositions *opi* and *epi* as one or two units on historical and semantic grounds. However, for our present argument, we are only interested in the fact that Myceanean *opi*, as well as Greek *opi-* stem and *epi* preposition, all combined the concept of futurity and the concept of being at the back or behind.

Levinson *et al.* 2002, 2003, or Pederson *et al.* 1998. If we pursue this analogy, then it seems that facing the past is a way of representing time in a relative perspective: the experiencer faces what is already experienced by him/her, what has already 'arrived' on the time line. In English, on the other hand, the experiencer is lexicalizing and conceptualizing time in absolute terms of the flow – *nota bene*, 'absolute' in terms of the experiential concepts of the A-theory, rather than 'absolute' in terms of the physical dimension of motionless (flow-less) real time. The direction of the experiencer is the same as the direction of the time flow. If this interpretation is correct and if the frames of reference indeed differ in this way, the question of linguistic relativity is much more justified. However, even on this interpretation the question of relativity only arises indirectly. This is so for the following reason. On this interpretation, we seem compelled to examine whether there is a correlation, as far as the frame of reference is concerned, between the way Maori speakers think about time in performing non-linguistic tasks and the way in which they speak about time. This is the strategy successfully used in Pederson *et al.* 1998 with respect to the conceptualization of space. But although they found such a correlation in their experiments, they did not jump to the conclusion of linguistic relativity. The correct methodological move is to assume that, once this correlation is found, linguistic relativity becomes merely a possibility rather than a corroborated fact – only a possibility because there is a long way from demonstrating a correlation to demonstrating causation. A correlation between the way we speak and the way we think does not yet warrant a move to the Sapir-Whorf hypothesis that the language we speak determines or affects the way we think and perceive reality.[30]

This parallelism with spatial frames of reference also seems to constitute an indirect form of support for the idea defended here that time is real and is an element of space-time, while the flow of time is psychological. There is a time dimension, just as there are dimensions of space in space-time, and in addition to this time dimension we have the experience of flow: either through the concept of absolute flow, or through the concept of relative flow as in Maori.

1.5　Concluding statement

Is time a series of positions on a line or is it a flow? Is it like a ski lift or like a washing line? Is time like space, or is it a departure from the certainty of *now*, i.e. a modal notion? There are no simple yes/no answers here. Nevertheless,

---

[30]　See also Gumperz and Levinson 1996, esp. Part I.

there are some preliminary conclusions that we have reached in this chapter. These conclusions are increasingly more frequently accepted by those who analyse time, be it from the physics, philosophy, or linguistic semantic perspective, and deserve to be stated succinctly. Hence, here is my proposal of a list of introductory statements for theorizing about time in any type of scientific enterprise and on any level of formality and sophistication:

  I. There is real (metaphysical) time which is a feature of the universe and there is internal (psychological, experiential) time which constitutes our consciousness of time.
 II. Both B-series and A-series resources are necessary: B series pertains to space-time (real time) and A series together with B series to psychological time (the concept of time).
III. Real time does not flow; the flow of time belongs to human experience (internal consciousness of time).

From now on I will focus on the concept of time and the semantic representation of time. This conclusion provides a suitable starting point for posing the main question of this book: *Is the concept of time a primitive concept and a primitive semantic notion?* We will reach the negative answer to this question in the process of comparing time with modality in Chapter 2, ending up with analysing time in terms of modal notions. The theses to be defended in the remaining chapters are:

 IV. The flow is best explained as detachment from certainty, and hence as modality.
  V. There is supervenience of the psychological on the real, explained in terms of degrees of modality.
 VI. For the purpose of semantic representation of time, duration is best conceived of as a concept that belongs to mental representations rather than to real time.

2

Time as modality

It has been pointed out that theories of time explain time either in terms of modality, as in Priorean logic, or in terms of space, where the moment or interval in time is understood analogously to a point or area in space (see Meyer 2002). We established in Chapter 1 that there is no real need to make such a choice: both the location and the detachment from the certainty of *now* are valid and important, albeit on different levels of analysis (physical world and human experience respectively), and are both used in current truth-conditional semantic theories. In this chapter, and in the remainder of this essay, I focus on the psychological time and present arguments in favour of the view that *humans conceptualize time in terms of certainty and possibility*. In other words, the concept of time supervenes on a more basic concept of modality. The way in which we represent time in semantic theory will then have to directly reflect our conclusion on how humans represent time in thought: semantic representation will follow mental representation, as is the case in all explanatorily adequate theories of meaning, including those where the degree of formalization would seemingly justify sacrificing psychological reality.[1]

Conceptualizing time has a long history and in many distinguished philosophers' conception time has had strong affinities with modality. I shall begin by giving a few examples, without attempting a presentation of a history or even all main landmarks,[2] in order to place my arguments for time as modality in a wider perspective. Since antiquity there have been two dominant views on time: time as a flowing river and time as a line on which states of

---

[1] To give some examples, [1] DRT sees formalization as subordinate to the main goal of providing mental representations of discourse (see Hamm *et al.* 2006). Cf.:

DRT's claim that there are features of natural language the analysis of which requires a distinct level of discourse representation is consonant with a cognitive perspective on the nature of natural language meaning: Meaning in natural language manifests itself as the semantic competence of the language user... (Hamm *et al.* 2006: 5–6)

[2] Jackendoff (2002; Culicover and Jackendoff 2005) claims that building a *conceptual* semantics is a superordinate objective and it only makes use of, rather than being a slave to, formal methods.

[2] See Øhrstrøm and Hasle 1995 for a detailed history of temporal logic in a wider background of the philosophy of time.

affairs are stationary points.[3] Zeno of Elea and Parmenides (fifth century BC) represent the static view of time according to which any appearance of temporal change is an illusion. Just as there is no absolute *now*, so there is no real change. Zeno's famous paradoxes are aimed at demonstrating that change is impossible. For example, in the 'Achilles' paradox, a fast runner can never overtake a slow runner who had been given a head start because he has to reach the point of the slow runner's start, then the point the slow runner had reached by the time the fast runner had reached the start, and so on, with all consecutive stretches. In the 'arrow' paradox, Zeno asks about a flying arrow whether in any smallest, indivisible instant of its flight the arrow is stationary or in motion. On one hand, it cannot move in an instant, and, on the other, if it is stationary, then it can never move. Aristotle (384–22 BC), like Heraclitus (fifth century BC) before him, had a dynamic concept of time, but with clear affinities with modality with respect to the future. In *De Interpretatione*, he lays the foundations for regarding propositions about the present and the past as true or false, and the future as modality or *potentiality* (see Aristotle 1928: 19a). He considers the by now famous example 'There will be a sea battle tomorrow' about which he observes that we are not in a position to know the truth value: the truth value depends on the time that the statement concerns. Since all statements must be either true or false, the future is understood as an expression of potentiality.

Diodorus Cronus (*c.*340–280 BC) was a philosopher and logician famous for inventing paradoxes, one of which was the Master Argument. According to this paradox, propositions [P1]–[P3] cannot all be true:

[P1]   Every proposition true about the past is necessary.
[P2]   An impossible proposition cannot follow from/after a possible one.
[P3]   There is a proposition which is possible, but which neither is nor will be true.

(adapted from Øhrstrøm and Hasle 1995: 15–16).[4] It is evident that time is thought of in the context of determinism and probability, and hence is clearly tied up with modality. He discusses time in terms of what is possible and necessary. When we assume that time is linear, this way of thinking leads directly to determinism about states of affairs. When we assume that time is a structure that branches out from *now* into the different possible 'futures', then the set [P1]–[P3] becomes more plausible: what is possible need not ever become true.

---

[3] This is the dichotomy reflected in the current discussions in McTaggart's A- and B-theories discussed in Section 1.3.

[4] Many thanks to Jiranthara Srioutai for pointing out the paradox by Diodorus Cronus to me.

In the Middle Ages discussions about time largely adopted the Aristotelian idea that the truth of a proposition is time-dependent. Time was discussed with reference to truth and the time of evaluation, for example in the writings of Jean Buridan (*c*.1300–*c*.1360) and Walter Burleigh (*c*.1275–*c*.1344). They were both concerned with the issue of time duration, unlike William of Ockham (*c*.1285–1347) who focused on time as the moving object. The emphasis on *now* for the purpose of truth-evaluation as well as discussions on the conventional assignment of duration to *now* also testify to the interests in certainty and modality. It has to be remembered that modality itself was in the very focus of attention of medieval logicians: we owe the contemporary research on modalities *de dicto* and *de re* to medieval disputes on necessity and substitutivity of statements *salva veritate*.[5] For Thomas Aquinas (1225–74), the relations of later-than/earlier-than and simultaneity do not require the presupposition of time; just as God is timeless, so 'time' itself does not require the past–present–future distinctions. This is a clear defence of what was discussed in Section 1.3 as McTaggart's B-theory of time and as phenomenological time consciousness: the flow of time is only present when humans conceptualize states of affairs. As we can see in the discussion in the remainder of this essay, even a clear-cut B-theory of time is compatible with, and supports, the concept of time as modality. Next, God's knowledge is timeless and certain; human knowledge is 'contaminated' by the egocentric perspective and detached from the ideal. Ockham, and, a few centuries later, Gottfried Wilhelm Leibniz (1646–1716) contributed discussions of human freedom which shed a great deal of light on the understanding of the future as conditional on human decisions rather than divinely predetermined. It is to Leibniz that we owe the central idea of contemporary formal semantics, that of possible worlds.

Taking a big leap, we arrive at the periods in philosophy when the internal representation of time came to the forefront. Kantian internal time, Schopenhauer, and the phenomenologists, notably Husserl and subsequently Heidegger, were discussed in more depth in Section 1.2. In Section 1.3, I also discussed some 19th – and 20th – century attempts to develop temporal logic, and in particular that of Arthur Prior. Charles Peirce considered it necessary to introduce time to logic explicitly – the task subsequently performed by Arthur Prior. Aristotle's views on the future were then taken up by Prior and another eminent logician, Jan Łukasiewicz: is the statement 'There will be a sea battle tomorrow' true now because the sea battle is possible, as Prior's

---

[5] See Jaszczolt 1999, 2000, 2002 Chapter 7.2, and 2006a for an introduction to modalites *de re* and *de dicto* and the semantic problem of truth-preserving substitutivity.

interpretation of Aristotle has it, or is it undetermined, as Łukasiewicz's version, in which he introduces the third truth value, claims?[6] Next, from 1958 and Saul Kripke's discussion with Prior there begins the development of logic with branching time. From that period onwards, temporal logic has come even closer to modal logic than ever before: as time passes, the number of possibilities is diminished. We have a clear link between the future and the lack of certainty, and, on some accounts, also the past and the certainty.[7]

As is evident from this set of examples spanning twenty-five centuries, the concepts of possibility, necessity, past, and future have been intimately connected. To understand the future is to develop a stance on the issue of determinism. To understand the past is to take a stance on what makes it a past state of affairs: the present moment or something that happened before *now*. Moreover, as we observed in Section 1.2, the concepts of duration and time flow are often conceived of as being dependent on the way humans understand causal relations among events and states. We seem to have a plethora of concepts: possibility, necessity, causation, experience, anticipation, retention, memory, which are all good candidates for the status of an *explanans* for the concept of time.

We established in Chapter 1 the crucial importance of experience, anticipation, retention, and memory in the concept of time. Now we can assume the concept of time defined with the help of these notions and build on these foundations while trying to answer the next question, which is the main question of this essay: is time a primitive concept or do humans conceptualize time in terms of something else more basic? To repeat, our main hypothesis for this investigation is that *possibility and certainty are such basic concepts out of which internal time is constructed*. In Section 2.1 I focus on the way time is expressed in natural language and hence on the *semantic* category of temporality, and present a selection of arguments that support the view that (i) temporality and modality are semantically akin, as well as more controversial views that (ii) temporality can be conceptually derived from modality, or even that (iii) temporality *is* modality. Supervenience of time on modality may as a result turn out to be replaced by identity. In the following sections devoted specifically to the concepts of the future, the present and the past (Sections 2.2–2.4), the discussion will be taken one step further. Just as the *semantic category of temporality* is not basic and can be traced back, both diachronically and synchronically (i.e. with respect to semantic properties) to the category of modality, so the *conceptual category of time* can be shown to be none other but a conceptual category of modal detachment. I provide

---

6 See Øhrstrøm and Hasle (1995: 151–2) for a discussion.
7 See, for example, Thomason 2002 on historical necessity and possibility.

further evidence from the semantics of expressions with future, present, and past reference in Section 2.5 and use it as a springboard for semantic representations of utterances with future-, present-, and past-time reference. The steps in this reasoning are as follows. We agreed in Chapter 1 that there is real time, which is of the B-theory type, which does not flow and respects the laws of the two theories of relativity. On the other hand, there is also psychological time, a concept of the A-theory type, that flows and reveals itself in the form of the past, present, and future. Next, in Section 2.1, I look at the *semantic* category of time, accepting the premise that it will provide a window on the *psychological* time, and ask the question as to whether this flow of time is the primitive concept or rather is supervenient on some more basic concept. I put together a collection of arguments in support of the semantic category of temporality that supervenes on the concept of modal detachment. From supervenience I move to entertaining the possibility of identity of time and modality on the level of semantic analysis. Having established that there are strong foundations both for (ii) and for (iii), and adding the premise that semantic temporality is a window on the conceptualization of time (i.e. the internal time), we can go further into separate investigations as to whether the internal future, present, and past also mean, on the most fundamental conceptual level, a detachment from certainty. This is pursued in Sections 2.2–2.4.

For the purpose of the argument I make use of the thesis introduced in Section 1.2 that time is conceptualized as degrees of commitment founded on the (often subconscious) assessment of certainty of states of affairs, and hence on perception of the *now*, memory of the past, and anticipation of memory of the future. But before we proceed, a brief recourse to psychology is necessary. We have to address the question: what is this *memory* that figures in the definition? Contemporary neuroscience tells us that memory consists of a pattern of connections formed between the nerve cells (neurons) that is stored in the brain.[8] A point of connection is called a synapse. The mechanism is this: a neuron releases a chemical neurotransmitter as a signal to another neuron and forms a synaptic connection. Synapses can be created, strengthened, or weakened when the person thinks a thought or remembers something. The number of such connecting neurons is in the range of a hundred billion and each neuron is capable of making between 5,000 to 10,000 such connections. Sensory information can be received by the cortex and held in short-term memory for fractions of a second, or in working memory where it is available

---

[8] See, for example, Guttenplan 1994 and Foer 2007 for excellent introductions to memory and memory loss. For a philosophical discussion of the content of memory see Fernández 2008.

for retrieval. Next, registered facts, after a few seconds, become encoded in the areas of the medial temporal lobe such as hippocampus and information 'flows' from short-term to long-term memory and is stored in the cortex. It can then normally be retrieved as working memory when it is required. Accounts of forgetting and especially serious clinical cases of memory loss tell us that 'our memories make us who we are' (Foer 2007: 36): not only does memory allow us to function in society, but it is also necessary in performing everyday solitary tasks. Patients who don't remember they had breakfast a few minutes before prepare and eat it again. Patients who can't remember that they began a simple task a few seconds before are not in a position to complete it. In this sense, memory is not only our past and future but also the *now* in the sense of current states and events, not unlike the specious present discussed in Chapter 1. Therefore, the claim that the concept of time, or internal time, is closely associated with memory does not require particular defence. The idea I am defending in this essay, that internal time is a modal, epistemic commitment, makes this association with memory into a definitional commitment: it builds memory into the very concept of time.

2.1 Certainty and degrees of commitment

The term 'modality' corresponds to a variety of interrelated concepts. For the present purpose it is useful to understand it in a way it is frequently understood in semantic analyses, as *qualifications of states of affairs*.[9] Following van der Auwera and Plungian (1998: 80), I shall use the term 'modality' as a concept comprising possibility and necessity where possibility and necessity are paradigmatic variants. Out of these variants, they construct four semantic domains:[10]

(i) participant-internal modality, with the paradigmatic variants (i.a) participant's ability and (i.b) participant's internal need, as in (1) and (2) respectively.

(1)   Tom can move his ears up and down.
(2)   Tom needs to drink five cups of coffee a day to be able to concentrate on his work.

(ii) participant-external modality, with the possibility and necessity paradigmatic variants as in (3) and (4):

---

[9] See Nuyts 2006 for an informative overview.
[10] See also de Haan 2006 on typological approaches to modality.

(3)   You can find the train timetable on the internet.

(4)   In order to find out the train timetable, you have to check the GWR website.

Participant-external modality also subsumes (iii) deontic modality, i.e. permissions and obligations as in (5) and (6):

(5)   You may speak now.

(6)   You must be silent during the performance.

Finally, (iv) epistemic modality refers to the speaker's judgement of a degree of certainty with which the proposition expressed is to be taken. In (7), the degree of probability is low (some possibility), while in (8) it is high (virtual certainty).

(7)   Tom may have arrived in London by now.

(8)   Tom must have arrived in London by now.

Only category (iv) concerns the entire proposition: it presents the state of affairs as more or less probable. And it is this category of epistemic modality that we shall use in representing time. Within the category of epistemic modality, just as modal expressions *may, can, might,* or *could* express a certain degree of detachment from the state of affairs expressed in the proposition, so the indicators of temporality in the form of the past or future markers express a certain degree of detachment from the certainty of *now*. And, just as modal expressions *must* or *have to* express a high degree of probability or even certainty on behalf of the speaker, so the indicators of present time express a high degree of probability that the state of affairs is in reality just as it is described in the speaker's sentence. In Chapter 4, linguistic expressions pertaining to the future, present, and the past will be further classified with respect to the degree of possibility within each of these three categories.

A brief disclaimer is due at this point. Some accounts make a distinction between *epistemic* and *metaphysical* modality. Epistemic possibility pertains to situations where the issue is settled but the speaker cannot express it with certainty.[11] Metaphysical possibility, on the other hand, describes future situations where the state of affairs is not settled. For example, (9) is ambiguous between these two types of modality, as the continuations in (9a) and (9b) indicate.

(9)   There may be a Halloween party on Friday.

(9a)   I have to check in my diary.

(9b)   We haven't decided yet whether to organize one this year.

---

[11] See, for example, Condoravdi (2002: 80).

For the purpose of this analysis we will not differentiate between the categories of epistemic and metaphysical modality. Since the subject of the analysis is internal, psychological time, it is the internal, psychological modality we want to pursue as a possible basis for supervenience. If the metaphysics is sometimes the culprit of epistemic uncertainty, then so be it: there is no harm in subsuming it, for our purpose, under the epistemological notion and epistemic modality. The difference between the epistemic and the metaphysical only demonstrates that the thesis of the correlation between real, ontological and psychological, internal time is further supported by, and arguably reflected in, the relation between these two types of modality. By the same token, for our argument, *logical* dependence or *logical* supervenience will suffice. But it has to be borne in mind that logical dependence of the concept of time on the concept of modality is directly associated with the logical supervenience of real time on probabilities and possibilities of events. And the latter may turn out to be of a stronger form, that of *metaphysical* supervenience. Further, just as the concept of time will next be identified with the concept of modality, so real time may be identified with possibilities of states and events. In short, the notion of supervenience may fall out as not sufficiently radical, even in the metaphysical *strong* sense (pertaining to all possible words) in the sense of Kim (e.g. 1987). To repeat, the exact nature of this dependency will not concern us here. The ultimate objective is to build semantic representations of temporality and to demonstrate that for doing this modal concepts will suffice.

The remainder of this essay is devoted to presenting various arguments in support of this view of the supervenience of the internal concept of time on the concept of perceived or assessed probability. In this section, we focus on the concepts that will facilitate discussing it. In addition to epistemic modality, we need here the concept of evidentiality. Evidentiality is a highly contentious category and therefore it is necessary to take a stance and spell out precisely what we will mean by it. We follow van der Auwera and Plungian (1998: 85) who define it as follows:

Evidentiality concerns the indication of the source or kind of evidence speakers have for their statements. The evidence is marked as, e.g., direct or non-direct, first-hand or second-hand, based on visual or auditory evidence, on hearsay or on reasoning.

This is a rather generous definition, according to which evidentiality and modality clearly overlap. Epistemic necessity in example (8) is at the same time an example of the so-called inferential evidentiality. The judgement in (8) contains an expression of conviction, virtual certainty, at the same time pertaining to the 'kind of evidence' that the speaker has for this judgement: this kind of evidence is inference from other judgements (van der Auwera and

Plungian 1998: 86). *A fortiori*, we shall not follow those accounts on which modality and evidentiality are strictly dissociated.[12] For example, we shall not follow the view that the source of information must be grammaticalized as the core meaning, as in Aikhenvald's definition according to which evidentiality means 'the grammatical means of expressing information source' (Aikhenvald 2004: xi) and '[t]o be considered as an evidential, a morpheme has to have "source of information" as its core meaning; that is, the unmarked, or default interpretation.' (*ibid.*: 3). She explicitly says that on her definition, '[e]videntiality is a category in its own right, and not a subcategory of any modality' (p. 7). We find that the more general definition of van der Auwera and Plungian offers a concept that is more adequate from the functional point of view in that the source of information and the degree of certainty are not kept separate but are shown to interact: inference from other judgements is a source of information and at the same time produces a certain degree of probability with which the speaker formulates and expresses his or her judgement. When cognitive, semantic, and pragmatic considerations are at stake, this construal is superior by far.[13] Alternatively, we could follow Palmer's (1986) construal of evidentiality as a subcategory of epistemic modality or his (2001: 8) classification of epistemic modality and evidentiality as subcategories of the so-called *propositional modality*, where the latter is contrasted with *event modality*. While propositional modality refers to speaker's judgement concerning the proposition, event modality refers to speaker's attitude towards a possible future event. Epistemic modality is then subdivided into *speculative* ('John may be in London now'), *deductive* ('John must be in London now', asserted on the basis of evidence), and *assumptive* ('John will be in London now', asserted on the basis of knowledge from experience), with the proviso that not all of these distinctions are made in all languages.[14] Similarly, evidential systems are more or less elaborate in different languages.

All in all, what matters most for the present discussion is that modality is a semantic and conceptual category broadly understood as detachment, qualification, of the state of affairs. Our adopted definition allows for evidentiality and modality to overlap as this construal seems to better reflect the fact that evidence may come from other accepted judgements: evidentiality and epistemic detachment are thus closely intertwined.

---

[12] For references see van der Auwera and Plungian (1998: 85). Also, McCready and Ogata (2007) clearly demonstrate that in Japanese there are expressions indicating the source of evidence which should be classified as epistemic modals.

[13] According to Nuyts (2006: 19) evidentiality is on a higher level of abstraction as a semantic category than epistemic modality.

[14] See Palmer (2001: 24–5).

Historical considerations testify to the close link between modality and time. In many languages, possibility markers have future meaning. For example, according to van der Auwera and Plungian (1998: 94, after Bybee *et al.* 1994), one of the paths of the historical development of futurity is from participant-external possibility, which in turn developed from participant-internal possibility and ultimately from expressions 'be strong', 'know', 'arrive at', 'finish', and 'suffice'. Another path is that from participant-external necessity. Epistemic necessity, in turn, may develop from a future, as in (10), where the future may develop from the expressions of desire and movement towards a goal.

(10)   (*doorbell*) That will be my taxi.

As they say (*ibid.*: 111), there is evidence for a remodalization cycle in the history of the future in that participant-external necessity gave rise to the (postmodal) future, which in turn functioned as a (premodal) basis for epistemic necessity. Bybee *et al.* (1994) investigate a large sample of languages and find out interesting contrasts in the domain of the future that are shared by various subsets of them. For example, some languages make a distinction into *immediate future* and *simple future*, where the latter can contain the meaning of epistemic possibility, as for example in Basque, Cantonese, or Tok Pisin. Some languages in addition make a grammatical distinction between *future certainty* and *future possibility* and some have a grammatically marked *expected (prearranged) future* (Bybee *et al.* 1994: 248–9). They discuss several different paths of historical development of the grammatical markers of the future, such as desire>willingness>intention>prediction; possession> obligation/predestination>intention>future; or attempt>intention>future; and also mental/physical ability>ability>root possibility>intention>future, with the alternative path from root possibility to epistemic possibility; and finally frequently observed paths from movement verbs such as 'come' and 'go' (*ibid.*: 267).

Palmer (1979: 5–6) observes that in most Indo-European languages, future tenses originated from expressions of non-factivity such as the subjunctive or expressions of intention and desire.[15] The English *will* testifies to this path of development:[16] the epistemic *will*, meaning 'what is reasonable to expect', co-exists with the deontic *will* (and *shall*) – an expression of obligation – as well as the *will* of volition and habitual *will*, as exemplified in (11)–(14). Although there are no clear-cut boundaries between these meanings, the salient, main meaning can be discerned.

---

[15] See also Palmer 1979, Chapter 7 and Lyons (1977: 809–23).

[16] Bybee *et al.* (1994: 24) also point out that 'the grammatical development of *will* in English spans the entire documented period of approximately one thousand years'.

(11)   There will be a Halloween party tomorrow.   (epistemic *will*)
(12)   You will go to her and apologize.   (deontic *will*)
(13)   I will look after the puppy.   (*will* of volition)
(14)   He will always come five minutes late just to annoy the teacher.
                                                          (habitual *will*)

Similarly, Fleischman (1982) demonstrates in the example of Romance languages that the future is closely related to *irrealis* or nonfactive modality and to deontic modality. She calls the historical development a bidirectional semantic shift: modal forms change to tense forms, and these in turn change into modals.[17] Furthermore, as Traugott (2006: 127) observes, there is a category of expressions called *semi-modals*, such as *need to, want to*, which testify to the plausibility of the theory that one can construe a cline of degrees of modality. A complete map[18] of such pre- and post-modal expressions of futurity is not our aim; suffice it to say that such historical interrelations are strong, frequent, and well documented in many languages.

Next, the category of English modals has been carefully scrutinized in semantics in order to check their compositional properties, and in particular to answer the question as to whether modals contribute directly to the temporal interpretation of the sentence or whether there is an implicit tense involved. One position, attributed to Hornstein (1990), is that temporality is externally assigned to modals which have otherwise the same meaning when applied to statements about the present and the past. The alternative view, defended among others by Condoravdi (2002), states that modals do not have tense in their scope. For example, (15) has the logical representation as in (15a) rather than (15b) because the backshifting is achieved by the perfect alone, without the help of tense:

(15)   He may have been sick.
(15a)   MAY (PERF (he be sick))
*(15b)   MAY (PAST (he be sick))

Similarly, the existence of the future orientation of a modal depends on the type of eventuality (state or event, see Section 3.2) that the sentence concerns. As she points out, 'modals for the present have a future orientation optionally with stative predicates and obligatorily with eventive predicates' (Condoravdi

---

[17] See also Traugott, e.g. 2006, for the examples of 'demodalization' (such as the English demodalized verb *dare*) which testify in favour of bidirectional semantic change.

[18] See van der Auwera and Plungian 1998 for the method of *semantic maps*: a map is a geometric representation of relations between meanings, that is it is a *semantic space* that contains grammars and lexicons of various languages, showing their interrelations, both synchronic and diachronic, in the form of a typological study.

2002: 69). For example, (16) may refer to the present or the future, while (17) is univocally future (*nota bene*, the unasterisked 'now' would also have to refer to the future).

(16)   John may be sick (now/tomorrow).
(17)   John may go to the concert (*now/tomorrow).

On this account, the time of evaluation of the statement in the scope of the modal is facilitated by the modal and the situation type, without a tense element being present.[19] This is yet another argument in support of modality as the basis for supervenience of temporality.

There is also a direct semantic parallelism between temporal and modal statements which reflects their conceptual affinity. In Section 1.3 I discussed Priorean tense logic and his sentential operators P and F that turn a sentence about the present into a sentence about the past or future. Analogously, modal sentences are founded on a simple, non-modal matrix by adding the indicators of lesser certainty:

…we have to see modal sentences as *constructed from* simple sentences by the application of modal operators to them. In this way we can analyse the ability to use and understand modal sentences as resting on two distinct abilities: the (modally innocent) ability to use and understand simple sentences; and the (modally sophisticated) ability to imagine other possible worlds and to contrast the actual world with them. (Recanati 2007a: 68)

Similarly, sentences about the past and the future are constructed from sentences about the present and to understand them we have to think of the world as it was or will be – or alternatively of other possible worlds with a *now*, the moment that is present to the thinking subject, which is different from our *now*. Recanati points out that the present tense is unlike the past and the future in that it is more fundamental, 'temporally neutral': one need not have a concept of the past or the future in order to use a present-tense sentence or have a present-time thought. There is of course an alternative way of representing temporality by postulating argument places for time instead of sentential operators P and F.[20] But, as Recanati (2007a: 69) observes, in the latter case adjectives would no longer denote properties and would have to denote relations between the objects and times: *the lemon* is yellow *at time t*. This construal, as had been pointed out by many before him, contains the

---

[19] This influence of situation type is also discussed in Gennari 2003, esp. pp. 34–46.
[20] See, for example, Enç 1987 on tenses as referential expressions denoting intervals and providing a temporal argument for the verb, and Hornstein 1990 on a similar view of tenses as adverbs.

position for time which is rather superfluous from the common-sense point of view, as well as from the point of view of methodological economy. Be that as it may, what matters for our purpose is that just as Prior's temporal operators select possible worlds that pertain to the past or the future, so modals are quantifiers over possible worlds.

Partial arguments in support of the supervenience of the concept of time on the concept of degrees of probability are ample. Moens and Steedman (1988) and Steedman (1997) contend that temporality is supervenient on the concepts of perspective and contingency and that tense and aspect systems are founded on the same conceptual primitives as evidentiality which, by our definition, is a concept overlapping with that of epistemic modality. Slightly more remote from our thesis is that of van Lambalgen and Hamm (2005) who argue that the past, the present, and the future are linked by means of the imposition of goals, planning, and causation. They propose that 'the *linguistic* coding of time is (. . .) driven by the future-oriented nature of our cognitive makeup' (p. 13). Temporality supervenes on what is intended, desired as *present*, as well as on the cause-and-effect relation between events and states that are arranged on the line with relations such as earlier-than, later-than, or overlap. Finally, Nuyts (2006: 19) proposes that modality occupies a higher place than time in the hierarchy of semantic categories, which means that it is of a higher level of abstraction.

It is by no means a new idea that time and modality are interconnected. But it is much less often claimed, and much more controversial, that time *is* modality. The positions I sketched in this section are the first step in the construal of time as modality when time is internal time – a concept we arrived at in Chapter 1. Leaving aside the medieval disputes, we can find plenty of other arguments in support of this view. In this section I briefly mention two views according to which time and modality *are one conceptual category*, before moving to my own proposal developed in Chapters 3 and 4.

Peter Ludlow (1999) argues that the future is predictability or potentiality, 'disposition of the world', and hence is to be regarded as a modal concept. He analyses the future-tense morphemes in Spanish as consisting of an *irrealis* marker *ar* and a 'future' ending. For example, *hablaré*, 'I will speak', is analysed not as *habl + aré*, but instead *habl + ar + é*. Moreover, as he points out, in Italian, to express futurity, one standardly uses a present tense form (e.g. *vado*, 'I go') reserving the future tense form (*andrò*, 'I will go') for situations of lesser probability or uncertainty. Similarly, in English, futurity can be expressed with any of the forms listed as (18)–(21), where the present-tense forms in (18) and (19) express higher certainty.[21]

---

[21] For an extensive discussion of futurity as modality see Jaszczolt 2005, Chapter 6 and Jaszczolt 2006a.

(18)   Peter goes to London tomorrow morning.
(19)   Peter is going to London tomorrow morning.
(20)   Peter is going to go to London tomorrow morning.
(21)   Peter will go to London tomorrow morning.

I discuss this gradation of modality in Section 2.2 but for now it has to be emphasized that such scales pertaining to degrees of speaker's commitment to the proposition and the degrees of certainty with which the speaker issues a judgement testify to a very intimate connection between time and modality. And since these scales are scales of modality, modality is the basis for temporal supervenience in the case of expressions of the future.

In spite of the rather unquestionable unreal character of the future, not all languages express it as equally 'unreal'. As de Haan (2006: 41–2) points out, a Native American language Caddo treats the future as a *realis* category. The future morpheme *-ʔaʔ* is combined with the *realis* prefix *ci-* as in (22):

(22)   cííbáw-ʔaʔ
       ci   yi   bahw   ʔaʔ
       Realis *1Sg* see   *Fut*
       'I will look at it.'   (adapted from de Haan 2006: 41)

In a Californian language Central Pomo, on the other hand, the future can be accompanied either by *realis* or by *irrealis*, depending on the speaker's judgement concerning the degree of probability of the described event (see *ibid.*: 42). This freedom of combination with *realis* or *irrealis* constitutes a strong argument in favour of the underlying modal character of the future: states of affairs are described as more, or less, certain. This explanation is further supported by the fact that there are languages in which there is a choice between different future morphemes to express different degrees of certainty (see *ibid.*: 50 for examples). The pairing with the *realis* category in Caddo, on the other hand, is more difficult to explain without a more detailed analysis of the devices available in that language. It may, for example, signal that in different languages there is a different degree of reliance on the epistemology of time. When the degree is high, the internal, psychological time and the *irrealis* prevails; when it is low, the ontology of time and the B series surface out as *realis*. The fact that generally in languages of the world the future pairs with modality (see van der Auwera and Plungian 1998) appears to testify to the strong cognitive reasons for the predominance of the internal time.

The past is governed by the same principle of supervenience (if not more) on modality. Although it is a little more difficult to see because, unlike the uncertain future, the past may seem to consist of what 'actually happened' and is subject to judgements of truth or falsity, the supervenience is there nevertheless. Ludlow (1999: 160) points out that 'in most non-Indo-European languages the so-called past is generally just some form of aspectual marker'. Similarly, in English the past-tense morpheme -*ed* is the leftover from a perfect aspectual marker. Next, past tense is used in counterfactuals to express an alternative present state of the world (or a certain *now* of an alternative possible world) as in (23).

(23)   If I *had* more time, I would meet my friends more often.

Ludlow (1999: 161) provides pertinent references to the accounts on which the past is taken to mean 'remoteness', 'remoteness from reality', and 'exclusion'. But here is where Ludlow's analysis differs from mine. For Ludlow, states of affairs can be 'remote in time' or 'remote in possibility'. Hence, he speculates that there is 'some deeper third element [that] underlies both tense and counterfactual modality' (p. 161). He proposes evidentiality as this underlying parent category: all past-tense morphology is morphology of evidential markers. This recourse to evidentiality is, however, superfluous when we redefine epistemic modality as inferential evidentiality. Evidence that we have *now* about what happened *in the past* allows us to use indicators of the past tense but by the same token we are detaching ourselves from the *now* in the sense of diminished probability as compared with that of a statement in the present tense. Hence, the situation with the past is analogous to that with the future described above: the truth of *now* is given *in* and *by* the *now*: the truth about the future and about the past is given *in* the *now* and by what we remember about the past, or anticipate about the future, *now*.[22] This is how the modal detachment is created and cannot be escaped.[23]

This construal derives from the Aristotelian view, taken up in the Middle Ages by Ockham, according to which statements can be true or false even though we may not be in a position to know the truth value. Varieties of this view will include the evaluation of anticipations and memories. But this is not the strongest argument for the modal status of temporality. In fact, modal

[22] Truth-makers for future and past statements gave rise to ample discussions in the philosophical literature. One of the core questions is: are statements about the past verified by a past event or by the present memory of it? I will have more to say about the truth-makers in Section 2.4 while discussing Michael Dummett's recent views. See also fn 20 in Chapter 1.

[23] De Haan (2006: 51) also reports research on the reconstruction of the tense-aspect-modality system in Proto-Uto-Aztecan by Steele (quoted in de Haan). The reconstructed *irrealis* morpheme is there proposed to be the same as the past tense morpheme and it is suggested that both are founded on an abstract conceptual feature called *dissociative*: past tense marks a dissociation from *now*, just as *irrealis* marks a dissociation from reality. According to the alternative view, expressed among others by Bybee, past tense alone does not produce the modal meaning: it has to be combined with a modal verb, imperfective aspect, or the subjunctive. See de Haan 2006 for detailed references.

detachment is intuitively even stronger on an alternative construal where the truth or falsity of a statement are settled not by how the states of affairs are now but by how they were, are, or will be at the time of the statement. This is the notion of truth that was propounded by Charles Peirce and is frequently called *Peircean*: it is the facts themselves that settle the matter of truth or falsity. On this construal, statements about the future come out as modal. To take Aristotle's famous example from *De Interpretatione* (1928), that there will be a sea battle tomorrow, this statement is neither true nor false now: it is a modal statement involving the operator of necessity. Thanks to introducing modality, the law of the excluded middle can be preserved. While p $\vee \neg$ p is problematic with respect to statements about the future, $\Box$ p $\vee \Box \neg$ p is not: they may both be false.[24]

In temporal logic, representing the past as modality has also been successfully attempted. Thomason (e.g. 2002) proposes to view pastness as *historical necessity*. The idea is essentially Aristotelian: a sentence S is historically necessary at a certain time *t* if it is true at *t*. No matter what the future development of the world, the truth of S remains. Historical necessity is founded on the model of forward-branching time: with the passage of time, *historical possibilities* diminish monotonically. If two possible worlds w_1 and w_2 are similar at time *t*, then this means that they share the same past up to and including *t*. They are historical alternatives at *t* but they may stop being historical alternatives at some subsequent $t + t_1$ where branching occurs. So, for example, a sentence 'It may rain on Sunday' is true in all branching worlds and at all times until the end of Sunday but ceases to be true when Sunday is over and it didn't rain. I discuss this view in more detail in Section 2.4 devoted to the concept of the past.

The second modal view of time to be mentioned in this section is that of Joshua Parsons. Parsons, a defender of a modal version of A-theory, proposes amending tense logic by strengthening the relation between time and modality: instead of representing time as similar to modality, using parallel syntactic and semantic devices, we can equate time with modality and say that time *is* modality (cf. Parsons 2003: 5). In practice, in tense logic, instead of relativizing truth to time, we simply relativize truth to a world. He suggests thinking of each possible world as associated with a certain time-at-this-world as it is at present. Then we can construct tense logic by considering not all possible worlds, but the worlds which differ in what time there is at this world. As a result, we can talk about the truth-in-a-world instead of truth-at-a-time because the worlds in our domain are already relativized to times. In what

---

[24] See also the introduction to this chapter and Kaufmann *et al.* 2006.

follows I develop an argument from the processing of natural language sentences that supports this suggestion and shows that it captures the intuition of thinking and talking about time.

Last but not least, it is necessary to mention languages in which formal indicators of time are optional. In such languages we should investigate not only expressions of time but also the semantic category of temporality which is often realized through pragmatic inference. In Thai, for example, both tense and aspect can be left out of the sentence and the specification of these can be left to the addressee's pragmatic inference. For example, $f_3on\ t_1ok$[25] ('rain fall'), can express a wide range of temporal and modal commitments from 'it is raining', through 'it was raining' and 'it will rain', to 'it might rain'. When a modal marker is present, its meaning can also vary and the contextual accommodation normally allows the addressee to recover the speaker's intentions without giving rise to ambiguity. A lexical item $d_1ay_1^{II}$ with the lexical meaning 'to receive', can perform the function of a modality marker expressing ability. Sentence (24) can be translated as a statement of Gremlin's (the cat's) ability but the temporal location is not specified, as (24a) and (24b) indicate. The example derives from a natural conversation recorded and discussed by Srioutai (2006).

(24) $k_1r_3eml_3in$ c_1ap ng_3u: $d_1ay_1^{II}$
        Gremlin   catch   snake   *d1ay1II*

(24a)   Gremlin *was able to catch* a snake (and he caught it).

(24b)   Gremlin *can catch* a snake (if he wants to).   (adapted from Srioutai
        2006: 109; see also Jaszczolt and Srioutai forthcoming)

Contextual information allows the addressee to opt for (24a) or (24b). In addition, as Srioutai (2006) demonstrates, $d_1ay_1^{II}$ comes with a salient, preferred meaning of past tense. In other words, when context does not suggest otherwise, (24) is taken to mean (24a). Pastness is the default, but cancellable, interpretation. It is not encoded, it is merely recovered as the preferred and more common interpretation. Similarly, a Thai word c_1a, normally translated as the English *will*, is not necessarily a marker of futurity. Just as the English *will*, *c1a* can assume the meaning of epistemic necessity (as in 25) or the habitual meaning, also called dispositional necessity (as in 26).

(25) $m_3ae:r_3i:^I$ kh_3ong c_1a d_1u: $'_1op_1e:r_3a:^I$ $y_3u:^I$ $t_1o'nn_3i:^{II}$
        Mary   may   *c1a*   see   opera   *Prog*   now
        'Mary will be in the opera now.'

---

[25] For transliteration system see Diller 1996. 1, 2, 3 and I, II stand for tone markers.

(26) b_1a:ngkh$_3$r$_3$ang^{II} m$_3$ae:r$_3$i:^{I} c$_1$a p$_1$ay$_1$ d$_1$u: '$_1$op$_1$e:r$_3$a:^{I}
      Sometimes   Mary   *cia* go   see   opera
      n$_3$ay$_2$ ch$_3$udw$_3$o'm
      in   tracksuit
      'Mary will sometimes go to the opera in her tracksuit.'

                    (adapted from Srioutai 2006: 125; see also Srioutai 2004)

Unlike the English *will*, c_1a incorporates readily into the Thai grammatical system and expresses modality with predominant future reference, just as $d_1ay_1{}^{II}$ expresses modality with predominant past reference. This behaviour of modals, combined with the situation in which the language itself does not have an obligatory marking of tense, provides a strong argument for the supervenience of temporality on modality in the sense of conceptual and semantic inheritance: modal detachment is grammaticalized, and temporal detachment follows as defaults or context-driven non-default interpretations.[26]

In Chapter 1 we reached the conclusion that the past, present, and future, the A-theory terms, are terms pertaining to human experience. While in reality time exists but does not flow, for human agents it is the *now* that has the privileged status; I am experiencing the symptoms of flu *now*, I perceive the clock on my mantelpiece *now*, I hear its ticking *as I am writing these words*. It is the privileged status of the *now* that forces us to conceptualize the *not now* not as experience but as an anticipation or a memory of an experience. Let us turn to McTaggart again:

Why do we believe that events are to be distinguished as past, present, and future? I conceive that the belief arises from distinctions in our own experience.

At any moment I have certain perceptions, I have also the memory of certain other perceptions, and the anticipation of others again. The direct perception itself is a mental state qualitatively different from the memory or the anticipation of perceptions. (McTaggart 1908: 127)

Unless they are illusory, perceptions are real and certain. Memories of perceptions and anticipations of perceptions are removed from this certainty to some degree, just as the past and the future are removed from the very central experience of the *now*. In this section I considered a selection of arguments in support of treating the semantic category of time as derived

---

[26] Srioutai (2006) presents a plethora of arguments from Thai that support the thesis of the modal character of the human concept of time, also addressing the issue of linguistic universals and relativity. We shall not repeat them here but it has to be pointed out that the analysis is fully formalizable in the framework of dynamic semantics such as DRT (Kamp and Reyle 1993; Kamp *et al.* forthcoming) or Default Semantics (Jaszczolt 2005). For an analysis in Default Semantics see Jaszczolt and Srioutai forthcoming.

from modality, or even stronger, as modality itself. We can now move to the next step in my main argument of this essay, namely the thesis that internal time itself, that is the psychological future, present, and past, are modalities. To repeat, for this step we will utilize the premise that semantic categories are a window on conceptual categories – in agreement with the rich tradition in various strands of semantic theory, from broadly defined cognitive (e.g. Jackendoff 2002; Culicover and Jackendoff 2005) to dynamic truth-conditional (Hamm *et al.* 2006).[27]

2.2 The concept of the future

In this section I will discuss various ways of expressing future-time reference and try to look at them bearing in mind the assumption that they express the internal, psychological time. I will try to establish whether this internal time is a primitive notion, or, just as the semantics of temporal expressions suggests, it is (at least) supervenient on modality. In the previous section I summarized a number of arguments for the modal underpinnings of time as a semantic category. In this section, and analogously in sections about the present and the past, I will go further and extrapolate from the semantic category to the cognitive category of internal future, and analogously internal present and internal past. The conclusion I reach will depict internal time as internal detachment from certainty. In other words, not only is it the case that real time does not flow while internal time does but also the internal time itself, i.e. *the time that flows*, is conceptualized as flowing from the probabilities of the future into the certainty of *now* and out of the certainty of *now* into the fragmented picture, and hence uncertainty, of the past.

Let us consider the following set of expressions in (27)–(33).

(27)   Tom will quit smoking tomorrow.
(28)   Tom is quitting smoking tomorrow.
(29)   Tom quits smoking tomorrow.
(30)   Tom is going to quit smoking tomorrow.
(31)   Tom is to quit smoking tomorrow.
(32)   Tom is about to quit smoking.
(33)   Tom is on the point of quitting smoking.

All of these sentences have future-time reference. They are not, however, synonymous, neither are they all unambiguous in themselves. Sentence (27) can express a prediction or a statement of volition. It may also express what we called in Section 2.1, with reference to modal *may*, an epistemic claim that to the best of the speaker's knowledge, tomorrow's world will contain non-smoking Tom, or a metaphysical claim that it is highly probable that in tomorrow's world Tom no longer smokes.

The diachronic relations between the future and modality are well documented. In Section 2.1 we referred to Bybee *et al.* 1994, Fleischman 1982, van der Auwera and Plungian 1998, and de Haan 2006, among others, to signal their historical interrelations. Conceptually, obligation and permission are directly related to the future: one can fulfil the obligation or make use of permission only at a time that follows them. In French, *devoir*, 'must', 'ought to' is often used to signal that an event will take place in the future rather than to signal obligation.[28]

Expressions 'be about to' and 'be on the point of' as in (32) and (33) express immediate future, 'be to' as in (31) expresses obligation or arranged future such as a scheduled plan. Next, present tense can also be used with future-time reference. The present tense, combined with progressive or nonprogressive aspect as in (28) and (29) respectively, is described by Declerck (2006: 181–8, 357) as representing situations that depend on present circumstances. Nonprogressive present signals according to him 'complete determination' or 'inevitability' (p. 182) as in (34)–(36).

(34)   The train leaves at 8.45 a.m. tomorrow.
(35)   The service begins at 9.00 a.m. next Sunday.
(36)   Tomorrow is 28 September.

While the labels 'completely determined' and 'inevitable' are possibly too strong, it is certainly correct to say that the speaker represents the situation as being beyond his/her control. Progressive present, on the other hand, signals the existence of a current plan from which the future situation stems as in (37)–(38).

(37)   Tom is going to China next month.
(38)   Jenny is staying with us tomorrow night.

The agent has some control over the future event and hence the certainty is lower than those of situations expressed by means of nonprogressive present. This sense of control and intentionality is also present in the case of nonhuman subjects: (39) means that it is the speaker's intention that the car stays where it is:

(39)   The car is staying in the garage tomorrow.

---

[28] See de Haan (2006: 50).

On the other hand, (40) and (41) are semantically and pragmatically ill-formed due to the clash between the sense of planning provided by the grammatical form and the impossibility of planning conveyed by the lack of intentionality in the verb *feel.*

?(40)   Tom is feeling unwell tomorrow night.
?(41)   Tom feels unwell tomorrow night.

Similarly, *be going to* is used for future situations that are predictable from the present moment, as in (30) above. Its use in the past form implies that this future situation was not actualized, as in (42).

(42)   I was going to go to London on Monday.

Unlike *will*, *be going to* is natural without the specification of time, as in (43).

(43)   The cat is going to fall off the roof.

But it can also be used as a pure future form, for example in weather predictions where it serves as the unmarked form, while the *will* construction seems to be more marked for having the grounds for a prediction, as in (44) and (45) respectively.

(44)   The weather is going to be warmer tomorrow.
(45)   The weather will be warmer tomorrow.

The question arises, do all the expressions that trigger future-time reference correspond to one single concept of futurity, perhaps expressing just its different shades or strengths? Or are they heterogeneous and require more than one conceptual basis? In the section entitled 'Does English have a "future tense"?', Declerck (2006: 102) observes that any sentence about the future is modal in virtue of being about something that is yet to come and hence uncertain. But he also observes that since '*will* + present infinitive' is used primarily to express future location, it is justified to call this form a tense form. He goes on to say that there are pure and non-pure uses of this tense form: the pure form is the least subjective in that it does not convey the speaker's will or expectation, as in (46).

(46)   The meeting will take place on Monday at 10 a.m.

The non-pure forms are those of *prediction* and *predictability.* For example, (47) can fall in either of these categories.

(47)   If there is a phone call, that will be my daughter.

Interpreted as a prediction, sentence (47) means that it is possible that there will be a phone call and that the speaker predicts that, if there is one, it will be from his/her daughter. Interpreted as predictability, the sentence means that since (as the speaker is informed) there is a phone call, it is predictable that it is from his/her daughter. The latter interpretation carries the strongest epistemic possibility. It is also about a present rather than future event.

However, the list of the categories is incomplete. It is also wanting in that it assimilates prediction and predictability too much. In practice, quite often prediction and predictability are distinguished by aspect: 'If the phone rings, . . .' (prediction), vs. 'if the phone is ringing, . . .' (predictability). Morevoer, predictability is not strictly speaking future, although Declerck (2006: 105) argues that it should be regarded as future due to the future-shifting focus: 'it will become apparent in the future that the situation was actualizing at (. . .) present', that is the sentence conveys that the statement will be evaluated at a future time. As we saw in Section 2.1, there are many more shades of meaning of the future *will*, as well as many non-future uses of it. So, can they all be subsumed under one conceptual category of, say, 'future is strong probability' and hence 'expression of a future-oriented statement means that the speaker considers the likelihood of the statement's being true to be high at some future time'? Declerck's aim is classificatory and he focuses on the types of verb phrases encountered in the English language rather than on the epistemic underpinnings. For example, the means of expressing futurity such as 'be about to', 'be going to', or present progressive are called by Declerck (2006: 106) 'futurish' tense forms. 'Be about to', 'be going to', or present progressive have on his account 'dual time reference': that of the present moment from which the predicted future stems, and that of the future situation. In addition, 'be going to' can also function as a pure future tense form when it does not imply a present state. There is no clear-cut boundary between these two uses, though. Neither is there a clear boundary anywhere to be discerned among Declerck's classes that would pertain to tense/non-tense distinction. It has to be pointed out that Declerck's definition of tense as 'the pairing of a morpho-syntactic form with a meaning, the meaning being the specification of the temporal location of a situation' (Declerck 2006: 94) overstates the importance of morpho-syntactic means of expressing temporality for the overall conceptualization of time in a language. His classification of expressions of futurity into pure and not pure also seems inconsistent with his claim that 'English tenses appear to reflect a mental division of time into past and nonpast' (p. 147) – a conclusion he reaches on the basis of the fact that there is no future tense morpheme in English, while there are past and nonpast/present morphemes.[29] The best way to proceed seems to be to reject

---

[29] See also the conclusions to Section 2.5 below.

any claims of categorial differences within our class (27)–(33) and allow a cline of probability instead: when a state of affairs is relatively certain, predictable, and can be planned, expressions (28) and (29) can be used, where (29) surpasses (28) in probability value. When certainty is high but planning is not a requirement, (30), (32), and (33) are utilized. (31) normally combines an element of deontic modality, while (27) is the most futurative of the future-time referring expressions: just as the future is uncertain, so the English *will* expresses the uncertainty that it requires. In other words, as I discussed in Jaszczolt (2005), it is the most modal of the modal expressions: probability is duly weak as compared with other forms, albeit sufficiently strong to justify a commitment in the form of making a statement. In the account of futurity in my Default Semantics (Jaszczolt 2003, 2005, 2006a), I also proposed a scale of modal detachment on which I placed the future *will*, the present progressive (called there 'futurative progressive'), and present nonprogressive called there, after Dowty 1979, 'tenseless' future. On this scale, (29) comes out as the expression with the weakest degree of modal detachment, and hence with the weakest modality and at the same time the strongest intention to communicate certain content and the strongest commitment on the part of the speaker to the content of the sentence. Next follow (28) and (27), where (27), the 'regular future' realized as Simple Future with auxiliary *will*, is the default way of expressing the futurity in that it is, so to speak, the 'most modal' form – a form that is suitably detached to express the uncertain future. We can also add here the periphrastic future in (30), as well as forms with future-time reference which are overtly modal, such as epistemic necessity future (in the sense of inferential evidentiality) in (48) and (49) and epistemic possibility future in (50) and (51).

(48)   Peter must be going to London tomorrow morning.
(49)   Peter ought to/should be going to London tomorrow morning.
(50)   Peter may go to London tomorrow morning.
(51)   Peter might go to London tomorrow morning.

Periphrastic future in (30) will occupy a place between futurative progressive and regular future as it comes with a lesser degree of detachment than regular future, as was discussed with respect to its historical development into the standard future form. Expressions (31)–(33) can also be added, on the proviso that tangential features of these, as well as of (27)–(29), such as planning, immediate or delayed actualization of the state of affairs, volition, and so forth are accounted for. Further qualifications by modal adverbs such as 'possibly', 'evidently', or 'certainly', combined with the information provided by the grammatical form, also help allocate utterances on a scale of epistemic commitment.[30] In the present discussion, and until Chapter 4, I am not concerned with graphic representations and producing multi-dimensional scales of probability. I propose more detailed clines of modality in Section 4.2.1, also incorporating such overtly modal expressions with future-time reference whose semantic representations are given there.

It is easy to observe that modal detachment, or alternatively the strength with which we commit ourselves to the proposition expressed, are a useful measure for comparing the meaning of these future-oriented expressions. We are returning now to the question: *Does the concept of the future in the internal time presuppose the flow of time as its basic constituent?* Or, does futurity rely on a concept more basic than that of a flow? The above discussion and the conclusion we reached, namely that there is no clear boundary among the constructions exemplified in (27)–(33) and (48)–(51), suggest that there is no time/modality boundary to be discerned. There is no one, default way of expressing futurity that relies on the flow of time and does not rely on modal detachment. On the contrary, the English *will*, which is still the most unmarked way of expressing futurity, in spite of forms such as *be going to* encroaching on its territory,[31] is 'the most modal' of the list of expressions in (27)–(33) and also fitting well with (48)–(51). At this stage of the investigation we have found no good reason to delineate time flow as the conceptual basis for the internal, psychological notion of the future, or to put it simply, for the human concept of futurity. Naturally, more arguments from other languages have to be brought in unless we make a big assumption of linguistic universalism in the domain of the correlation between expressions and concepts of time. Some of them were already aired in Section 2.1, others will have to wait for Section 2.5.

In the remainder of this section I take a closer look at the arguments for the mental representation of time as modality that pertain to the interpretation of utterances in discourse. Some of them will rely on the formal methods of providing a theory of meaning for temporal expressions, others will take a more psychological line of the analysis of utterance processing itself. As I argued in Jaszczolt (2008), notwithstanding Frege's fierce arguments against psychologism in logic, psychological considerations must not be excluded from a theory of natural language meaning.

---

[30] See Simon-Vandenbergen and Aijmer 2007 for an extensive corpus-based study of English adverbs of modal certainty.

[31] In English, and also in French, simple future forms are becoming increasingly modal, while their basic future-time reference function is taken over by *go*-constructions. See, for example, Fleischman (1982: 97–8, 135) and Eckardt (2006: 91–127). Future *be going to* is, however, restricted to certain grammatical contexts and literary genres. For example, it is rare in the antecedent of a conditional or in adverbial clauses. For a detailed discussion see Wekker 1976.

There is no better place to start than Prior's tense logic again. For Prior (1957: 9), as for Aristotle, the truth in the present moment of a future-time statement is equivalent to the truth at some future moment of a present-time statement. A future-time statement is part of the larger concept of possibility: when *p* is possible, then it either is or will be the case that *p*. When *p* is necessary, then it is and always will be the case that *p* (*ibid.*: 12). Tense logic is thus a modal system. Now, in the latest discussions on metasemantics it has often been pointed out that any theory of discourse meaning should aim at fulfilling two objectives: to provide mental representations of discourse, and to back them by a formal account of the compositional semantic structure. Discourse Representation Theory and its offshoot Default Semantics both see formalization as subordinate to the main objective of providing such mental representations of discourse fragments. Both of these theories make some use of Prior's tense logic: although temporality is accounted for by means of the B-series devices, it is accounted for on the propositional, sentential level rather than an argument level, and with the use of an A-series device of the deictic centre. Discourse representation is then seen as a level of mental representation, additional to the level of discourse structure (see Hamm *et al.* 2006). This applicability of Prior's tense logic for the conceptual modelling of discourse is yet another supporting pillar in our construction of a modal basis of thought about time.

There are numerous accounts of future-time reference which make a direct use of the notion of future tense. It is therefore necessary to ask whether they constitute a counterargument to our modal account. Parsons (1990: 28) regards simple future as tense and employs a sentential operator FUT in the logical form according to the rule that '. . . a formula may be preceded by FUT, in which case it is true now just in case the part governed by FUT will be true at some time later than now'. So, in his subatomic, Davidsonian semantics, sentence (52) obtains the logical form in (53), where 'Cul' stands for culmination and 'e' for an event.

(52)   Brutus will stab Caesar.
(53)   FUT ($\exists$e) (Stabbing (e) & Subject (e, Brutus) & Object (e, Caesar) & Cul (e))

However, the truth condition for a formula preceded by FUT is clearly Aristotelian and allows for a modal interpretation. In other words, the semantic basis for the future tense is modality. Similarly, Dahl (1985: 103) proposes FUT as a universal category that underlies most of the forms called in different languages future tenses. His analysis is founded on the investigation of sixty-four languages representing a wide range of genetic groups. His argument is that while future-time reference is a constant feature of such forms, other elements, such as intention, are not. For example, 'He will go' expresses the speaker's prediction even when the subject may not have an intention to go, while 'He intends to go' expresses the subject's intention when the speaker is not necessarily predicting that he/she will go (see pp. 106–7). So, modal elements such as intending are not necessary parts of the meaning of a future construction, while prediction is. Again, just as in the case of Parson's account, it would be wrong to consider this to be a counterargument to the modal foundation of futurity. Epistemic modality understood as the evaluation of the likelihood of a situation is not undermined. Our notion of epistemic modality is semantic and conceptual, understood as speaker's judgement about the degree of certainty of the proposition (van der Auwera and Plungian 1998) and as an attitude, mental operation on a state of affairs (Nuyts 2001). Modality so conceived can be placed one level higher in the conceptual hierarchy than that exemplified by Dahl's intentions: while modality in the sense of intending may be absent from a future-referring statement, modal detachment certainly is not. Moreover, he also finds out that the most typical uses of the future involve intention and planning rather than pure prediction – to reflect the root, dynamic meaning 'to act on one's will, desire, want, hence insist on doing something' (Allan 2001: 358).

Next, Wekker (1976) provides a careful analysis of the expressions of futurity in contemporary British English and attempts a classification. He discerns the categories of pure futurity, volition, characteristic (which we called dispositional necessity use in Section 2.1), inference (which is a subcategory of epistemic necessity, e.g. 'Oil will float on water'), and epistemic (which we called epistemic necessity). What he couldn't identify is a pure category of future tense. While the expression of a future state of affairs is, naturally, the main purpose, it is interwoven with the purpose of expressing a degree of probability, hypothetical status of the statement, element of volition, and so forth. As he says, the meaning of *will* may differ from speaker to speaker. The differences stem from the fact that speakers issue utterances based on various degrees of certainty: sometimes it is reliable knowledge, and at other times merely a vague belief or reasoning from assumptions. But this variation is bound within certain limits in that the main, salient function is to convey futurity, such as the concepts of prediction and anticipation. Moreover, since predication and anticipation are closely connected with volition, the modal colouring of volition can also be present (*ibid.*: 67). Other conditions that may affect the degree to which various meanings of *will* are mixed are the influence of negation, animacy of the subject, possible intentionality of the action denoted by the verb phrase (the action may be intended or agreed), conditional and interrogative expressions, and so forth. Since, as Wekker observes, it is often impossible to dissociate various uses even in the case of one single speaker, it is best to resort to assessing the overall force of *will*. In short, it is best to resort to the graded concept of modality.

One possibility we have not yet explored is that the English *will* is ambiguous. This is a position supported by Hornstein (1990: 38) who considers *will* to be on some occasions of use a future tense marker, and on others a modal associated with an imperative and akin to *must*. His main reason for postulating ambiguity is to preserve the intuition that English has a future tense and a morphological marker of this future tense. It also allows him to dissociate the present-time uses as a separate category. In view of the fact that in real use the dissociation is often impossible, as our discussion of Wekker signalled, Hornstein's argument appears rather weak. Moreover, it is a well-acknowledged and widely accepted methodological principle in semantics and pragmatics not to multiply senses beyond necessity: proposed by Paul Grice (1978) under the powerful name of Modified Occam's Razor, it proved very successful in the analyses of semantic properties of many problematic constructions such as negation, where wide and narrow scope were demonstrated to be related through semantic underdetermination rather than ambiguity (see Atlas 1977, 1979, 1989; Kempson 1977), other sentential connectives, or the relative scope of quantifiers (see Jaszczolt 1999, 2002 for an overview). Leaving the semantic representation of an expression underspecified and allowing for further modifications to be provided by pragmatic inference in the process of utterance interpretation respects this principle of parsimony and, more importantly, allows us to separate the analysis of the devices of the language system from the analysis of meaning construction in discourse. The latter advantage is important for those of a contextualist orientation for whom these further inferences intrude into the semantic representation itself and into the truth-conditional content. It allows them to dispose of the notion of ambiguity which does not seem to be corroborated in the experimental testing of the process of utterance interpretation. This is the direction I will follow in the Default Semantics analysis of temporal expressions in Chapter 4. For those with more minimalist sympathies, separating sentence meaning from utterance meaning is a methodological requirement and is also greatly facilitated by exorcising ambiguities: a sentence is a sentence, full stop (Bach 2004, 2006; Atlas 2006; Horn 2004, 2006) or, on an alternative construal, a sentence is a sentence plus further unspecified minimal elaborations that are necessary to derive a proposition (Borg 2004) or further, specific but grammatically highly restricted, elaborations (Capellen and Lepore 2005).[32] Moreover, what Hornstein calls a future-tense

---

[32] Versions of semantic minimalisms are compared and assessed in Jaszczolt 2007.

marker seems to be closely related semantically to the modal marker not only in virtue of expressing probability but also in its grammatical behaviour. Although this marker refers to the future, undeniably modal markers such as *must* also refer to the future, as (54) demonstrates.

(54)   You must come to dinner on Friday.

Will also patterns with modal markers rather than with tense markers in the sequence-of-tense circumstances. As Enç (1996: 350) observes, while (55) can have a reading on which saying and being hungry are simultaneous, as well as a reading on which the state of being hungry is 'shifted' into the past with respect to Tom's expressing it, (56) allows only for the shifted reading.

(55)   Tom said that he was hungry.
(56)   Tom will say that he will be hungry.

Similarly, in (57) 'is' refers to the time of speaking, while in (58) it refers to a future time. (58) patterns with future-shifting modals, and hence with (59), rather than with (57).

(57)   Tom said that Mary is hungry.
(58)   Tom will say that Mary is hungry.
(59)   Tom may say that Mary is hungry.

Even the most forceful appeal to possible worlds does not bring about the desired ambiguity view. The ambiguity view would require that a sentence with *will* as a future-tense marker should refer to one world, while one with *will* as a modal marker should refer to other possible worlds. However, it cannot be denied that (60) is modal and yet it refers to the actual world (see Enç 1996: 348).

(60)   It is certain that Mary was hungry.

The ambiguity view or the tense marker view are therefore founded on dubious grounds.

Moving now to arguments from etymology and diachronic processes, *will* can reasonably be expected to retain some meaning of volition in that it derives from Old English *willan*, meaning 'to want'. The fact that in the context of a sentence referring to the present time *will* signals an intentional present and not futurity, paired with the fact that in future-oriented sentences it frequently conveys intentionality, is a strong argument in favour of the volitional basis for all of its meaning. As Werth (1997: 112) observes, strong intentionality results in strong probability: the expression of the future often is the result of the expression of the intention. In other cases, it is the expression of the result of inference: an expression of 'near-certainty of deduction based on experience or available information' (p. 112) – a modal notion through and through. In a more universal perspective, as was discussed in more detail in Section 2.1, future tenses arise historically out of (i) inceptive or inchoative aspectuals, (ii) modals, mostly of obligation, volition, uncertainty or unreality, or (iii) goal-oriented categories such as verbs of motion meaning 'go' that function as auxiliaries (see Fleischman 1982: 23; Ultan 1972: 114). In addition, in many languages, referring to future states of affairs is grammaticalized as mood rather than tense. Fleischman (pp. 84–5) offers the following generalization. Analysed in a cross-linguistic perspective, the future is either (i) temporal and aspectual, or (ii) temporal and modal, or (iii) temporal, aspectual, and modal. The relative significance of each of these components is subject to historical change, where the change is motivated by the 'division of labour' in the verbal system at any time in the history of the language.

There are ample cross-linguistic studies of expressions for future-time reference, some involving a great number of languages. In addition to Dahl already discussed, we have to mention Ultan's (1972) study in the tradition of implicational universals in which he points out the greater markedness of future forms as compared with the past forms in world languages and proposes a diachronic universal of unidirectionality of neutralization of tense in subjunctive constructions: the future-nonfuture contrast disappears first, and the past-nonpast last. Moreover, sometimes the future form disappears in negative constructions, while the past form remains. This tendency testifies, according to him, to the conceptualization of the future as uncertainty. He says that the relatively frequent occurrence of neutralization of future tenses as attested in subjunctive and negative constructions has a rational explanation. It is directly related to the degree of uncertainty, called by him 'indefiniteness', 'the unknown quality' (1972: 101) that is conveyed by futurity, as well as by the subjunctive and by negation. He concludes that it is very plausible to consider the future as a modal category – more for some languages than for others, though. The English future auxiliary *will* behaves similarly to modal auxiliaries (*can, must,* etc.), derives from a volitional verb, and testifies to the uncertainty discussed above. French, on the other hand, uses the subjunctive for the expression of uncertainty. In this sense, as Ultan (p. 109) observes, the subjunctive in languages such as French, replaces the future. Moreover, as was mentioned in Section 2.1, in many languages the future is realized as *irrealis* morphemes. But, on the other hand, there are also languages where the future is realized as *realis*. De Haan (2006: 49) explains this state of affairs as a mismatch between ontology and epistemology: in the ontology, the future is not yet there, it has to come. In epistemology, future events are not yet known to the speaker. But since this uncertainty is a graded concept, in some languages it may surface as a grammaticalized concept that is situated more towards the certainty end than towards the uncertainty end of the spectrum. Just as a future event is going to 'come', so the certainty of a judgement is going to 'increase' with the passage of time. This hypothesis is compatible with the one I put forward in Section 2.1, namely that the semantics of time expressions may rely to a greater or lesser extent on metaphysical, real time: some languages follow the concept (internal time), and some follow reality (real time) – just as some languages tend to conceptualize space in absolute terms of reference (west, east) and others in relative (the speaker's left and right) or intrinsic (*x* faces *y*).

It has to be noted that I have used here the A-series devices, both for the ontological and epistemological domains: 'coming' and 'increasing' presuppose the flow of time. This observation forces us to return again to the question of the flow of time. Does the human concept of futurity, as expressed in natural language, presuppose time flow as a conceptual primitive?

Fleischman (1982: 8) gives an indirect answer to this question while discussing tense: tense does not express the flow of time but rather expresses the sequence of events – a sequence that is organized in our mental representation of the world and that need not necessarily mirror the real order of events. It may be so organized either for the purpose of our mental representation or even for the purpose of adding expressive power to the utterance. For example, (61) and (62) correspond to the present time of events.

(61)　Michel n'est pas là.　Il *sera* toujours au lit.
　　　Michael is not here. He's probably still in bed.

(62)　There's the doorbell: that *'ll* be the delivery boy. (from Fleischman 1982: 9)

Tense is understood here as a semantic (and deictic) category whose role is to order events in sequences. Future forms, therefore, reflect the cognitive space in which such sequencing is present. At the same time, they reflect modal detachment. The present and the past (i) are acquired sooner by children and (ii) are present in a large percentage of languages. Future-tense forms are less common in natural languages and, where they are present, are slow to acquire. Fleischman suggests that they are a second-order category. The fact that they are modal in origin adds to the plausibility of this construal of the concept of futurity. Combined with the earlier arguments from diachrony, the grammaticalization of future-time reference as mood in some languages, and the analysis of the semantic categories that combine in various uses of future-time expressions in English, we can conclude that the concept of the future is detachment, prediction, graded commitment – in agreement with Husserl's and Heidegger's anticipation, but without any clear indication of the reliance on the concept of time flow. If the underlying concept for the concept of time pertains to modality but not flow, then it is plausible to entertain the hypothesis that time flow is itself a *complex concept*, composed out of the underlying modal time and the emergent property of movement.

The location vs. flow argument is also indirectly supported by the formal analysis of *will* and *would* construction in Abusch (e.g. 1988). She proposes that in the logical form there is an element *woll* which is itself tenseless but guarantees that the event or state it helps express takes place subsequently to some deictic centre. Then, *Pres* or *Past* operators make it into *will* and *would* respectively as in *Pres* [woll [V]], accounting for the time location with reference to the utterance time. This is an improvement on the way the future was analysed in Montagovian semantics in which it was represented by a future-tense operator W. The introduction of tenseless *woll* allows her to deal with the sequence-of-tense phenomena and intensionality of temporal constructions.[33] The proposal follows the conceptual assumptions of Hans Kamp's two-dimensional tense logic, where definition of truth in relation to time is replaced with truth in relation to a pair of times: reference time and speech time (after Reichenbach 1948; see Dowty 1982). This is an essentially B-theory solution to what for Prior's A-theoretic operators was an insurmountable problem. The stumbling block is best exemplified by (63) and (64).

(63)   A child was born who would be king.
(64)   A child was born who will be king.

While Prior's operators can account for (63) as in (63a), (64) remains problematic until we introduce a B-theoretic notion of sequence of events and prefix the operator F with a qualifier that the future has to count from *now* (N), the moment of speech, as in (64a).

(63a)   P $\exists$x (Child (x) $\wedge$ Born (x) $\wedge$ F King (x))
(64a)   P $\exists$x (Child (x) $\wedge$ Born (x) $\wedge$ NF King (x)) (adapted from Dowty 1982: 31)

B-series devices become more diaphanous in Kamp's DRT where the relation of precedence ($t < n$, where n stands for 'now') is used for representing temporal relations.

Does the fact that semantic, and thereby in DRT mental, representation of temporality uses ordering of events constitute a supporting argument in favour of dissociating the concept of time from time flow? Unfortunately, the answer cannot be given so readily. The deictic component of speech time, the *now*, is at the same time an A-series resource when we interpret it in the way it is interpreted in presentism: there is real change and only present events

---

[33] For further developments of this account see, for example, Ogihara 1996.

exist. What makes an event past or future is the *now*: the world at the present moment. This Priorean, and also Augustinian, conception of time is added to the B-theory devices of earlier-than/later-than relations. The answer to our question will require a careful scrutiny of the concept of *now* attempted in Section 2.3.

We also have to mention a puzzle which was originally discussed to exemplify the variable scope of tense operators. (65) and (66) differ in the 'scope' of futurity.

(65)   Every boy will be a man.

(66)   Every player will have a partner.   (from Ladusaw 1977: 94; see also
              Ogihara 1996: 178–80 for so-called *double-access sentences*)

Each sentence has two possible interpretations ('double access') but in each case one interpretation is much more natural than the other. While (65) tends to refer to a set of people who are boys now at n and will be men at some subsequent time $t > n$, (66) normally refers to a set of people who will act as players at some $t > n$ and will have partners while so acting. What interests us here is the conceptual representation of such examples. One obvious solution is this. Being a boy and being a man are states which can be represented by standard DR-theoretic means and then ordered by the relation of precedence as in the DRS in Fig. 2.1.

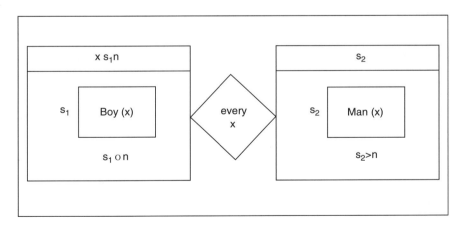

Figure 2.1 DRS for example (65)

As in the previous examples, there is no need to represent the flow of time directly: ordering states using B-series devices supplemented by n is again sufficient.

Finally, let us briefly address the fact that forward-facing future is by no means a universal concept. Most Indo-European languages are like English in that their speakers conceptualize the future as lying ahead, in front of them; the future is the unknown which they are facing. There is a plethora of metaphorical expressions that testify to this orientation, such as 'don't look back, look ahead into the future', 'face the future', etc. However, this orientation is not present in all languages of the world, as was discussed at length in Section 1.4 in the examples of Maori, Aymara, Hausa, and Ancient Greek. This variation may provide a supporting argument for the symmetric modal treatment of time. While the modal *character* of the future is independent of the position of the speaker on the time axis, the *degree* of commitment may be affected: facing the past conveys the intrinsic concept of time, while facing the future can be relative or absolute, depending on whether it is *realis* or *irrealis*. In other words, facing the past the speaker is positioned 'face to face' with experiences. Facing the future he/she is confronted either with anticipations of experiences or with independent facts.

2.3 *Now*: The concept of the present

The concept of the present does not have a real, worldly equivalent:

According to relativity, there is not really such a thing as the 'now' at all. The closest that we get to such a concept is an observer's 'simultaneous space' in space-time (. . .), but that depends on the *motion* of the observer! The 'now' according to one observer would not agree with that for another. Concerning two space-time events A and B, one observer U might consider that B belongs to the fixed past and A to the uncertain future, while for a second observer V, it could be A that belongs to the fixed past and B to the uncertain future! (Penrose 1989: 392)

Equally, for the equations of physics, the direction of time can be reversed: they work in both directions, so to speak. The past and the future are symmetrical, and, since there is no 'now', there is no 'past' or 'future' once and for all either. It is, however, quite obvious that humans make an essential and quotidian use of the concept *now*, just as they make an essential and quotidian use of other concepts associated with indexical expressions such as *here*. In this section I discuss this concept, its compatibility with different representations of time, and remark briefly on its utility for semantic theory.

In the current state of semantic theory, it can be safely said that the B-series devices perform the core of the required functions for representing time.

Earlier-than/later-than relations, captured in the Reichenbachian model of event time (E), speech time (S), and reference time (R), allow us to model the core of temporal relations.[34] But there is also additional information that can be conveyed by temporal systems grammaticalized in natural languages. As Eckardt (2006: 114–15) observes, to remain in the familiar Indo-European territory, there is imminent future of *be going to*, as well as immediate past of the French construction *venir de faire*. She demonstrates that the extant devices of E, S, and R suffice for representing their meaning. In the case of *be going to*, the reference time R is not in the future but in the present: the sentence with *be going to* is about the present time and what is imminent in it (see p. 124). While the notion of imminence may have to be conceptualized as speaker's judgement, closely related to the degree of certainty rather than to the time interval, the analysis itself is quite convincing: I say 'I am *going to go* to Shanghai in eight months' time' rather than 'I will go to Shanghai in eight months' time', although the time interval is quite long, just because the decision has been taken and I want to inform the addressee about this presently obtaining decision. Similarly, if I use *be going to* in the antecedent of a conditional as in (67), I signal that the situation is in some way related to the present moment: because the current weather forecast is very reliable or because the sky is already overcast.

(67)   If it is going to rain, we will have to stay at home.

The ease of substitution of 'since', as compared with the equivalent construction in (68), should also be noted. While in (67a) 'since' is readily substituted with the effect of a slight enforcement of probability (arrived at through inference or other evidence), in (68a) it is not: we have to resort to the leap in probability to (68b).

(68)   If it rains, we will have to stay at home.
(67a) Since it is going to rain, we will have to stay at home.
(68a) ?Since it rains, we will have to stay at home.
(68b) Since it will rain, we will have to stay at home.

In short, we need not even resort to the path of grammaticalization and the shift from the verb of motion to the temporal expression in order to represent this 'imminence'. It is so because we have access to the magic device of speech time, or *now*, which acts as an accelerator for the modal value of future statements: direct reference to *now* as proposed on Eckardt's account brings

---

[34] See also Bennett and Partee 1978.

the expression closer to the certainty of *now*. But this is where our problem lies: *now* is not a B-series device. It situates the speaker in time. Does it also necessitate the conceptualization of time as *a flow into now* and *away from now*? Or, rather, is time flow a complex rather than a basic concept?

Unlike the future discussed in Section 2.2, or the past discussed in Section 2.4, the present moment does not display such a striking contrast between the virtual and the actual. It is of a different ontological and epistemological status altogether when compared with the future and the past. While the time when I am typing this sentence (word, letter, etc., depending on the assumption as to whether we are considering a moment or an interval and how each of them is construed) is real, its reality is not its most important characteristic. The most important characteristic is that it is also virtual, internally represented as someone's (in this case my own) *now*. In the more poetic language of David Mitchell's *Cloud Atlas*, what makes the real present virtual is the very fact that it moves from being the future to being the present. So, being actual and being virtual have to coincide, unlike in the case of the future and the past:

One model of time: an infinite matrioshka doll of painted moments, each 'shell' (the present) encased inside a nest of 'shells' (previous presents) I call the actual past but which we *perceive* as the virtual past. The doll of 'now' likewise encases a nest of presents yet to be, which I call the actual future but which we *perceive* as the virtual future. (Mitchell 2004: 409)

It is worth noting that this conceptualization of time is not identical to the one of branching past and branching future where the present moment is the only certainty. This conceptualization differs significantly from the more standard branching future model in Fig. 2.2 and the branching past and branching future that underlies the modal conceptions of the past discussed in Section 2.1 and depicted in Fig. 2.3.

FIGURE 2.2 Branching future

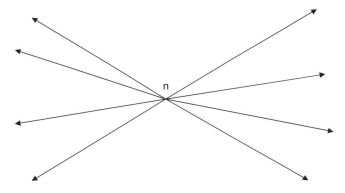

FIGURE 2.3 Branching future and past

In the virtual past/virtual future model we can retain the linear conception of time, making an additional assumption that the line need not, but may, correspond to the line of the actual future and the actual past. The protagonist of *Cloud Atlas* who writes his thoughts about time in a notebook is about to die in a plane crash: while the virtual future includes him, the actual future does not. Similarly, while in the actual past he had a 'real' part to play, the virtual past includes him on a par with Santa Claus and Snow White:

> The detonator is triggered. The C-4 ignites. The jet is engulfed by a fireball. The jet's metals, plastics, circuitry, its passengers, their bones, clothes, notebooks and brains all lose definition in flames exceeding 1200 C. The uncreated and the dead exist solely in our actual and virtual pasts. Now the bifurcation of these pasts will begin. (Mitchell 2004: 409)

The current state is the most certain one of the three: as was discussed in Section 1.2, the past and the future are the remembered and anticipated *now*s. This way of thinking about temporal location is reminiscent of the departures from certainty represented as modality. In formal representation of sentences, temporal operators and modal operators are added to predicate logic on an analogous basis, both types achieving the effect of a detachment from *now*. The point of evaluation of sentences is usually considered to be similarly shifted in that modal operators shift it from the present state of affairs to a different state accessible from the current one. As Recanati (2007a: 65) points out, there is a qualitative distinction between the currently obtaining state and the modal detachments in that the current state is given, while the targets for such modal shifts are merely representations. Or, in other words, the *now* is certain, while modal and temporal shifts are second-order concepts that assume this certainty of *now*. What differentiates this concept from that in

Figs. 2.2 and 2.3 is that time need not flow: there is no need for the time arrow in the representation. All we need is departures from certainty guaranteed by *now*. If we were to provide a graphic representation, it would have to consist of a point for *now*, nothing else: every judgement that is not about *now* is the complementary set. In fact, even some judgements about the present, expressed in the present tense without the use of a modal, will have to be placed in this complementary set; there are uses of irony, hyperbole, and litotes which will have to be placed there.

Husserl (1928) describes this status of *now* as a *mode of temporal appearance* with a privileged status as compared with that of the past and the future. It provides the point of reference for temporal experience: it is from the perspective of *now* that events are experienced as past or future. Also, they are past because they once were *now*, and they are future because they will be *now*. *Now* is not an independently existing moment; Husserl calls it 'a mode of appearance' of something. It is not even capable of independent functioning as a theoretical construct but rather has to be accompanied by the horizon of the future and the past. We discussed the boundaries of the *now* while analysing the notion of specious present in Section 1.2 and will not ponder the size or boundaries of the dot that we have just postulated for representing *now*. We will not make any further use of the notion of specious present in William James's version either because our objective is to search for a construal that would not necessitate direction or flow. The only way we could make use of specious present and avoid time flow is to follow Husserl's retention and protention. The experienced present merges into these two features of cognition.[35]

Let us agree that the concept of the *now* is not a point in the mathematical sense but rather a fuzzy set of judgements, made with a commitment closely approaching and including certainty; a set without clear boundaries but rather merging into its complement of graded uncertainty. The use of overtly modal expressions such as *may be* + V-*ing*, *may* + V, *could be* + V-*ing*, *could* + V, as well as modal adverbs such as 'possibly', 'probably' accompanying present tense forms testifies to this gradation of certainty. In other words, although scales of epistemic commitment and thereby also degree of modality can be constructed just as they can be constructed for the future and the past, they are of lesser theoretical importance due to the inherently indexical, or at least 'focal' as we will argue below, character of *now*. What is important here is that it is not a real *now*: it is the *now* of our conceptual representation, the internal *now*. Therefore, it is not constituted by the present states of affairs as

---

[35] See also Cram (2007: 193).

it would be in ontology, but rather by the judgements issued usually with a low degree of modal detachment and beliefs held with a high degree of commitment. In the semantics of indexicals, we would refer here to the judgements as the content that corresponds to the character, the linguistic meaning of *now*, discussed below.[36]

Prior's (e.g. 1968b) defence of the redundancy theory of the present tense, according to which *p* and *It is now the case that p* are the same proposition, is another way of expressing this privileged status of the present. He introduces operators for the past and for the future, leaving the present as the springboard from which they work. Somewhat paradoxically, he also attempts to retain *now* in his logic. Although idiomatic *now* is plagued by complications with its indexical (deictic) characteristic presented in (69), the concept of the deictic present should remain: replacing 'now' by 'then' changes the sense; in both occurrences 'now' refers to the time of speaking and at no time in the future will the speaker be able to assert 'I am glad that I am ϕ-ing now'.

(69)   It is now the case that I will later be glad that I am ϕ-ing now.

(from Prior 1968b: 105)

Following Hans Kamp, whose introduction of *now* to formal semantics was discussed in Section 2.2, he opts for preserving this concept in tense logic, at the same time showing how it *could* be dispensed of even for the analysis of examples such as (69).

One question to ask is whether *now* is required by a formal system for representing natural language meaning. Another is how its sense is determined. We can start here with Kaplan's (1989) content and character distinction used for the analysis of indexicals. *Now* has a very limited linguistic content. Its content is on Kaplan's account a mapping from situations, real and counterfactual (called by him circumstances of evaluation) to an appropriate extension, where the extension will be the present moment for these circumstances. In other words, the content is a concept, or an intension which provides an extension. How is this content determined? Kaplan's answer is that it is determined by linguistic conventions, or, in other words, for our current purpose, the linguistic meaning of *now*. This linguistic meaning is in turn a mapping from various contexts to those concepts or intensions (Kaplan's contents). In other words again, the word 'now' as used in various contexts will produce the concept of the *now*. The context is composed out of an individual, a time, a location, and a possible world. Context contains the speaker: it contains the cases in which the speaker means by *now* some point

---

[36] See, for example, Kaplan 1989; Perry 2001; Recanati 1993, 2007a.

in time which is not the time of speaking as for example in (70). The sentence in (70) is the ending of a letter which an addressee reads some time after it was written and posted.

(70)   You know the whole truth now.

It has been argued recently (Predelli 2006) that such occasions of deictic shift should not be regarded as special cases to be relegated to pragmatic inference. They fit well in Kaplan's semantics of indexicals and show that *now* is not token-reflexive: it has a meaning provided by mappings from contexts to contents. In other words, Predelli argues against Reichenbach's proposal according to which *now* conforms to the token-reflexive rule that for any token 'now' of *now*, this token 'now' refers to the time when this token was uttered. But if Predelli is right and the meaning of *now* is flexible to such an extent, then what is the concept that we make use of in thinking about time? It must be the concept of the present, but this concept of the present is separated from the concept of the time of speech: time of speech is only one of its instantiations provided by the context. Conceived of along these Kaplanian lines,[37] as the 'current' *now* or a 'shifted' *now*, it seems to fit very well in our proposed theory of temporal concepts in that it can be easily explained by modal detachment. *Now* is not a moment in the time flow: it need not even be the present moment in the sense of the time of speaking or time of my writing this sentence. It is the concept that pertains to the *focal point* with respect to which statements are assessed. If they are about the present, they remain close to the focal point in the sense of reliability of judgement. If they are about the past or the future, they have to be marked – just as they are marked by the operator P or F in Priorean tense logic. But let us now try an alternative construal, according to which *now* is a point in the time flow. It is easy to see that it will not work. We would have to revert to token-reflexivity of *now* and face all the problems it engenders, such as regarding the deictic shift as a special case which eschews explanation. While on the modal ('focal point') theory it is easy to discern the *now* as a point of reference for all kinds of statements and judgements, on the flow construal there is no such unique *now*. Next, on the focal point construal, we

---

[37] Balaguer (2005) offers an interesting account on which referents are picked not just by Frege's senses but by senses plus context – thereby allowing for one of the possible senses to be selected. His account is similar to that of Predelli (2005a, 2006) and thereby to Kaplan's content-character distinction. It works against token-reflexivity and proposes the sense of 'now' as 'the present moment':

…what I am proposing is that the word 'now' has *one* sense that's operative for all of its (literal) uses; i.e., the word *type* has one meaning. This, I think, is very intuitive: the word 'now' always *means* the same thing; it's just that in different contexts, it *refers to* different times. (Balaguer 2005: 330–1)

benefit from a *now* as a point of reference for ordering all statements and judgements on a scale of modal detachment, implementing the undeniable fact that direct experience is more reliable as a foundation for a judgement than memory or anticipation of past and future experiences respectively.

In view of this superiority of the focal-point account of *now*, how are we to understand and evaluate the concept of *now* used in DRT, arguably the most successful current dynamic semantic theory? The semantic representations of DRT have the status of mental representations and hence the discourse referents postulated there have to have conceptual reality. To repeat, for representing time, DRT uses discourse referents t, for the time of the eventuality (state or event), n, for the utterance time, and the relations of precedence (e.g. $e < n$ for an event located in the past), overlap (e.g. $s \circ t$ for a state that obtained at some specified time) and inclusion (e.g. $e \subseteq t$ for the event being temporally included in some specified time). The discourse referent n is defined as always referring to 'the utterance time of the discourse that the DRS is taken to represent' (Kamp and Reyle 1993: 511). DRT subscribes to token-reflexivity of n. It also subscribes to the linear rather than modal structure of time, and that includes a linear representation of the future: Kamp and Reyle say that the future tense refers to one particular continuation of the time line (p. 535). But it is easy to observe that the discourse referent n is just a subordinate concept to our *now*: it is a concept which is formed only with the subset of contexts on which 'the present moment' is the moment of the utterance. This move is justified when one tries to represent the structure of sentences and uses Reichenbachian reference points S, R, and E: having R at one's disposal, one is free to use the indexing to the moment of speech. Moreover, DRS represents tenses rather than internal times and hence the linear structure of time is just a theoretical construct that works for this purpose. One should not write into it epistemological or ontological commitments. As Kamp and Reyle (1993: 512) say, 'The algorithm must represent the temporal information that is contained in the tense of a sentence and in its temporal adverb (if there is one)'. They introduce a feature TENSE whose value is *past* when the main verb is in the simple past, *pres* when it is in the simple present, and *fut* when there is the auxiliary *will* (*ibid.*: 512–13). Our starting point is different. As I demonstrated above, tense is not a reliable guide to conceptual temporality: the future can be represented by a wide array of means, including the present tense combined with progressive or nonprogressive aspect. As we will see in the following section, the same can be said about expressing the past and the correlation of the conceptual past with grammatical past tense. While the account of tense proposed in DRT deals with the standard, default temporal links encoded in grammar and lexicon, it does not give us the option of representing the shades of meaning that come with different expressions of futurity or pastness. The only way to account for those shades of meaning is to treat them in the Aristotelian manner, as modality. It may prove to be a valuable exercise to add this modal perspective to the DRT account in order to check whether the authors are really anti-Aristotelian as they proclaim to be or rather they appear to be anti-Aristotelian because branching time is simply not required for their task at hand. In my view, the modal account of time can be incorporated in DRT, bringing the benefit of accounting for a larger fragment of English and for presuppositions present in the preceding discourse.

2.4 The concept of the past

> Time is what stops history happening at once; time is
> the speed at which the past disappears.
>
> David Mitchell, *Cloud Atlas*, 2004, p. 244

The past as memory, juxtaposed and contrasted with the actually occurring events, is best summed up by one of the protagonists of David Mitchell's *Cloud Atlas*:

Exposition: the workings of the *actual* past + the *virtual* past may be illustrated by an event well known to collective history such as the sinking of the *Titanic*. The disaster as it *actually* occurred descends into obscurity as its eyewitnesses die off, documents perish + the wreck of the ship dissolves in its Atlantic grave. Yet a *virtual* sinking of the *Titanic*, created from reworked memories, papers, hearsay, fiction – in short, belief – grows ever 'truer'. The actual past is brittle, ever-dimming + ever more problematic to access + reconstruct: in contrast, the virtual past is malleable, ever-brightening + ever more difficult to circumvent/expose as fraudulent. (Mitchell 2004: 408)

David Mitchell's exquisite novel is composed out of interwoven stories where the lives of the protagonists belong to very different epochs, going far into the past and far into the future of our planet, connected by the hint of genetic and cultural inheritance and a near-repetition of events combined with an experience of *déjà vu* on the part of the characters. What is particularly interesting for the purpose of my argument is that the virtual past prevails, brought into existence by the demands of the present:

The present presses the virtual past into its own service, to lend credence to its mythologies + legitimacy to the imposition of will. Power seeks + *is* the right to 'landscape' the virtual past. (He who pays the historian calls the tune.) (Mitchell 2004: 408–9)

This virtual past makes temporality symmetrical with respect to the *now*:

Symmetry demands an actual + virtual *future*, too. We imagine how next week, next year or 2225 will shape up – a virtual future, constructed by wishes, prophecies + daydreams. This virtual future may influence the actual future, as in a self-fulfilling prophecy, but the actual future will eclipse our virtual one as surely as tomorrow eclipses today. Like Utopia, the actual future + the actual past exist only in the hazy distance, where they are no good to anyone. (Mitchell 2004: 409)

We have here a simple exposition of the phenomenological idea of internal time consciousness, combined with the reality of time: the past and the future are more powerful than our memories and predictions but they are useless, 'no good to anyone'. In fact, they are both equally detached. Or, in the language of this essay, they are both characterized by some degree of modality, and what in Section 4.2 we will analyse as a degree of *acceptability*, rendered in semantic representation by a sentential operator ACC indexed with a value of epistemic modality:

Q: Is there a meaningful distinction between one simulacrum of smoke, mirrors + shadows – the actual past – from another such simulacrum – the actual future? (Mitchell 2004: 409)

The virtual time is all too well known from fiction. It is a little more unconventional when it is combined with the first-person perspective: 'Shot myself through the roof of my mouth at 5 a.m. this morning…' (Mitchell 2004: 487). However, this view seems to find ready support in theories of physics: as Hawking (2001: 153) says, time travel cannot be excluded in principle. Although the probability that one will 'travel back' and, say, kill one's own grandmother is 'less than one in ten with a trillion trillion trillion trillion trillion zeroes after it' and the possibility for building an actual time machine is zero, time loops are in principle possible for universes with certain properties of directions of expansion and for microscopic objects. Time is a component of space-time and this space-time can be construed in a variety of ways, only some of which are available to human comprehension, as the anthropic principle explains: we see the universe in a certain way because we exist in it in a certain way, with the properties and abilities we have. As to the actual histories of the universe, there may be many. In other words, the world as it is now can be described with the help of many combinations of parameters. The world we pick as 'real' seems to correspond to the highest degree among probabilities of modalities we discussed. I had fish pie for lunch but I might have had a steak. Moreover, I only *think* I had fish pie for lunch: there is some small chance I may be mistaken and in fact I had fish pie a day before and fish fillet today. When I say 'I am eating a fish pie at the moment', my experience is less likely to deceive me though. Still, this is only the way *I* see the situation of sitting at the table and performing the activity of eating.

Cram (2007: 202) discusses an excellent perspective on this relativity of the past when he observes that future-in-the past, the way people anticipated the *then* future, does not always coincide with what actually happened. Let us take the example of the World War II. In the autumn of 1939, people in occupied Poland lived and acted under the conviction that war would not last much longer. Their everyday actions, directed at the future, were directed at the future that did not happen: the future of imminent victory. They had to wait until May 1945 for the desired liberation. When we reconstruct the history of that period, it would be irrational to criticize people for acting unwisely when, for example, remaining in Warsaw until they were killed or until they were captured in the street and taken to Auschwitz, instead of devising a plan of better hiding and escape. Similarly, they cannot be reproached for not dividing their dry food and valuables sensibly to make them last until 1945. In the *now* as it was *then*, different histories of the world were being constructed, only one of which became true. At the same time, it has to be remembered that most histories *are* (re)constructed in the light of what happened next and in the light of the present consequences of the past decisions and actions.

Husserl (1928: 71) says that '[e]very perceived time is perceived as a past that terminates in the present'. This phenomenological perspective ties in very well with the anthropic principle: all we have access to with reasonable certainty as human beings is a past that is constituted by current experiences. They are current but they have duration and hence they become past while they are still ongoing, so to speak: they overlap with the *now* but they are not limited to it. Then, there is also the past that is not experienced now and the past that was experienced by other agents and related to us in some form or other. Again, the best way to order such types of the past is according to their certainty. What we obtain then is the flow of time as a concept that supervenes on a more basic concept of detachment. Considering the facts that (i) the conceptual metaphor of space seems to be a constitutive metaphor for time (see Lakoff 1987; Ungerer and Schmid 1996) and that (ii) real, ontological time is a dimension of space-time, this supervenience is not as deplorable a hypothesis as it may first appear. Time flows, people are born, get older and die, but the concept that underlies this feeling of the flow of time is the movement along a dimension that is in itself very much like space: it does not run away from us but we move along it. Just as we walk to the newsagent or take a plane to New York, so do we move along the dimension that is in itself perfectly stationary. And just as, when we walk or fly, what we saw before and what we are going to see is blurred, so, when we move along the temporal dimension, what we did experience or will experience is not given to us with utmost certainty. Finally, just as I can halt at any point of my walk, or the plane can land in emergency before reaching the destination, so can I, only in theory of course, slow my travel along the time line when I move with the required speed. If not for this anthropic constraint, the whole areas of philosophy and semantics would be redundant: our perception of time is precisely our anthropic limitation. But the question is, how deep is this limitation, or, in other words, does it extend to primitive constituents of thought. As our discussion so far suggests, it is not that deep. Grammatical and lexical means that languages employ for expressing temporality suggest that modality is the bottom level: we think in terms of certainties and graded possibilities. Whether this is an evolutionary characteristic, developed for the preservation of the species, or rather the result of the second law of thermodynamics and the world's entropy, is too big a question to address in this predominantly linguistic-semantic enquiry. Suffice to say that it might be both, on two different levels of explanation.

The past and the present are thought of in strict association: 'My style of dressing is *beautiful*; Mother's style of dressing is *ugly*; Grandma's style of dressing is *quaint*. The rest is history' (Cram 2007: 197–8, after James Laver). The past is thought and talked about from the perspective of *now*, as detached experiences. This brings us to the problem of evaluation of statements about the past. There is a view called *temporalism about truth*, according to which truth and falsity are properties of objects thought of or uttered (propositions, statements, sentences, utterances, according to one's favourite orientation) which they don't have eternally; they can lose it (see Künne 2003: 295). This is the most common view in truth-conditional semantics, according to which propositions are evaluated with respect to a model and a time (see, for example, Kaplan 1989; Kamp and Reyle 1993). And at a certain time a state of affairs that truly took place may, at least according to so-called anti-realists about the past, cease to be true. For example, if John Brown murdered his brother in 1892 and no one remembers this crime any longer in 2010, the proposition that John Brown murdered his brother in 1892 ceases to be true; it becomes neither true nor false. Or, as Łukasiewicz (1961: 126) put it, the event of committing the crime by John Brown becomes only *possible*.[38] Łukasiewicz argues that while the law of the excluded middle holds, bivalence does not apply to all sentences. In other words, it is not true that every proposition is either true or false. To use Aristotle's famous example again, the alternative 'Either there will be a sea battle tomorrow or there will not be a sea battle

[38] See Künne (2003: 304) for further discussion.

tomorrow' must be true according to the principle of the excluded middle. But the separate sentences 'It is true at time *t* that there will be a sea battle tomorrow' and 'It is true at time *t* that there will not be a sea battle tomorrow' are not contradictory. *A fortiori*, when *t* equals the present moment, the sentences are not contradictory. Łukasiewicz (p. 124) also distinguishes between two scenarios: a scenario on which it has already been decided that there will be a sea battle and a scenario on which it has not yet been decided. On the latter scenario, he says, we can only 'suspend judgement'. On his scenario, we need a formal tool of a third truth value which he calls *possibility* and which is used for propositions which are neither true nor false. As he says, in this new logic there is no place for determinism: the future is not determined by the past or present either by the law of the excluded middle or by laws of causation. What is also interesting is that, on this account, the past and the future are conceptualized along the same lines: as possibilities. As Łukasiewicz says, just as only that part of the future is real which is determined by the present, so only that part of the past is real which still exerts effects on the present. His view has both theoretical and moral implications and therefore I think the passage deserves to be quoted in full:

We should not treat the past differently from the future. If the only part of the future that is now real is that which is causally determined by the present instant, and if causal chains commencing in the future belong to the realm of possibility, then only those parts of the past are at present real which still continue to act by their effects today. Facts whose effects have disappeared altogether, and which even an omniscient mind could not infer from those now occurring, belong to the realm of possibility. One cannot say about them that they took place, but only that they were *possible*. It is well that it should be so. There are hard moments of suffering and still harder ones of guilt in everyone's life. We should be glad to be able to erase them not only from our memory but also from existence. We may believe that when all the effects of those fateful moments are exhausted, even should that happen only *after* our death, then their causes too will be effaced from the world of actuality and pass into the realm of possibility. Time calms our cares and brings us forgiveness. (Łukasiewicz 1961: 127–8)

In short, determinism is rejected both with respect to the past and with respect to the future, and so is bivalence. Both are rejected with reference to internal time, the concept of time. This is the address that Łukasiewicz delivered as Rector of Warsaw University at the inauguration of the academic year 1922–23 and which he had subsequently been revising until 1946. By 1946 Łukasiewicz was aware that the theory of time propounded by atomic physics and the theories of relativity was in agreement with his anti-deterministic account of time. We can only observe then that, while his account, and the formal support in three-valued logics that he gives it, correlates well with our findings on the modal conceptual basis of the human concept of time as expressed in natural languages, its importance is not confined to that perspective. The fact that it is compatible with the physicists' concept of real time makes both his account of possibility, and our theory of the modal basis of internal time, even stronger.

Dummett (2004), being an antirealist himself, defends the position as follows. Let us begin with his theory of meaning called justificationism. For Dummett (2006), the notion of a proposition is not important for the semantics of time; instead, it is the utterance and the time of speech that play the crucial role. What matters is the position from which we evaluate utterances about the past and the future and the strength of evidence that we can obtain in their support. For him, 'proposition' is not a term that belongs in semantic theory. He adopts instead the *content of an utterance*, understood as a belief that arises in the addressee as a result of accepting the speaker's statement (cf. Dummett 2006: 30). This acceptance proceeds according to the justificationist theory of truth – the methods interlocutors actually use for judging the utterance to be true or false. These include deduction, empirical methods, and a mixture of the two.[39] In short, according to justificationism about truth, to be able to tell whether a statement is true or false means being able to do so on the basis of reasoning and observation when such are available. As can easily be inferred, the justificationist approach rejects the principle of bivalence and therefore the law of the excluded middle in logic.

Now, the justificationist theory of meaning, as Dummett says, is interested in what makes a statement true – and what makes a statement true is, on a radical version, something that exists. This leads to anti-realism about the past, about events and states of affairs that took place in the past. But, Dummett argues, such a strong version is not plausible. Instead, justification-ism has to be moderated slightly in the direction of realism about the past: realism to the extent that we must admit memories and evidence that are now present or are now present through being certain at some point in the past and surviving until now:

For all the messages that have been lost, it remains that statements about the past must count as having been directly established, and therefore as true, if someone observed them to be true at the, or an, appropriate past time. (Dummett 2004: 68)

But only those statements about the past are true for which we can find present truth-makers such as memories, accounts of past testimonies, and

---

[39] See Dummett (2006: 59).

other reliable traces.[40] If there are no such memories, for example concerning, say, the number of teeth that Socrates had at the time of his death, then there are no past states of affairs either. What is interesting about this perspective is that it is so appealing to common sense, so acceptable, and at the same time so unusual as judged by methodological criteria: in the philosophy of time, one tends to be either a realist about the past or an anti-realist, rather than an anti-realist overall, but making advances towards the realist position. But perhaps we should acknowledge the fact that the world is precisely that: there is the past, but only to a degree.

The effect of this moderate anti-realism about the past on semantic theory of natural language is significant. If all past events were certain, we would have a simple evaluation of propositions as either true or false. As Dummett (2004: 69) says, in an imaginary language in which every sentence can be reliably judged as true or false the difference between justificationism and truth-conditional theory of meaning disappears. Unfortunately, not all statements we make are decidable: some are just probable to a sufficient degree to be issued. In fact, on the account adopted in this essay, no statements are *fully* decidable: they are all modal, approaching the truth (approaching the least modal end of the scales proposed earlier with respect to the future, i.e. the highest degree of commitment).[41] In other words, Dummett's common-sense approach to the past offers a pertinent and constructive argument for the modality of the expression of temporality: statements cannot be framed as true or false; they can be framed as necessary and possible – or, on our account, possible to a greater or lesser degree.

Just as the past makes use of the *now* as discussed above, so the linguistic means pertaining to the present perspective can be imposed on the expression of the past in order to bring it to the focus of attention, make it more vivid or credible – in other words, to make it more probable, as in the past of narration in (71).

---

[40] The question as to what extra-linguistic facts make a statement true or false is pertinent for the understanding of the correspondence theory of truth. As Patterson (2003) points out, a correspondence theory is to be understood in terms of a relation between truth-bearers in semantics and the structure of reality. Correlation with any other extra-linguistic entities does not yet warrant the name of a correspondence theory of truth. On this reasoning, neither Aristotle nor Tarski were correspondence theorists. The effect this argument has on our analysis of the past and the future is that when the truth-makers are not part of reality but rather memories or anticipations, the meaning of the sentence is not analysed in terms of a correspondence theory of truth. In our account of internal time as modality, this effect can be accommodated: truth-conditional semantics need not be correspondence-theory-based semantics.

[41] See also Section 4.2.3 for the graphic representation.

(71)   This is what happened last Monday. Tom, Jane and their dog Flossie go for a cliff walk in Eastbourne. Jane is looking at the scenery and Flossie starts pulling her over the edge. John runs up to her and saves her life by catching her at the last moment.

Expressions in (72)–(75) all refer to an event in the past.

(72)   Jane went to Scotland yesterday.
(73)   Jane would have gone to Scotland by then.
(74)   Jane may have gone to Scotland yesterday.
(75)   This is what happened. Jane goes to Scotland, meets this dashing bloke from Edinburgh, falls in love, and, before you know it, they are married and settled in a cottage by a Scottish loch.

Sentence (72) makes use of the most standard way of expressing pastness, that is simple past, called here regular past. (73) exemplifies the use of the *epistemic necessity past*, also referred to as *inferential evidentiality*: judging by some other facts we have knowledge of, it is likely that Jane went to Scotland at the time referred to. (74) exemplifies *epistemic possibility past*: it is probable to a sufficiently high degree to be declared, that Jane went to Scotland yesterday. Finally, (75) is a variation on (71) and uses the *past of narration*, making the situation vivid and creating an illusion that the story is happening in front of the interlocutors' eyes, that is is being experienced *now*.

It is easy to represent these ways of expressing the past on a cline of graded commitment to the certainty of the situation conveyed in the proposition. The cline will order the past of narration and regular past before epistemic necessity past, and finally epistemic possibility past as the form which corresponds to the lowest degree of commitment and at the same time the highest degree of modality. I present a detailed scale in Section 4.2.3 (Fig. 4.19) while discussing the semantics of English expressions with past-time reference. These representations will be analogous to the ones proposed for the future (in Section 4.2.1). This is so due to the fact that expressions of the past-time reference and expressions of the future-time reference both prove to have modal properties and allow for degrees of detachment from the proposition in their scope. Analogous observations concerning the inter-action with modal adverbs such as 'possibly' or 'probably' also apply here. As Dummett (2004: 73) points out, there are four possible standpoints on the reality of the past and the future: both are real; both are unreal and only the present is real; only the past is real; or only the future is real. Dummett presents a detailed discussion of these metaphysical stances and we shall not attempt to add anything new to his arguments. But let us focus on the view that both the past and the future are real. Surprisingly, we will find it equally commensurate with our view of the concept of time as modality as we did the view that both are unreal. If they are both *unreal* and exist only to the extent that they have traces in the present, then the modality view is a direct translation of this metaphysical stance onto the level of concepts and *a fortiori* (for us) onto the level of semantic representations of natural language sentences, because the concepts are reflected in the lexicalized and grammaticalized expressions of time. If they are both *real*, then they are like a map: we travel through the past, present, and future, occupying various spatial locations, and the location at which we speak of the given location, let us call it the location of speech, is the one at which we speak with evidence, from experience. We can also remember or plan locations on the map and point to them with lesser or greater certainty. On this conceptualization, time is an element of four-dimensional (for us, bound by the anthropic principle) space-time. Juxtaposed with the arguments from the principles of relativity, it seems that there is every reason to adopt the reality conception. It is compatible with the modality of the concept of time and it is, as we are told, the stuff there is. But Dummett disagrees. He argues that, on the four-dimensional conceptualization, the explanation of what for us is 'past' and 'future' is circular and the meaning of change is lost. On this conceptualization, the past and the future are 'regions of reality' that are established by our own perspective, our own concept of time (Dummett 2004: 87). Now, when we move from place to place, our spatial perspective changes with our change of location in space. But it is faulty reasoning to argue by analogy that our temporal perspective changes with our change of location in time. Time, Dummett argues, depends on location and on the state of things that surround us, and this is something that the four-dimensional concept cannot capture. In short, it cannot capture change. It supplies instead a static reality and a concept of a dynamic agent moving along the time dimension, and this is not, for Dummett at least, an adequate concept of reality. We shall not enter into the argument on the meaning of *change*. In the ordinary sense of the word, the world does indeed change. But what matters is the concept of time flow, and that can be easily excluded from the metaphysics of time, as well as from the human concept of time and the semantics of natural language. Reality need not be 'static': space-time is not a perspective on reality. Four-dimensional space-time is, but space-time is reality itself and changes have to be described in terms of the histories of the world calculated with the help of its possible dimensions. Unlike Dummett, we do not therefore limit reality to 'the totality of what can be experienced by sentient creatures and what can be known by intelligent ones' (*ibid.*: 92). But we will follow Givón (2005: 1) who says that chunks of reality are 'artifacts of their framing, arbitrary time-slices of the experiential continuum'. The view that such time-slices are reality itself can be accepted on the anthropic principle, but, from what we are led to believe by modern physics, not for reality at large. In short, we are able to accept the reality of time, reject the reality of time flow, and build upon this picture the human concept of time as 'diluted certainty': graded modality. There is no need to conclude from the modal conception of time and modal semantics of time that the past and the future (and perhaps even the present) are unreal.

Let us now juxtapose this radically modal conception with the formal account of the past proposed by Thomason (2002) as historical necessity, mentioned briefly in Section 2.1. Thomason (2002: 209) models what is understood as the flow of time as the loss of possibilities. A state of affairs that is present or past is *necessarily* so:

$\phi \leftrightarrow \Box \phi$ provided ϕ contains no occurrences of F. Also,

$P\Box\phi \rightarrow \Box P\phi$

To repeat, he suggests that, as time passes, the number of possible states of affairs diminishes monotonically. In other words, as we move along the time line, the number of branches that can be drawn from every subsequent point will be smaller by a predictable amount from the number pertaining to previous moments. Sentence (76) exemplifies this.

(76)   In 1932 it was possible for Great Britain to avoid war with Germany; but in 1937 it was impossible.   (from Thomason 2002: 207)

This is so because what in the past was a possibility about some subsequent *now*, at the point of this *now* became reality: historical necessity. He fits this model in the times and worlds framework and stipulates that if world w is similar to some w' at a time t, then w and w' share the same past up to, and including, the time t. In other words, for any $t' < t$, the formulas have to mean the same thing for w and w' (see Thomason 2002: 209). This account revolves around the concept of probability, understood as modality (see p. 205), but probabilities culminate in necessity when a state of affairs becomes present and then past. On the other hand, our view of the psychological past is founded on a degree of irrealism about the metaphysical correlate of this concept of the past: what makes statements about the past true is how things are now, what memories and evidence we hold at the present moment referring to the past time in question. In other words, although we agree that the concept of the past supervenes on real past, this supervenience is construed in the Dummettian way by means of being coloured by and restricted to memories and evidence. Real past needs B-theory, not A-theory, resources. Now, in order for this type of a formal account to support our view on psychological past, the notion of historical necessity would have to be replaced with a formal model of possibility including approximation to necessity. While not everything can function as evidence, not everything that really happened can be present in internal, psychological time. The number of teeth Socrates had at the time of his death is a real number and there was a state of affairs that, were it that time now, would give us an answer, but the fact is not part of our available truth-makers and the notion of historical necessity that it engenders is of little use for internal time. It is of use for metaphysical time but there the concept of necessity is undermined by quite another consideration: that of allowing reality to be present without the anthropic (and Dummettian) point of view. So far, so good. We can now climb down and have a closer look at the nitty-gritties of time expressions: tense and temporal adverbials.

2.5 Temporal markers in discourse

2.5.1 *Tense*

There is no doubt that the main marker of temporality in Indo-European languages is tense. We have to begin therefore with some terminological remarks concerning tense and time. Just as modality will be distinguished from mood, so temporality will be distinguished from tense. Tense is a 'grammaticalized expression of location in time' (Comrie 1985: 9). Tense is a grammatical category, while time is ontological and psychological, giving rise to our earlier notions of external (real, metaphysical) time and internal (conceptual, psychological) time.[42] Henceforth, it is time that is modelled in semantic representations. The dependence between external and internal time was the subject of Chapter 1 in which we concluded that time is both real and psychological, but for the purpose of semantic analysis of linguistic expressions it is the psychological time, pertaining to the internal consciousness of time, that we should consider. Since the purpose of this essay is an investigation into the semantic representation of time, tense will be addressed only tangentially, as one of the linguistic devices used to express temporal distinctions. This device is neither necessary, as tenseless languages as well as tenseless utterances in tensed languages demonstrate, nor sufficient, as the heavy reliance on temporal adverbials in tensed languages shows.

---

[42] See also Kuhn and Portner 2002 on tense, time, and temporal orientation in their survey of the literature on the semantics of time. They distinguish prospective and retrospective orientations from which a past, present, or future event can be taken.

This distinction into grammatical tenses and ontological, psychological, and semantic time is clear and intuitive but not entirely uncontroversial. For example, Declerck (2006: 94) offers the following definition of tense:

> A tense is the pairing of a morpho-syntactic form with a meaning, the meaning being the specification of the temporal location of a situation. Thus, in the future tense, the form '*will* + present infinitive' is paired with the meaning 'location after speech time'.

On this definition, tense is a grammatical but also a semantic category: it is a pairing of the morpho-syntactic form with meaning. However, this construal leads to many insurmountable difficulties. As we saw in Sections 2.2–2.4, temporality of a described situation is inferred from many different sources, some left unuttered. It also has to be pointed out in this context that the temporality of the noun phrase and the temporality of the verb phrase of a sentence may have to be interpreted separately: in (77), the reference of 'my grandfather' cannot be interpreted with reference to any time prior to the speaker's birth (since the referent was not his/her grandfather at any time prior to that event), while the event described in the verb phrase is temporally included in such a prior time interval, namely 1903.

(77)   My grandfather was born in 1903.

Incidentally, this separate temporality of the noun phrase has been employed in the wider argument to the effect that there are so-called *nominal tenses*. In Paraguayan Guaraní, for example, there are nominal markers that signal the past and the future orientation of the noun phrase (*kue* and *rã*, respectively). It is sometimes claimed that such markers are nominal tenses. However, as Tonhauser (2007) convincingly argues, they are better defined as, simply, nominal temporal markers. They do not affect the temporality of the verb phrase, as (78) demonstrates. In the simplified translation, *Ref* stands for a cross-reference marker, 3 for the third person, *la* for the definiteness marker (borrowed from Spanish), and *re* for argument marker.

(78)   O-ho   peteĩ arriéro o-jeruré-vo   la   h-embireko-rã-re.
        Ref 3-go one   man   3-ask.for-at   *la* 3-wife-*rã-re*
        'A man went to ask for his future wife.'
                                            (adapted from Tonhauser 2007: 833)

These markers do not determine the temporal location of the noun-phrase time: in (78), the future is the future with respect to the past time of the event. Neither can *kue* and *rã* be equated with the adjectives *future* and *former*: their relative distributions in contexts do not coincide. We conclude with

Tonhauser that temporal nominal markers are a separate phenomenon from tense and should be added to the list of linguistic markers of temporality.

Next, Mocoví, a language spoken in Argentina belonging to the Guaykurúan (also referred to as Waikurúan) family, has no morphological tense marking in the verbal system but uses certain classifiers (also analysed as determiners) which help in conveying temporality. For example, 'the dog' can be translated as 'na pyoq', 'so pyoq', or 'ka pyoq'. The determiner 'na' signals the present time, while 'so' and ka' the recent and the remote past respectively (see examples in Manni 2007: 130). Further, when the speaker talks about a dog that is dead at the time of speaking, the determiner 'ka' is obligatorily used. We can stipulate from the extant studies (see Manni 2007) that determiners in Mocoví have an evidential function and thereby help achieve temporal reference to situations. Evidence from languages such as Mocoví is pertinent to my argument for the modal supervenience of temporality in two ways. Firstly, it acts as evidence in support of the thesis of interaction of information from various sources in constructing temporal reference. This thesis is more formally developed in Chapter 4 where I demonstrate how information about temporality coming from various carriers of meaning is merged. Secondly, it provides a supporting argument for the dependence of the category of temporality on that of evidentiality, and thereby also epistemic modality.

Further, we must recognize the importance of the contribution from the pragmatic component in the form of pragmatic inference and pragmatic defaults. To repeat, in Thai, one form, corresponding to, for example, 'rain fall' ($f_3$on $t_1$ok) can convey a wide range of temporal locations, depending on the context and shared assumptions. Although there are indeed regularities in that '*will* + present infinitive' more often than not pertains to future orientation, this claim can be made only with reference to *default situation types*. We find it more adequate, therefore, to draw the boundary between tense and time in a more intuitive way and say that tense is the grammatical means of conveying temporality of the situation and leave semantics out of the definition of tense, 'kicking semantics up', so to speak, to the level at which all available information and assumptions about the temporality of the situation presented in the utterance combines. Merger representations of Default Semantics employed in Chapter 4 are precisely such semantic structures where information coming from various sources interacts. As a result of this allocation of semantics to a higher level, we will also make a very cautious use of Declerck's (2006: 94) claim that tense can be credited with specifying the temporal location of a situation by relating it to some point of reference. The claim is correct with respect to presumptions of temporality that can be drawn from situation types ('*will* + present infinitive' normally refers to the future) but for our purpose of representing utterance meaning it has to be qualified with precisely this proviso: *normally, commonly, unless other sources of information signal otherwise.* For example, while Declerck (2006: 103) agrees that future-oriented sentences are always modal precisely *qua* being future, he adds that the high probability with which we can pair '*will* + present infinitive' with the future justifies its status as a future tense. We will have no objection to this statement because Declerck's aim is to provide a comprehensive grammar of the English verb phrase and therefore typical, fairly reliable pairings of morpho-syntactic forms with meaning are his main objective. But, precisely because our aim is utterance interpretation, we will have to adopt a different angle where tense figures less prominently.[43]

In short, grammatical means of expressing temporal distinctions are neither necessary nor sufficient to place in time a situation to which an utterance pertains. Therefore, although it is true that grammaticalization of temporal distinctions is an important part of conceptualizing time, it does not suffice to look at tense while drawing conclusions concerning the concept of time. Declerck, for example, suggests the following conceptualization for the English language:

English tenses appear to reflect a mental division of time into past and nonpast. The main evidence for this is that all tenses carry either a past or a nonpast (present) tense morpheme. There is no future tense morpheme. We will represent this division of time as involving two time-spheres: a past time-sphere and a present time-sphere. (Declerck 2006: 147)

In view of the fact that grammar alone does not determine temporality, paired with Declerck's (2006: 102) own claim that future, although modal ontologically, is rendered in English as a future *tense* ('*will* + present infinitive'), we consider this conclusion too strong.

We will also treat with caution the privileged position that grammatical tense is awarded in the semantic representation of time in some formal semantic theories. DRT is one of such approaches:

[The feature] TENSE has three possible values, *past*, *present*, and *future*, signifying that the described eventuality lies before, at, or after the utterance time, respectively. The value of TENSE for a given sentence S is determined by the tense of the verb of S. When the main verb is in the simple past, TENSE = *past*; when it is in the simple

---

[43] N.B. Philosophers sometimes use *tense* in a more restricted, and at the same time, liberal, sense, speaking of 'tensed facts' and 'tensed reality'. For Kit Fine (2005), being *tensed* is dissociated from the linguistic means of expressing information about temporality but pertains to temporality. Being *tensed* is also differentiated from the *passage of time*.

present, TENSE = *pres*; and when the verb complex contains the auxiliary *will*, TENSE = *fut*. (Kamp and Reyle 1993: 512–13)

As the examples of mismatches between grammatical tense and temporality discussed earlier in this chapter demonstrate, this strategy may only be adopted when the objective is to represent the default uses of grammatical forms in a natural language system. It will not suffice for our more philosophical objective of relating semantic representation to the concept of time at large.

It also has to be observed that, although it is past tense that is normally credited with information about the past, this information may be extracted from aspect. The English perfect contributes temporal information to the truth conditions. As Portner (2003) points out, various types of perfect carry information about precedence of the state of affairs the sentence is about with respect to the time of speech. Sometimes this precedence is complete, as in (79), at other times it includes overlap with the time of speech, as in (80).

(79)   Tom has read *Cloud Atlas*.
(80)   Tom has been in Cambridge since Monday.

The semantic content of the perfect does not differentiate between such continuative (80) and non-continuative (79) readings. As Portner (2003: 461) suggests, there is an additional pragmatic component to the perfect that adds pragmatic presuppositions of current relevance to the communicated content. Although there is no doubt that there is more to the meaning of the perfect than the past orientation, this pastness is an essential component of it. The essential component is current relevance of a past state of affairs and it can be derived from the perfect form and the common ground, a pool of shared presuppositions. Adding past adverbials as in (79a) is not compatible with sentences in Present Perfect, not because they don't convey pastness but because of this common-ground presupposition of current relevance.

*(79a)   Tom has read *Cloud Atlas* yesterday.

To support this claim further, it has been extensively argued that a Thai expression *kh₃oe:y*, which used to be regarded in traditional grammars as a marker of past tense, is better analysed as an aspectual marker with the default past-time reference.[44] In a similar spirit, Gennari (2003) gives a detailed account of how tense and other sources of information such as lexical or sentential aktionsart and pragmatic inference 'conspire' to render the required

---

[44] See Srioutai 2006.

temporal information. For example, past sentences of eventive aktionsart as in (81) receive only a sequential interpretation and never an overlapping one, while stative sentences allow for both, as in (82).

(81)   Tom said that Mary broke her leg.
(82)   Tom said that Mary was ill.

As was discussed briefly in Section 2.1, this 'conspiracy' is also present in future and other modal constructions, where only stative sentences allow for an overlapping reading as in (83) as opposed to (84).

(83)   Tom will/may/must be in London.
(84)   Tom will/may/must leave.

As she says, 'tenses have the same meaning in all contexts but aktionsart properties lead to the overlapping readings' (Gennari 2003: 46). Analogously, pragmatics and grammar can conspire. A complement sentence in the scope of a future-time marker can obtain an interpretation which is wholly future or future overlapping with the time of speech, depending on the addressee's assumptions and background knowledge concerning the state of affairs it concerns. For example, since talking on the phone is of a relatively short duration, (85) is likely to receive a non-overlapping interpretation. Since writing a book is of a relatively long duration and is likely to have commenced before the utterance was issued, (86) is likely to receive an overlapping interpretation.

(85)   When he gets home, John will think that Mary is talking on the phone.
(86)   John will announce today that Mary is writing a new book.

(adapted from Gennari 2003: 63)

All this testifies to the accuracy of Dowty's (1986: 350) observation, generally acknowledged nowadays in Gricean pragmatics, that temporal ordering of events in discourse relies not only on the processing of sentence meaning by the addressee but also on the result of pragmatic inference that may interact with the output of syntactic processing. It also testifies to the adequacy of our decision to 'kick semantics up' to the level of interaction between various sources of information about meaning. In the spirit of contextualist semantics, we can easily replace 'implicature' with pragmatic inference that contributes to the semantic, truth-conditional representation of the communicated content, without losing the gist of the 'conspiracy' view. This conceptual assumption, culminating in the idea of pragmatic compositionality, will be followed in my semantic representation of temporality in Default Semantics in Section 4.2. This 'conspiracy' is also utilized in an offshoot of DRT worked out by

Asher and Lascarides (e.g. 2003) who propose a set of so-called discourse relations, or rhetorical structure rules, which account for the relations between chunks of information in discourse and thus for discourse coherence. There are relations such as Explanation, Elaboration, Narration, Contrast, or Background, among others, which 'glue' information about particular events or states, having truth-conditional effects in the form of constraints on an interpretation. For example, if two utterances are about events and the second event occurred later than the first, the relation between them is likely to be Narration. They call this 'glue' a 'logic of information packaging' and point out that it has to be nonmonotonic: it relies on default rhetorical links 'If A, then normally B' which are cancellable when background knowledge so dictates. Temporal relations can thus be pragmatically captured in this formal system by the addition of such nonmonotonic 'glue logic'.

What happens when neither tense nor aspect is a compulsory component of the sentence and many temporal orientations can be represented by the same grammatical form? I mentioned this situation briefly in Section 2.1 with reference to Thai. In Thai, expression $d_1ay_1^{II}$ that normally refers to the past is better regarded as modal in that it is by no means restricted to past-time contexts and there is ample evidence that the default sense of pastness can be overridden. Similarly, the marker c_1a, traditionally classified as an auxiliary conveying future tense, was found to convey epistemic possibility and in default scenarios communicate future-time reference.[45] Next, Matthewson (2006) observes that in Lillooet Salish, also referred to as St'àt'imcets, a language spoken in British Columbia in Canada, there is a morpheme *kelh* which, although it is used for futurity, is not a tense morpheme but rather a marker of modality. Its behaviour resembles that of Abusch's (1988) theoretical construct *woll*[46] which signals that an event or state follows another in a sequence but does not overtly signal future tense: in addition to being realized as *will*, it can also refer to the past and be realized as *would*. Since St'àt'imcets has only one tense morpheme, restricting reference time to being non-future, Matthewson suggests that the future is always marked as modality. Evidence from St'àt'imcets for the modality thesis may, in fact, be even stronger than she suggests. The non-future morpheme proposed by her is phonologically null and in effect what she does is analyse a tenseless language *as if* it were a tensed one, albeit minimally so. Be that as it may, there is no overt tense marker in St'àt'imcets and the only marker of futurity proves to be modal, just as the Thai c_1a did on Srioutai's (2006) analysis.

---

[45] Srioutai 2004, 2006; Jaszczolt and Srioutai forthcoming.
[46] See Section 2.2.

Srioutai (2006: 247) demonstrates that blocking of the default interpretation commonly takes place when shared background knowledge dictates it or when the default reading is incompatible with the adverbs and other markers with temporal significance. As a result, she concludes that temporal information in Thai 'resides in pragmatics': it is pertinent to the understanding of sentences but it is not obligatorily inherent in the sentence's lexicon or grammar. In order to propose a semantics for a language such as Thai that would reflect the conceptualization of time, one has to move from sentences to utterances and adopt a theory in which compositional meaning is the output of the interaction of information coming from various sources, including, but not restricted to, the lexicon and grammar. The semantic (and conceptual) representation also makes use of situational defaults and of pragmatic inference performed during utterance interpretation by the addressee, and predicted as necessary by the speaker. Srioutai presented such an analysis of temporality in Thai in the framework of Default Semantics in that this framework allows a suitable account of the interaction of sources to produce a representation of time and offers a model of suitably pragmatic compositionality. To repeat, the framework of Default Semantics will be further extended and used in Section 4.2 but, before this can be done, we have to propose the semantic equivalent of the state of affairs that is to be utilized in this semantics. This will be the topic of Section 3.2.

It has often been assumed that, although natural languages differ in the types and numbers of grammaticalized distinctions pertaining to tense, aspect, and mood, there exists a functional equivalence between the grammars of various languages (see Dahl 1985; Tynan and Delgado Lavín 1997). In other words, various devices present in a language conspire to render temporal, aspectual, and modal information to the degree to which it is required for communication. No system is worse in this respect than any other. Only by broadening the semantic perspective to include tense–time mismatches as in (87) and the Spanish equivalent (88) below, and cases of underspecified temporality as in Thai, can we account for this property of communicative adequacy of language systems.

(87) Mary is leaving tomorrow.

(88) María se   marcha   mañana.
      María *Refl.3Sg* leave *3Sg Pres Ind* tomorrow. (adapted from Tynan
                                             and Delgado Lavín 1997: 117)

As Tynan and Delgado Lavín (1997: 117–18) observe, there are two types of explanation of the behaviour of verbal tenses: (i) tenses can be used to refer to more than one temporal orientation, for example the present tense need not be used to refer to the present, and (ii) tenses can convey epistemic meanings in that their usage relies on the type and strength of evidence that gives rise to the speaker's utterance. On their construal, the mismatches between the tense and time referred to, as in (87) and (88), convey modal connotations, with the proviso that there is always an unmarked form that conveys purely temporal information.

Now, for Givón (2005: 149), modality is a shell that 'encases' but 'does not tamper with' the kernel of propositional information. This shell encodes the speaker's attitude, coloured, as Givón argues, with the addressee's attitude. With reference to temporality, this means that the speakers assume that the addressees have a representation of the temporal structure of the situation of speech within which they can locate the events and states that are mentioned in discourse. For example, Swahili has a so-called consecutive tense which signals that the clause continues the temporal location assigned to the preceding one. So, the passage becomes temporally grounded as past, future, progressive, or perfect and the following clauses continue the assigned orientation. The speaker uses this device in order to orient the addressee to the chain of temporal reference. Example (89) demonstrates how the consecutive-tense marker *ka* follows the grounding in the past established initially.

(89)   a.   ... wa-Ingereza   wa-**li**-wa-chukua   wa-le   maiti,
            3*Pl*-British   3*Pl*-***Past***-3*Pl*-take   3*Pl*-*Dem*   corpses
            '... then the British took the corpses,

       b.   wa-**ka**-wa-tia   katika   bao   moja,
            3*Pl*-***Cons***-3*Pl*-put.on   on   board   one
            put them on a flat board,

       c.   wa-**ka**-ya-telemesha   maji-ni   kwa   utaratibu   w-ote...
            3*Pl*-***Cons***-3*Pl*-lower   water-*Loc*   with   order   3*Pl*-all
            and lowered them steadily into the water...'
                                              (adapted from Givón 2005: 154)[47]

The usual translation of -*ka*- when it follows the past tense marker -*li*- is 'and', 'and then'. It is therefore a straightforward marker of the order of narration. However, when -*ka*- follows a marker of future tense -*ta*-, its meaning tends to be 'so that', 'in order to', and thus it is coloured to involve causation as in (90).

---

[47] Many thanks to Lutz Marten and to Andrew Smith for discussing this example, as well as basic Swahili grammar, with me.

(90) Ni-**ta**-kwenda soko-ni,   ni-**ka**-nunua   ndizi.
      1Sg-***Fut***-go   market-*Loc* *1Sg*-***Cons***-buy   bananas.
      'I will go to the market and/to buy some bananas.'
                                  (from Lutz Marten, personal communication)

This causal colouring of the future can be construed as supporting evidence
for the modality of the future in that a future state of affairs is likely to be
expressed when it has a causal connection with the present or some other
form of present significance. In other words it has to be *justified as possible*.

Restricting the discussion to the typology of grammatical or lexical markers
of time or to their properties in the language system does not cover the
required spectrum of strategies commonly used in discourse that is essential
for adequate representation of utterance meaning. One has to view them in
the light of interlocutors' strategies in discourse in order to properly understand their functioning. For example, it is important to understand the
correlation between the relative social status of the interlocutors and the
epistemic strength with which the statement is made. This correlation differs
from culture to culture. Givón (2005: 176) refers here to the principle he calls
subjective certainty vis-à-vis higher authority: 'In communicating to an inter-
locutor of higher status, one downgrades one's own subjective certainty'.
Various models of politeness offer different explanations for this phenomenon but we will not be concerned with theories of politeness here.[48] What is
important is the existence of a correlation between epistemic modality and
especially the strength of the epistemic commitment expressed, and strategies
of effective communication.

2.5.2 *A note on some relevant adverbials*

It need not be argued that 'time words' are of primary importance in
specifying the temporality of a situation. While the grammatical expression
may leave the temporality open for further specification, or even be misleading when taken on its own, time adverbs and adverbial clauses express it
beyond doubt. In (91), it is the adverb 'now' that directs away from the default
future reference, and, in (92), repeated from (18), it is the adverb 'tomorrow'
that directs the interpretation away from the default present-time reference.

(91)   John will be in London now.
(92)   Peter goes to London tomorrow morning.

In languages where tense or aspect need not be present in the sentence, time
adverbs are often of crucial importance, especially when, as in English, the

---

[48] See, for example, Leech 1983; Brown and Levinson 1987; and also Jaszczolt 2002, Chapter 15,
for an overview of approaches to politeness.

default reading is to be overridden. In English, they happily co-exist with tense markers but not always with temporality markers of an aspectual character: to repeat, as Portner (2003) points out, various types of perfect in English (e.g. present perfect) carry information about pastness but do not interact with past-time adverbials as (93), repeated from (79a), demonstrates.

*(93)   Tom has read *Cloud Atlas* yesterday.

This is so because, in addition to pastness, perfect also carries other kinds of information such as current, present relevance, effect or interest.

Time adverbs not only specify the temporality of the state of affairs but can also link states of affairs by producing presuppositions. 'Again' is a good example of such a function. 'Already' and 'still' also trigger presuppositions but while *again* pertains to aspect (iterative) as well as to temporal ordering, the latter two are more clearly aspectual.[49] *Again* has been widely discussed in the Satisfaction Theory of presuppositions where presuppositions are regarded as conditions that have to be verified before the verification of the sentence that gives rise to them takes place. Presupposition associated with *again* is verified by means of what was already accepted as part of the semantic content of the discourse.[50] For example, in (94), the presupposition associated with *again*, namely (94a), is added in virtue of the content of the first sentence. Block capitals stand for accenting.

(94)   Last night our neighbours played their new stereo set. Tonight they made a lot of noise AGAIN.

(94a)   Our neighbours made a lot of noise last night. (from Kamp 2007: 25)

In the Binding Theory, adopted for example by DRT, on the other hand, presupposition triggers are anaphors and they require an explicit and accessible antecedent in the representation of discourse (a DRS). So, the presupposition associated with *again* in (94) requires that a representation of (94a) is accommodated – added as part of the discourse – on a par with explicitly uttered statements.[51] Be that as it may, Moltmann (2006: 192) concludes that *again* requires a proposition with the content of the presupposition, such as (94a), to be coindexed with the sentence under consideration, such as (94), as its background. While not all presuppositions are anaphoric in this way, *again* presuppositions seem to be.

Again can also be associated with the cyclic conception of time. To repeat, internal time, as lexicalized and grammaticalized in various natural languages,

---

[49] For an excellent analysis of these adverbs in DRT see Smessaert and ter Meulen 2004.

[50] See Moltmann 2006 for problems associated with this theory.

[51] The literature on presupposition in formal semantics is vast. See, for example, Beaver 1997; Kamp 2001; and Geurts 1999. See, for example, Moltmann 2006 for problems associated with Satisfaction Theory and Binding Theory.

can be conceptualized either as linear (horizontally or vertically) or cyclical. The presuppositions of *again* are, of course, valid for both, and the two conceptualizations seem to be capable of co-existing in one system. They are both active in contemporary Mandarin Chinese and Japanese,[52] and they are both attested in English. My example comes from literary English and in particular from David Mitchell's *Cloud Atlas* (again):

> Certainties. Strip back the beliefs pasted on by governesses, schools and states, you find indelible truths at one's core. Rome'll decline and fall again, Cortazar'll sail again (...), you and I'll sleep under Corsican stars again, I'll come to Bruges again, fall in and out of love with Eva again, you will read this letter again, the Sun'll grow cold again. Nietzsche's gramophone record. When it ends, the Old One plays it again, for an eternity of eternities.
>
> Time cannot permeate this sabbatical. We do not stay dead long. (Mitchell 2004: 489–90)

'Certainties' and the concept of reiteration captured in *again* are clearly linked. The modal role of time adverbs is well attested in the literature. In their corpus-based study, Simon-Vandenbergen and Aijmer (2007) consider modal adverbs of certainty within the framework of the semantic field they express. They are regarded as truth-intensifiers that developed through the grammaticalization process from adverbs with semantic content such as manner adverbs or adverbs of measure (see Traugott 2006; Traugott and Dasher 2002). Attested from Old English onwards, Early Modern English added to them increasingly frequent adverbs with different degrees of probability such as 'probably', 'presumably', 'possibly', or 'conceivably'. In addition to purely modal adverbs, where the intensification of truth is expressed from the speaker's perspective, we can also distinguish those expressed from the addressee's perspective ('obviously'), as well as epistemic modal adverbs with evidential component ('clearly'). Simon-Vandenbergen and Aijmer (2007) investigated their use through a search of the British component of the International Corpus of English (ICE-GB) and British National Corpus (BNC), as well as parallel translation corpora with Dutch, French, German, and Swedish, describing their semantic and pragmatic properties. The category of modal certainty was found to be closely related to that of evidentiality (and English evidential adverbs are modal, see *ibid.*: 32) and mirativity. Mirativity is the semantic category for marking the novelty of information or surprise on receiving it. Since these two dimensions are added to 'pure' modality, it comes with no surprise (no pun intended) that the

---

[52] See, for example, Evans (2003: 235) and further references there.

attested modal adverbs are either subjective or intersubjective.[53] Moreover, it has to be noted that modal adverbs have to be non-factive: neither the groups that signal higher degree of detachment ('supposedly', 'allegedly', 'probably') nor those signalling certainty ('undoubtedly', 'certainly', or evidentially tinted 'clearly') necessitate the truth of the proposition which they qualify. In contrast, evaluative adverbs are factive: the presence of 'regrettably' or 'surprisingly' entails that the proposition qualified by them is true.

What is important for our purpose is that such modal adverbs do not have rigidly determined semantic functions. Instead, they have a *rhetorical function* in discourse. When a speaker utters an unqualified sentence, for example, stating that 2008 is a leap year, in accordance with Grice's maxim of truthfulness or any other post-Gricean principles of rational communicative behaviour, the addressee assumes that the statement is true. Adding 'certainly' seems to have the opposite effect to the definitional intensification of truth. Instead, it signals that there is some initial doubt in the truth of the statement, either on the part of the speaker or the addressee. In short, as various versions of the Manner heuristic predict (Grice 1975; Levinson 2000), a marked expression signals a marked situation: the addition of a modal adverb of certainty signals such a marked case (cf. Traugott and Dasher 2002: 162; Simon-Vandenbergen and Aijmer 2007: 33). Similarly, 'no doubt' signals initial doubt as a reason for using the qualifier.

Next, the contribution of modal adverbs to the expression of certainty has also been thoroughly investigated with reference to their co-occurrence with epistemic verbs such as 'know', 'believe', 'doubt', or 'assume'. In the data-based study based on the British National Corpus, Cappelli (2007) identified frequent collocations in which the speaker's commitment to the evaluation encoded in the epistemic verb is further modulated by the adverb. For example, in her data, 'think' co-occurs with sixty-one modulating adverbs such as 'certainly', 'definitely', 'clearly' or 'truly' (cf. Cappelli 2007: 190). The phenomenon is analogous to that of the adverbial modulation in the case of temporal expressions, which further testifies to our thesis of the supervenience of temporality on modality.

I shall not be further concerned here with clearly modal adverbs such as 'possibly', 'certainly', 'probably', 'necessarily', or modal *qua* evidential such as 'evidently' or 'obviously'. As was pointed out earlier in this chapter, they modify temporal expressions and allocate to them specific degrees of epistemic commitment, just as grammatical forms including overt modal verbs do. There is nothing specific to their behaviour that would affect our argument

---

[53] See also Nuyts (2001: 65–6): '...the corpus data (...) [for English and Dutch, KJ] reveal that in the large majority of expressions with the modal adverb there is no inherent suggestion whatsoever as to whether the epistemic evaluation is subjective or intersubjective: it is simply neutral in these terms'.

here. It is not my aim to provide a detailed analysis of their semantic properties, neither is it my aim to compare the distribution of temporal devices across
languages. If it were, we would have to observe, for instance, that, where in one
system a grammatical form provides the indicator of the degree of commitment, in another language it may be the adverb, and yet in another there may
not be an overt marker but instead there will be a stereotypical association,
made through pragmatic processing, of a default degree of commitment with a
vague, semantically underdetermined form. All we need to attest at this stage is
that adverbials perform a variety of functions while contributing to the
semantics of time and they have to be analysed as interacting ('conspiring')
with the other sources of such temporal information which contribute to the
one, sole level of the semantic merger. Cappelli's (2007) study mentioned
above, which demonstrates the extent of this 'semantic conspiracy' for an
analogous and related phenomenon in the epistemic domain, shares the
main theoretical assumptions with the framework of Default Semantics
adopted in our analysis in Chapter 4.

2.6 Conclusion

The terms 'past', 'present', and 'future' belong to two different discourses. One
concerns real time and its ontology, as it is present in the theories of physics.
The other one deals with the human concept of time, which we called
internal or psychological time. In this chapter I investigated the properties
of this concept of time and defended the thesis that time is not a primitive
human concept but instead it is at least supervenient on, if not identical with,
the concept of modal detachment or epistemic possibility. I have also looked at
the concepts of futurity, the present (*now*) and pastness and how they are
realized in natural language expressions and concluded that both futurity and
pastness are conceptualized as degrees of modal detachment. I have also
tentatively suggested that this conceptualization of temporality is compatible
with the notion of real time as an element of space-time: neither presupposes
that time flows and both allow for modalities with respect to the past and the
future: different histories of the world and different anticipated futures on a par.

The remainder of this essay concerns semantic representation of temporality as conveyed in utterances, mainly utterances of English sentences. I propose
a category about which temporality should be predicated, scrutinizing in the
process the notions of event, state, proposition, sentence, and utterance, and
finish by developing such semantic, and at the same time conceptual, representations in a framework of Default Semantics which will be modified for this
purpose.

3

Semantic representation of time: A preamble

3.1 Semantic structures and cognitive reality

It is reasonable to begin this discussion with the assumption that the semantic representation of temporal expressions requires a perspective that reflects the cognitive reality of the human conceptualization of time and at the same time offers a formal account of meaning. We shall also assume, following the well-tested and successful tradition of contextualism in semantics and pragmatics,[1] that this formal theory of meaning should apply the tool of truth conditions not to abstract objects such as sentences or propositions physically expressed in speech or writing but instead to utterances, intended meanings, or thoughts that were intended by some model speaker and subsequently expressed, and at the same time thoughts that are recovered by a model addressee in the process of communication. In this way we can offer a representation, cognitive and semantic, of temporality that is not only encoded in the lexicon and grammar but also temporality that is part of the linguistic community's world view in that it can be left unsaid in the utterance, relying on the salient, common strategies of inference used by its members, as well as on default interpretations. We can also offer an account that is not concerned with ambiguities engendered by the lexicon or syntax but instead represents the result of the total process of meaning recovery. I shall refer to such units of analysis as utterances and talk about truth conditions of utterances. The semantic representation will therefore be a representation that subsumes the result of pragmatic inference, along the general lines worked out in the post-Gricean tradition (Sperber and Wilson, e.g. 1986, 1995; Carston, e.g. 1988, 2002; Recanati, e.g. 1989, 2004). Where post-Griceans differ is largely in the allocation of such inferences to the explicit content or implicit content, the number and character of the principles that account for these inferences (see, for

---

[1] For expositions of contextualism see Recanati 2004, 2005, 2007a, b; Jaszczolt 2002, Chapter 11 and forthcoming. For a defence against semantic minimalism see also Montminy 2006.

example, Levinson 2000 for an alternative view to the ones above), and the nature of the processes that lead to such contextual modification of the output of syntactic processing (see Recanati 2004, 2007c, and Carston 2007 on conscious and automatic processes). They also differ on the object of study: *whose meaning* is to be modelled, the speaker's, the addressee's, or the result of some statistically valid interaction between a model speaker and a model addressee. I devoted careful attention to these theoretical issues elsewhere and they need not be discussed in much depth for the present purpose. Suffice it to say that I will follow the assumptions suggested in my *Default Semantics* (Jaszczolt 2005) and adopt a contextualist position according to which some such pragmatic modifications to the encoded content are conscious and some automatic, and what is modelled is the meaning derived by a model addressee as that intended by the model speaker. Needless to say, the primary objective for such a model will be striving towards cognitive reality: a plausible, and testable, representation of the human concept of time. The subsidiary aim will be formal elegance: the representations will have to be analysable in a truth-conditional, model-theoretic framework. There is a significant difficulty, however, that this combination of aims, and the attempt to represent intended meaning, brings about as compared with formal, post-Montagovian representations of discourse. Standard dynamic approaches aspire to compositionality of meaning that is founded on the syntactic composition. What it means for temporality is that approaches such as DRT will rely on the tense of the verb phrase and on the coded content of time adverbials. Although such dynamic approaches differ among themselves in how 'strongly compositional' they are, i.e. in allowing or disallowing the level of representation that is intermediate between natural language and the syntactic algebra,[2] they don't go as far as 'kicking compositionality up', as we said in Chapter 2, to pertain not to the sentence but rather to the intended content, or utterance meaning. This is what has been attempted in post-Gricean pragmatics (Recanati 2004; Jaszczolt 2005). In Default Semantics, compositionality means compositionality of utterance meaning that is derived from various sources, not only the string of sentences but also what can be reasonably assumed as intended by the speaker. Therefore, pragmatic compositionality is the best tool to deal with languages where all markers of tense and aspect can be left 'in the mind', assumed, but not explicitly expressed. To repeat, it proved to be a successful framework for the analysis of temporality in Thai, for example.[3] But also, for the same reason, pragmatic compositionality is often criticized by formal semanticists for trying to achieve

---

[2] See, for example, Groenendijk and Stokhof 1991; Partee 1984; Dekker 2000; Zeevat 1989.
[3] See Srioutai 2004, 2006.

the impossible: an algorithm for the combination of total recovered meaning that comes not only from language but also from social customs, traditions, assumptions about how humans reason, inferences from the particular situation, and the like. I don't think this means achieving the impossible. Clear patterns can be discerned of how these different types of information interact. Although the theory of Default Semantics, which is founded on such pragmatic compositionality, is still some way away from a complete algorithm, it has been successful in modelling the recovery of meaning from a wide variety of what were traditionally considered to be ambiguous or, since the 1970s, underspecified expressions.[4] In Section 4.1, I present the idea of pragmatic compositionality and the merger of information about meaning. The purpose of this section is more preliminary: to justify an approach to meaning that subsumes the goal of formal elegance under the main goal of psychological adequacy. Time is probably the best example, on a par with propositional attitudes such as belief or doubt (to which I devoted almost two decades of my earlier work[5]), to argue for the plausibility of such preferences. What we want to know from the semantic theory of time is how the meaning of temporal expressions is constructed, but this construction of meaning would be of very limited interest if it aimed at the formal simplicity and power to account for a greater fragment of a language, without paying attention to the question as to whether this representation can function as a plausible model of how the speakers really conceptualize time.

The payoff in the direction of cognitive reality is not a new idea. DRT (Kamp 1981; Kamp and Reyle 1993; Hamm *et al.* 2006; Kamp *et al.* forthcoming) has always been explicit about the expectation that the representation structures it proposes resemble mental representations constructed in people's brains.[6] Similarly, Jackendoff's conceptualist semantics (e.g. Jackendoff 2002; Culicover and Jackendoff 2005) goes in the direction of cognitive reality as the superordinate goal even more explicitly. The orientation of the proposal that follows should be viewed as sharing this desideratum.

---

[4] See Part II of Jaszczolt 2005 for applications of Default Semantics.

[5] See, for example, Jaszczolt 1999.

[6] Cf.: '...discourse representations can be regarded as the mental representations which speakers form in response to the verbal inputs they receive' (Kamp 1981: 5). Also, '...this description is conceived as an (idealized) analysis of the process whereby the recipient of an utterance comes to grasp the thoughts that the utterance contains' (Kamp and Reyle 1993: 8) and, already quoted in Chapter 2 (see fn 1),

DRT's claim that there are features of natural language the analysis of which requires a distinct level of discourse representation is consonant with a cognitive perspective on the nature of natural language meaning: Meaning in natural language manifests itself as the semantic competence of the language user... (Hamm *et al.* 2006: 5–6)

The family of approaches to meaning that have taken this psychological status of semantic representations particularly seriously is of course cognitive linguistics. For Langacker (e.g. 1987, 1991, 1999, 2006), 'meaning resides in conceptualization' (Langacker 2006: 1). For example, he explains the use of the present tense as conceptualizing the situation as coinciding with the time of speaking. Following Brisard (2002), he subsumes this prototypical sense of the present under a general modal concept of 'epistemic control'. This is contrasted with the use of modal expressions which do not signify control but rather 'epistemic striving'. The present is associated with the concept of epistemic immediacy which refers to the cases of mentally experiencing present-time states and events. As Brisard puts it,

Instead of emphasizing the purely temporal functions of the present tense, I will rather propose that it is primarily concerned with a degree of *immediate* ('present') *givenness* that warrants the attribution of epistemic certainty to a state of affairs. (Brisard 2002: 263)

He demonstrates with a series of examples that the English present relies either on direct perception of a state of affairs, coinciding with the time of speaking, or on generality: a state that is always present, as he says, 'out of time, as a structural part of our model of reality' (*ibid.*: 265). In short, instead of tense and time, conceptual semantics models people's construals of situations and their apprehension of time. This apprehension fits very well under the label of modality, as an epistemic relation towards the situation. In the case of the present, it is epistemic immediacy, co-occurrence with the time of speaking (see also Langacker 2006; Brisard 2006).[7] Temporal location is therefore regarded as conceptually modal (epistemic) but can be instantiated as, among others, temporal coincidence. The benefits of this perspective are ample: tense-time mismatches can be easily explained, and the availability of alternative temporal expressions for describing one and the same situation can be directly related to the modal detachment pertaining to the speaker's particular construal of reality. Up to this point, this perspective on the semantics of time is very close to what I propose in this essay: conceptually, time supervenes on modality or even is modality. The main differences lie in the access to extra-mental reality and to formal tools for representing meaning. In the perspective I am propounding here, we go a bit further in the modal construal of time. It is not only the speaker's mental construal of reality that suggests the characterization of time as modality but also what we called

---

[7] See also Langacker 2001, esp. pp. 268–9 where he argues that what is linguistically modelled is the 'represented event' rather than the 'actual event'. In other words, the present tense can be used for past and future eventualities when the way they are represented to the speaker warrant the use of this tense because of the particular point of view that engenders their 'virtual occurrence'. See also Section 4.2.

the real, metaphysical time in Chapter 1 where I argued for a form of supervenience of the concept of time on real time. While the mental construal
utilizes epistemic detachment, reality utilizes alternative histories of the
universe which are also modal in character. These histories have scientific
explanations. For example, they are modelled in string theory as multidimensional time. Mathematicians constructed models of macro-reality according to
which the world has such multiple histories: there is no end and no beginning,
the model of space-time is a sphere where we always reach the point of departure
and where nothing outside the sphere exists. The fact that one history is 'real'
has to be qualified as 'real *to us*': in accordance with the anthropic principle
which I discussed in Section 2.4, we see the universe as we do because we are
human.[8] In quantum mechanics, particles have so-called 'multiple histories',
multiple ways of moving from one location to another, all of which are to be
regarded as equally real, according to Richard Feynman's theory that won him
the Nobel Prize. In this essay we are discussing the idea of supervenience of time
on modality in two ways: predominantly as supervenience of the concept of
time on the concept of epistemic detachment, and, where required for the
purpose of the argument, as supervenience of the concept of time on the
properties of time-space. At the current stage of our discussion, it seems safe
to suggest that these two strands are closely connected. We have found a
correlation: just as the concept of time is founded on a more primitive concept
of uncertainty, probability, and detachment, so it is founded on the probability
and relativity of real time. Therefore, it is not the *construal of reality* that requires
modality as conceptualist semanticists have it. It is *reality* itself. Our concept of
time reflects the properties of time of space-time. Time is a highly malleable and
undeniably modal construct in contemporary physics: it allows for multiple
dimensions in current models of the universe, it is dependent on the gravita-
tional field and possibly, if Stephen Hawking and Roger Penrose are correct,
breaks down at the point of singularity/big bang, where laws of physics and
predictions cease to work. Possibility and agent (speaker/observer)-dependence
are essential properties of real time and internal time alike.

The question arises how are we to reconcile the desideratum that semantic
representation has to have conceptual reality with the fact of significant
differences in the ways languages express temporality through their grammatical and lexical means. So far we have been silently adopting the initial

[8] I am timelessly grateful to Rachel Padman, an astrophysicist and a fellow member of
Newnham College Cambridge, for discussing Feynman's theory and anthropic principle with
me. She also made me aware of the fact that the sensational explanations of time loops and time
travel present in popular scientific books have a perfectly respectable explanation that substi-
tutes as an *explanans* antimatter for going back in time.

hypothesis of linguistic universalism and discussed internal time as a concept that has the same modal foundations for all cultures and languages, superficial differences notwithstanding. But this initial, silent hypothesis was warranted: we have found ample support in Chapter 2 for the modal conceptual foundations for the expressions of the past, present, and future, making frequent recourses to genetically unrelated languages. The strongest argument comes, however, not from typological studies but from supervenience on real time: time concept is epistemic and hence modal, because real time is probability and hence modal.

The implications for semantics of natural language are easily deducible. Let us leave aside cognitive approaches which, in spite of having the idea of human construct of reality excellently worked out, as exemplified in Langacker's conceptual semantics, are wanting in formal detail and perspicacy. Let us focus on the consequences of the equation of the conceptual and the semantic for formal semantic theories founded on various types of generative grammar. In Chomsky's minimalism, there is no semantic module separate from syntax; there are syntactic/semantic representations that are interpretable by conceptual-intentional systems (see Chomsky 2004). The syntax/semantics system is universal, and so are the conceptual-intentional mechanisms. However, as Ramchand and Svenonius (forthcoming) convincingly argue, this model can only be sustained when we add contextual, presuppositional and other 'negotiable' information to the meaning module, thereby shifting this model (halfway, in my view) in the direction of DRT or Default Semantics where such information is treated on a par with the output of grammar. In particular, they propose that such contextual information can be provided by the lexicon but it is different from the universal syntax/semantics system. It is, however, made available to the conceptual-intentional mechanisms for interpretation. So, although they don't go as far as integrating these sources of meaning with syntax/semantics, they integrate them under the label of the lexicon and underdetermined aspects of meaning that have to be read out from elsewhere for the conceptual-intentional system to get it right. They exemplify this model with the semantics of time. While the semantics is universal, the amount of information provided by the lexicon/grammar can vary from language to language, as their contrast between Lillooet Salish and English demonstrates.[9] Big paradigmatic splits in the field notwithstanding, their version of minimalism is, therefore, not far off our identification of semantic and conceptual structure. Cognitive conceptual semantics of Jackendoff or Brisard, dynamic representational semantics such as DRT, and Chomskyan minimalism are all slaves to the same desideratum after all.

[9] I have discussed tense in Lillooet Salish in Section 2.5.1 above.

One of the important characteristics of the concept of time is its affinity with the concept of space. Expressions of motion such as 'passing', 'approaching', 'flowing', 'arriving', 'coming', 'standing still' are frequently used accompanying the word 'time', as in (1) and (2).

(1)   Time has come to tell the truth.
(2)   Time passes quickly.

This affinity with space has been extensively discussed in the literature, particularly in cognitive semantic frameworks.[10] However, we have to regard this affinity with extreme caution. Motion verbs such as 'pass' or 'arrive' are not entirely spatial terms and therefore do not directly testify to the spatial conceptualization of time. Instead, they pertain to space-time: movement can occur on any of the many space-time dimensions proposed in mathematical models of the universe such as those of the string theory. Neither does it seem justified to propose polysemy of the lexeme *time*, as in Evans's (2005: 72) 'the lexeme *time* constitutes a lexical category of distinct senses instantiated in semantic memory'. Evans (2003, 2005) proposes the conceptualization of time as: duration, moment, instance, event, commodity, measurement system, matrix, and agent. For example, (3) pertains to the event sense of time, where 'time' is identified with 'death', and (4) to the agent sense where time is reified as a physician or, say, therapist.

(3)   The old man realized his time has come.
(4)   Time is the best healer.

We see little support for the polysemy view. The word 'time' is primarily associated with the concept of time *tout court* and only secondarily with other related concepts. While event, agent, duration, or measurement are undoubtedly related to the concept of time, they are not identical with it. They pertain to further characteristics of the state of affairs that the utterance is about, often rely on the metaphorical, *ad hoc* concept of time, and should not be confused with temporality itself. Further, Evans seems to be contradicting himself in saying on the one hand that one of the senses of the word 'time' is *event*, and on the other that '...time appears ultimately to derive from perceptual processes which in fact may enable us to perceive events' (2003: 9). If time is a means for perceiving events, it seems difficult to accept simultaneously that one of the senses of the word 'time' is *event*. In short, we should be wary of the approaches where the concept of time is analysed

---

[10] See, for example, Lakoff and Johnson 1980, 1999; Lakoff and Turner 1989; Evans 2003 and extensive further references in Evans (2003: 13).

through assembling the corpus data on the use of the word 'time'. While this is in itself a valuable source of information about the collocations this word enters into and the interaction between the concept of time and other concepts such as event, state, change, agent, it misses the centre of the enquiry into the concept: time in language and thought has to be looked at through a careful investigation of lexical and grammatical means for expressing it such as time adverbials, tense, aspect (where appropriate), and modality, rather than merely through the collocations the word 'time' enters into. It seems much more plausible to delimit the concept of time to location in time, in terms of instances or intervals, as appropriate, and relegate the related concepts to linguistic constructs that would represent the object which temporality is predicated about. The standard way of doing this is introducing events into semantics. I shall now move to this topic and try to answer the questions (i) what exactly should be construed as temporal for the purpose of conceptual/semantic representation of time: a state of affairs, an event, a proposition, a sentence, an utterance, and (ii) if any of these fits the purpose, then how it is to be defined, with what degree of granularity, from whose point of view, and bearing what kind of relation to the real world.

3.2 Situations and eventualities

We have now concluded that both real time and the concept of time are underlyingly modal. We also know that modality pertains to states of affairs and to conceptual and semantic representations of states of affairs. In other words, modality as probability pertains to situations in the world, and modality as degree of acceptance pertains to conceptual and semantic representations of situations. The next question to ask is, what are these conceptual and semantic representations of states of affairs? We agreed that time is a degree of detachment from the expressed state of affairs, but the state of affairs is represented as the content of *what*? Should this object be the proposition, the sentence, the utterance, the event or state? And if event or state, how are these to be defined? Let us first consider events as possible candidates. Events are directly related to reality: the opening of the session of the British Parliament, the launch of a spaceship, the birth of the first cloned sheep are all events. But is the birth of the first cloned sheep the same event as the birth of the famous sheep Dolly? Is the opening of the session of the British Parliament by the Queen the same event as the opening of the session of the British Parliament by Elizabeth II? If so, then events can be thought of as actual facts or possible states of affairs. But then, is the opening of the session of the British Parliament by the Queen the same event as the pompous opening of the session of the British Parliament by the Queen? Or the opening of the session of the British Parliament by the ceremoniously dressed Queen? If the answer is 'yes', then how do we draw the boundary between events if they can be narrated in such a variety of ways? If the answer is 'no', then events become a sentential correlate of states of affairs. However, they have to obey the rule of temporal continuity and manifestation in a single object (see Taylor 1985: 85): my eating breakfast and my eating dinner can't be construed as one single event, and similarly my writing Chapter 3 of my book and your writing Chapter 3 of your book cannot be construed as one event. If this is the case, then (5) is a sentential correlate of two different events and cannot count as an event on the understanding that events are sentential correlates of states of affairs.

(5)   Last week Kasia and Jenny wrote chapter 3 of their respective books.

It is well acknowledged that 'it is not very useful to study tense and aspect at the sentence level' (Hamm *et al.* 2006: 9). We can go further: studying temporal location of a situation taking sentential correlates as objects would be misguided from the start. We could follow DRT and assume that the level of discourse, represented in a DRS, provides the correct unit. Temporal location is then recovered from tense, aspect, but also from world knowledge of causal relations between events which is automatically added to the representation and executed as pragmatic inference. As Hamm *et al.* (2006: 10) correctly emphasize, the objective of formal semantics is not exhausted in providing an adequate truth-conditional analysis of sentences and giving an account of entailments between sentences; semantics also has to explain language comprehension and production. The formalism chosen in a semantic theory has to be compatible with this cognitive desideratum: it has to reflect the limitations of memory and the computations of which the human brain is capable. The best way to represent temporality is as a component in construing the structure of the entire chain of situations pertaining to the discourse rather than associate situations with particular sentences. Hamm *et al.* give an example of the combination of the French *Imparfait* with *Passé Simple* as in (6)–(8). In (6), the situation described in the *Imparfait* provides the background to the action of taking off the sweater, in (7) it terminated before getting a speeding fine, and in (8) it was initiated by pushing the button.

(6)   Il faisait chaud. Jean ôta sa veste.
       Imparfait   *Passé Simple*
       It was hot. Jean took off his sweater.

(7) Jean attrapa une contravention. Il roulait trop vite.
Passé Simple   *Imparfait*
Jean got a ticket. He was driving too fast.

(8) Jean appuya sur l'interrupteur. La lumière l'éblouissait.
Passé Simple   *Imparfait*
Jean pushed the button. The light blinded him.

(adapted from Hamm et al. 2006: 10)

Tense alone does not provide enough information to differentiate between these relationships: the combination of tenses is the same for all three. It has to be some other human ability that makes the addressee infer the relations. Hamm *et al.* (*ibid.*: 11–13) suggest, following Steedman (1997), that the ability to use a tensed language is directly connected with the ability to form and execute plans in order to achieve certain goals. They say that the present time corresponds to the current model of reality in which this plan is to be constructed, the future to the set of goals, and the remembered past is attached to them as a set of past goals and actions. The authors formalize this hypothesis elsewhere (van Lambalgen and Hamm 2005) as the so-called event calculus, in which they distinguish *event* (action) *types* ('break', 'come') and properties (called *fluents*) such as breaking or walking. Let us take the event type *run* (something that *happens*) and the fluent of *running* (that *holds* at a certain interval). The event type is formalized as $\exists t\ run\ (x,t)$ and the fluent as $run\ (x, \hat{t}\ )$. Such eventualities are not aspects of real situations but are rather conceptual, and therefore semantic, constructs. As conceptual constructs, they can be directly introduced as discourse referents in the DRSs. They are the building blocks for a computational model of meaning. As they say, '[t]he basic building block of the human construction of time is the event' (p. 15). To repeat, it is so because human concept of time is directly related to planning. While the present is normally subject to direct perception, the further we go into the future the more essential the element of planning and intention becomes – as the form *be going to* exemplifies.[11]

Van Lambalgen and Hamm are definitely correct in claiming that a semantic representation has to be cognitively real and involve a cognitively real construal of time. They are also correct in pointing out that the internal time is one of the crucial tools for gluing events and states together. But, as I briefly argued in Section 1.2, explaining time in terms of causation does not conform to the physicalist picture of the universe. Wheeling in causation and goals also

---

[11] See van Lambalgen and Hamm (2005: 118–29) on the formalization of various forms of expressing the future in terms of goals.

involves one basic mistake, namely they are categories of a different level of explanation; they are not epistemically more primitive than time, they assume time. Event tokens as cognitive correlates of states of affairs must involve temporal location, and it is event tokens rather than types that we use in representing reality. Here is where my event construal will have to depart from the practice of DRT adopted and extended in van Lambalgen and Hamm's event calculus. I want a conceptual correlate of states of affairs, real and imaginary, certain and probable, that will not abstract from any aspects of the state of affairs which are really present in the concept. Temporal location has to be present not only in the DRS, as an addition to the event structure, but in the event itself. Time is not just glue for events: it is their essential component in that, as the arguments in Chapter 2 suggest, it makes these events (and states) more, or less, probable: more, or less, detached from reality. In other words, it is the modal character of internal time that necessitates its status as a component of events rather than an external characteristic and glue between them.

With this assumption at hand, it will be best to resort to a new label for such a cognitive/semantic correlate of a state of affairs. It is not an event, a state, a fluent, neither can it be properly dubbed an event token because on my construal there can be no corresponding event types as temporality is inherent in the mental construction of reality and in the mental representation of a state of affairs. Before we name this unit, it is necessary to probe more the granularity of this construct, beginning with granularity of events. In other words, we have to reopen the old discussion between Davidson and Kim on the fineness of detail of events – after a brief resumé of the classic positions. Even if we abandon the label 'event', the granularity problem still applies.

Events were first introduced into semantics by Frank Ramsey (1927) who distinguished abstract facts (that Brutus stabbed Caesar) from (real) events (Brutus's stabbing of Caesar, at a certain spatio-temporal location).[12] Next, since the publication of Davidson's (1967) article 'The logical form of action sentences', followed by, among others, 'The individuation of events' (Davidson 1969) and 'Events as particulars' (Davidson 1970), semanticists have began to appreciate the importance of having an event-like construct in the logical form.[13] In sentence (9), in order to represent the adverbials 'slowly', 'deliberately', 'in the bathroom', etc., we can add new argument slots to the predicate 'butter', and keep adding them potentially indefinitely in order to accommodate 'with a knife', 'at midnight', and other possible qualifications.

---

[12] See also Pietroski 2005 for an overview.
[13] See also Higginbotham 2000 for a defence of events in semantic theory.

(9) Jones buttered the toast slowly, deliberately, in the bathroom, with a knife, at midnight.   (from Davidson 1967: 106)

This strategy, however, makes the predicate 'butter' infinitely ambiguous as it can take different numbers of arguments on different occasions. Moreover, it is not just 'buttering' that is slow but rather John's buttering of a piece of toast. Therefore, Davidson proposed that action sentences refer to events and this event occupies an argument position of the predicate. Adverbials of time, manner, etc. are then added as conjuncts predicating about the event. The logical form looks as in (9'), where *e* stands for the event.

(9') $\exists e$ (Butter (Jones, toast, e) $\land$ Slowly (e) $\land$ Deliberately (e) $\land$ In (e, bathroom) $\land$ With (e, knife) $\land$ At (e, midnight)

In post-Davidsonian so-called *subatomic semantics* (Parsons 1990, extended by, for example, Landman 2000; Schein 2002), the semantic roles became explicitly assigned in the logical form, making the first conjunct more explicit but to the detriment of the intuitive understanding of what counts as an event. In (9''), argument slots for subject and object are replaced with new 'subatomic' predicates – subatomic in that they do not figure in the actual English sentence.

(9'') $\exists e$ (butter (e) $\land$ Subject (Jones, e) $\land$ Object (toast, e) $\land$ Slowly (e) ... etc.

Or, in Landman's (2000: 43) formalization, (9) is represented as (9'''), where 'Ag' stands for Agent and 'Th' for Theme.

(9''') $\exists e \in$ BUTTER: Ag(e)=j $\land$ $\exists x \in$ TOAST: Th(e)=y $\land$ DELIBERATE (MANNER(e)) ... etc.[14]

The advantage of this method is that we can capture temporality by means of such subatomic explanatory predicates as in (10') which is a logical form of (10).

(10) Caesar died.
(10') $\exists e$ Dying (e) $\land$ Object (e, Caesar) $\land$ Culminate (e, before now)
                                         (adapted from Parsons 1990: 6)[15]

---

[14] See also Landman 2000, Chapter 3, on intensional adverbials. Some adverbs, such as 'reluctantly', are attached to the role. Cf.: 'Mary kissed John reluctantly but John was not kissed by Mary reluctantly'. They are also intensional with respect to the theme: Mary kissed John reluctantly but she didn't kiss the winner of the marathon (=John) reluctantly.

[15] For an application of Davidsonian semantics see Higginbotham, e.g. 1985, 1995. For an excellent introduction to events see Pianesi and Varzi 2000.

This opened up a plethora of questions concerning the metaphysical status of events, their status as types or tokens, and, most importantly, what exactly counts as an event, how finely-grained these units are, and by what criteria they are delimited. In formal semantics, events have been conceptualized as properties of time: something that pertains to moments or intervals (Montague 1960). For example, the property of the sun rising is instantiated by an interval or moment *t* in a possible world. Sun's rising is thus an event, or an *event type*. This concept of an event, initiated by Davidson and introduced into formal semantics by Montague, is therefore a theoretical construct that is considerably removed from real situations: the event that is of importance for formal semantics is the sun's rising rather than the sun's rising this morning. Further, the sun's rising slowly is a different event from the sun's rising; as Chisholm (1970) argued, this is so because it is conceivable that for someone the first one can be the object of thought while the latter is not. But while for Chisholm this explanation is naturally linked with construing events as types (sunrise can recur), for Davidson (1970) they are particulars.[16] Davidson's notion of event, further elaborated by Higginbotham (1985) and Parsons (1990), has now become the standard in semantic theory, extended from events to all eventualities (and therefore including at least states on a binary distinction) and applied to all predicates: all predicates are allowed an argument position occupied by an eventuality.[17]

Early Davidson (1969) considers events which have the same causes and effects to be identical. Events are concrete particulars; they are located in space and time, but in order to be able to call two events identical, it will not suffice to say that they occupy the same position in space-time. The advantage of adding the cause-effect criterion is that, for example, (11) and (12) can refer to the same event of Amelie's playing the clarinet in a performance of a sonata.

(11)   Amelie played a sonata.
(12)   Amelie played the clarinet.   (from Pianesi and Varzi 2000: 21)

When one allows events to be more finely-grained, as in post-Davidsonian subatomic semantics, this identity ceases to be an option: 'a sonata' and 'the clarinet' become two different arguments of the predicate 'play'. While Parsons considers this to be an advantage of his subatomic semantics that it provides a means of distinguishing between (11) and (12), it seems that the problems overshadow the benefits: we are moving away from real situations in the

---

[16] See Maienborn 2005 for an analysis of Davidson's position and implications for current semantic theory.

[17] See Maienborn 2005 for a critical discussion.

direction of sententialism, where the notion of an event becomes so heavily dictated by the linguistic form that it ceases to be an event and becomes simply a proposition or some other semantic correlate of the grammatical string. But while 'linguisticky' events and linguistic criteria for their individuation that Parson provides make the notion of event look superfluous, to the advantage of linguistic units, this is not necessarily a bad thing. It seems that a finely-grained construct that relies heavily on the syntactic unit of the sentence and on pragmatically conveyed information that comes with the utterance of this sentence is a good candidate for an event's replacement. And this is the position which, ultimately, we are going to adopt, following the foundations provided by Jaegwon Kim but opting out of the label 'event'.

Kim (1973) goes further than Davidson in the granularity of events: for him events exemplify properties and relations. Since the sun's rising slowly and the sun's rising exemplify different properties, they are different events. An event is on his account a concrete object or n-tuple of objects which exemplifies a property or n-adic relation at a certain time. Event is composed of objects and of properties; it also includes constituent fragments, and it is said to have a propositional structure: 'the event that consists in the exemplification of property P by an object x at time t bears a structural similarity to the sentence "x has P at t"' (Kim 1973: 8). Events (and states) are therefore almost linguistic constructs in that they depend on the logical form of the sentence describing them. They are particulars and have locations in space and time. But they are not totally sentential: Socrates' drinking hemlock at t is the same event as Xantippe's husband's drinking hemlock at t due to the identity criteria Kim proposes.[18] This level of granularity is supposed to attend to problems with the delimitation of events where an adverb is involved. While the sun's rising slowly may not trigger strong intuitions in either direction, (13a) and (13b) do. While (13a) uncontroversially reports on a situation described there, dropping the adverb in (13b) changes the sense.

(13a)   The traffic jam caused Pat's cooking spaghetti late.
(13b)   The traffic jam caused Pat's cooking spaghetti.

(from Pianesi and Varzi 2000: 21)

Examples of this kind can be easily multiplied: 'filling the glass halfway' does not warrant inference to 'filling the glass', and so forth. Such examples also testify against the early position adopted by Quine (1960) according to which events are delimited by what happens in space-time: real and potential

---

[18] But Socrates' dying is a different event from Xantippe's becoming a widow. See Kim (1973: 9).

'happenings' can pertain to infinite numbers of linguistic descriptions and are not sufficiently finely-grained as constructs for semantic representations of sentences or utterances. Events are therefore particulars, located in space and time, and are delimited by strict criteria of identity. They are also real:

... I find it plausible to think of the constitutive substance of an event as essential to the identity of that event. The fact that someone other than Sebastian could have taken a stroll in his place does not make it the case that the very stroll that Sebastian took could have been taken by someone else. If Mario had been chosen to stroll that night, then there would have been another stroll, namely Mario's. (Kim 1976: 48)

Just as one's pain cannot occur to someone else, he adds, so one's stroll cannot be performed by someone else: '[o]nly Socrates could have died *his* death' (*ibid.*: 48). Similarly, Sebastian's stroll, taken at a different time, is simply a different stroll. We can then pursue Kim's construal further and agree that events such as cooking spaghetti late are related to 'generic events' such as cooking spaghetti: they are subsumed under them as their exemplifications. It seems best to regard adverbs as predicates on events and assume that events require the description that the sentence provides; in fact, it seems safest to assume that the state of affairs pertains precisely to the description the utterance of the sentence provides (namely 'filling the glass halfway') – allowing for various forms of pragmatic enrichment, both from contextual inference and from cultural and other stereotypes. This pragmatic enrichment will then rely on world knowledge which subsumes information about identity conditions such as that between Socrates and Xantippe's husband.

   In short, we will opt for a finely-grained construal of events. On this account, however, the need for the label 'event' on such a semantic construct becomes questionable. 'Events' so construed are no longer states of affairs, either real or probable, because the latter will not give us sufficient amount of information for the purpose of constructing a semantic representation. Since we are interested in meaning in discourse, we need a unit that pertains to states of affairs that utterances are about but at the same time makes distinctions between playing the clarinet and playing a sonata, or cooking spaghetti and cooking spaghetti late: a causal link à la Davidson will not suffice. Should we follow Kim and his extreme version of finely-grained event constructs? In my view one should go even further. Going further is necessary if we want to have a complete, working account of what enters into the required unit of semantic representation of utterances. We agree that having a spatio-temporal location is an essential part of the event. But in order to make events suitable for semantic representations, we also need means for deciding on this spatio-temporal location. Equally, we require means for relating the sentence to the description of a state of affairs as intended by the speaker, albeit perhaps not to some 'objective' state of affairs. For all this we need pragmatic enrichment, also known as modulation (Recanati, e.g. 2004, 2005). We will have to use a theory of meaning that explains the interaction of the meaning provided by the lexicon and grammar with that provided by pragmatic inference and salient world knowledge that provides default scenarios. Such a compositional, pragmatics-rich semantics will be employed in Chapter 4. At this point I want to flag the point that Kim's finely-grained, token-based account will be our starting point. Following Kim, I shall also apply analogous reasoning to states, understood widely as including processes.

Asher (1993, 2000), who is Davidsonian about eventualities, distinguishes them from facts, which have to be true about the real world, and propositions, which exist in all possible worlds, independently of whether they are true. Events can be distinguished within fact-denoting expressions in that temporal location of an event is a fact, or, in other words, temporal location is a constitutive part of a fact. Events, on the other hand, are allocated temporal location externally. Events, so to speak, make up facts. Asher says that '[f]acts do not exhibit dynamicity because they are atemporal' (2000: 147). They are also abstract and bound to the world (Asher 1993). For example, the fact that it rained in Cambridge on 18 November 2006 is eternal: it will not change in the future, whereas the event of raining in Cambridge acquires temporal specification through introducing special discourse referent that relates it to a particular time (see Asher 2000). In the analysis in Chapter 4, I adopt a form of an external allocation of temporality that reflects the degree of epistemic commitment. I presented numerous arguments in Chapter 2 in favour of temporality as detachment from certainty of a state of affairs. The state of affairs is precisely such an event-like unit, with modal detachment acting as the 'temporal' qualification. The details will have to wait until Section 4.2. Instead, it is the granularity of this unit on which modality operates that should concern us now, as it appears from the discussion so far that it should be more finely-grained than Davidsonian eventuality allows. In other words, the external allocation of temporality should operate on a unit that is not an event in any legitimate sense of the term. It is a proposition but a proposition that pertains to the intended meaning that the utterance conveys, in the sense of being intended by the model speaker and recovered by the model addressee as that intended by the model speaker, in agreement with the pragmatic orientation already adopted. Let me spell this out in more detail. Our analysis will be performed in the framework of Default Semantics which is founded on the general principles of DRT and the 'event-like' concept applied in Default Semantics will follow the general principles set out in DRT and its offshoots such as Segmented Discourse Representation Theory (SDRT, Asher and Lascarides 2003). In DRT, events are Davidsonian constructs and they are temporal in the sense that they acquire temporal specification externally, so to speak. However, we do not see advantages of introducing into semantics a special entity called event or state, such as for example raining in Cambridge, in addition to what is already there in the form of the sentence with its structure, lexical concepts, and the output of pragmatic modulation from contextual and other world knowledge. One may try to argue that since there are concepts such as 'Mary's telling a story', 'John's winning a competition', they should correspond to a special semantic unit. But the fact that some sentences contain a gerundial form as in (14) does not warrant a conclusion that such a gerundial form stands for a unit of a significant semantic status.

(14)   John's singing the Marseillaise bothered Mary. (from Asher 2000: 134)

As Asher says, in DRT, events in expressions about facts obtain temporal specification from the semantics of the relevant predicates, namely from the predicates for which these expressions function as arguments. In (14), for instance, the semantics of *bother* triggers the temporal location of John's singing the Marseillaise that overlaps with the temporality of bothering Mary. His main argument comes from the so-called *evolutive anaphora*: verbs of destruction should make it impossible to refer to the destroyed object in subsequent clauses as in (15). However, this constraint is not universal: anaphoric continuation is frequently possible as in (16).

*(15)   The fire in the museum consumed a beautiful painting$_i$. The curator then tried to restore it$_i$.

(16)   The bomb vaporised the VW$_i$. It$_i$ disappeared in a flash.
                                        (adapted from Asher 2000: 136)

He explains the relations between the presented facts as discourse relations between such timeless events, written into their semantics and represented in DRSs by means of, for example, the rule of Narration for (15) and Elaboration for (16). He says that the conditions for well-formedness of such continuation are best captured by a semantics in which temporality is kept separate from the structure of the state or event: there is a discourse condition that states that the event e_1 took place before event e_2 as in (15) or that $e_2 \subset e_1$ as in (16). However, the relations between events are not the same thing as spatio-temporal location of the single eventuality. It seems that nothing is lost, and, indeed, simplicity of semantic representation is gained, when we construe the situation presented in the utterance as a propositional content on which some illocutionary force of the speech act operates. Davidsonian events alone, in spite of being particulars rather than types,[19] do not contain enough information about temporality to enter into relations necessary to explain anaphoric links in (15) and (16): the verb, such as the verb of destruction, or the relative temporal location, such as that indicated by pluperfect, has to make them into finely-grained constructs with time, place, thematic roles filled in by particulars. This seems a strong argument in favour of linguistic criteria of individuation of 'events' (or, since we rejected the term 'event', of 'semantic correlates of states of affairs') as well as in favour of propositionalism about objects for epistemic possibility (*qua* temporality) operators: temporality, realized as modal detachment, operates on propositional content intended by the (model) author of the message and recovered by the (model) recipient. Let us call this unit a *merged proposition*. I explain this concept in what follows.

The question to ask is, how exactly does this merged proposition figure in the semantic representation? This unit will be an object for modal operators, and in particular for the epistemic possibility operator that will represent the modal character of time. I mentioned above that finely-grained, token-based events as constructs for semantic representation become very close to the notion of proposition. This is certainly so when we understand proposition in accordance with the contextualist tradition as a modulated or enriched proposition: the meaning of the sentence that is pragmatically enriched, be it through pragmatic inference alone, as some post-Griceans have it (e.g. Sperber and Wilson 1986, 1995), or inference plus default interpretations (e.g. Levinson 2000; Recanati 2004; Jaszczolt 2005).[20] The modulation that affects the merged proposition is of a somewhat more radical kind than that proposed by Recanati in that, in accordance with the principles of Default Semantics, the logical form provided by the uttered sentence can be overridden by the output of some other sources of information about meaning, to be discussed at length in Section 4.1. The unit we will adopt will thus be based essentially on event particulars in that it will correspond to the particular state of affairs, with particular individuals but with spatio-temporal location assigned externally: merged propositions have externally assigned temporality in the form of a marker of epistemic commitment – a modal operator on the merged proposition. But, to repeat, this correspondence with event

[19] See Davidson 1970.

[20] The term 'modulation' is wider in scope than 'enrichment' in that it also subsumes cases of predicate shift, for example, as in 'The ham sandwich is getting impatient'. See Recanati 2005. Our merged proposition will be constructed on the principles of merger representations of Default Semantics and this distinction will not concern us. The terms 'modulation' and 'enrichment' are used here only for explanatory purposes in order to demonstrate the contextualist assumptions with which our concept will have many affinities.

particulars will not mean identity. We will require a construct that reflects the representation of a state of affairs by a model speaker, as recovered by a model addressee in the process of conversation or other linguistic interaction. In other words, we require a cognitive construct of a representation of a state of affairs, represented formally as a predicate-argument structure. But this structure is not solely sentence-based, or even 'sentence-plus-spatio-temporal location'-based, but allows for this information from sentence structure and word meaning to interact with, and even on some occasions be overridden by, information from other sources of utterance meaning such as contextual and other word knowledge. For the purpose of semantic analysis we will identify this construct with that of a merged proposition, with identity conditions provided from extensional semantics, further restricted for intensional contexts in accordance with instructions from world knowledge and pragmatic inference. Such a construct is necessarily highly linguistic, propositional, but propositional in the sense of a proposition which is fairly independent from the matrix of the uttered sentence. This means in practice that, for example, coreferential expressions such as 'The winner of the 2006 Nobel Prize for literature' and 'the author of *Snow*' can be rendered not substitutable *not* by the properties of the linguistic construction, such as being a subject of a *that*-clause embedded in a propositional attitude report as in (17), but in virtue of what we know about the situation of discourse.[21]

(17)   Mary believes that <u>the author of *Snow*/*the winner of the 2006 Nobel Prize for literature</u> is highly overrated.

We can easily envisage a scenario on which Mary has read *Snow* and doesn't think very highly of the novel. She doesn't know that the author, Orhan Pamuk, received the Nobel Prize for literature and, say, judging by the quality of the novel she read, she would not even believe it if she heard it. On our construal, however, such lack of truth-preserving substitutivity is not delimited by grammatical constructions. It may equally well occur in a sentence which is of a traditionally extensional type such as (18a), where a substitution as in (18b) produces a change in meaning.

(18a)   Yesterday he was (merely) the author of *Snow* and a few other novels; today he is the winner of the Nobel Prize for literature 2006.

?(18b)   Yesterday he was (merely) the winner of the Nobel Prize for literature 2006; today he is the author of *Snow* and a few other novels.

---

[21] Saul (2007) argues along the similar lines for the constraints on substitutivity of proper names across a range of constructions that lack standard triggers associated with intensional contexts such as embedding under an attitude verb or temporal adverbial.

The identity criteria for our 'events', understood as merged propositions, will respect this diversity of construction types that characterizes the set of cases in which the departure from the physically uttered expression may not be permitted.

It becomes evident at this stage why applying the term 'event' to our pragmatics-rich construct would be misleading, even if we provided a new definition of the term. 'Merged proposition' is a much more adequate label. In Chapter 4, we will unpack and identify it with a representation of meaning that draws on information from various sources and composes it according to principles of pragmatic compositionality. In other words, we will identify it with the so-called merger representation of Default Semantics (see Section 4.1). But until this construct is properly introduced, let us refer to it simply as Σ – because the Greek sign for summation well renders the idea that such units sum up information about meaning that comes from a variety of sources. We will show in Chapter 4 that the system of embedding of Σs, loosely modelled on embedded DRSs, combined with the appropriately qualified operator of epistemic possibility, suffices for representing temporal discourse, without the need for halfway units of events and states.

To sum up, I have argued that a 'linguisticky' equivalent of a state of affairs, called now a merged proposition and represented by a symbol Σ, is a more useful construct for mental representations of states of affairs than an event. If we still wanted to call it an event, then events would have to be construed as semantic/pragmatic entities rather than, as common sense dictates, as part of the ontology or of the *experience* of the world. Such a terminology would be rather misleading. The next question will be to assess the relation Σ bears to its metaphysical correlate. And the best place to start is to ask how do we extrapolate from Σ's location in time to situations, states of affairs, events, or other such parts of reality? Firstly, one has to acknowledge that the unit of time is not just a point on the time line, not a moment, but rather, for many occasions, it has to be a unit of an extended duration, notably an interval. Intervals were introduced into formal semantics by Bennett and Partee (1978). Cf.:

John will eat the fish α is true at interval of time I if and only if I is a moment of time, α refers to an interval of time I' and there exists a subinterval of I', I'', such that either I is an initial point for I'' or $I [<] I''$ and *John eats the fish* is true at I''. (Bennett and Partee 1978: 37)

where $[<]$ stands for 'wholly precedes'.[22] Then, for sentence (19) we obtain the representation of the situation as in Fig. 3.1.

---

[22] See also Binnick 1991.

(19)   John will eat the fish tomorrow.

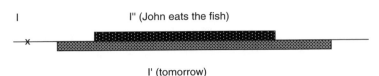

FIGURE 3.1 Graphic representation of (19) in terms of intervals
Source: adapted from Binnick (1991: 256)

Just as real time in space-time allows for real chunks and regions, so temporal location of the conceptual equivalent Σ allows for conceptual intervals.

There is a need for a disclaimer at this point. For the purpose of this essay I am interested only in some aspects of the event-like construct. I am interested in the question as to whether the conceptual equivalent of the situation (state of affairs) is better construed as a linguistic, some other abstract theoretical, or directly as an ontological, real entity. I have opted here for the first possibility. I am also interested in the follow-up question, namely, if the unit is linguistic, then how is it put together? What sources of information make it a conceptual equivalent of states of affairs, namely as a functional representation of a state of affairs represented by the model speaker *and* recovered by the model addressee in discourse as that represented by the model speaker? There are many questions, actively discussed in the current literature on events, which I will have neither opportunity nor direct need to answer in this essay, the first of which is the important problem of the individuation of events where different quantificational dependencies are possible as in (20) or where there is an ambiguity between the group event vs. singular events as in (21).

(20)   Five philosophers wrote seven articles for three journals.
(21)   Five philosophers gave a talk.

The proposals for a solution in the literature are ample (see, for example, Landman 2000;[23] Schein 2002; Rothstein 2004; Pietroski 2005). The semantic mechanisms proposed for, for example, shifting from singular to group interpretation of (21), while of central importance in formal semantics, are replaced in my conceptual semantics with principles that a process of utterance interpretation follows in producing one, unique representation. So, for example, in deriving the collective interpretation of (21) our Σ draws on

---

[23] Landman (2000) develops a theory of a semantic shift from the distributive (sum of events) to the collective (a group event) interpretation of plural noun phrases through type shifting.

sentence structure and the lexicon, but also on contextual clues such as that the discussion concerns, say, an informal event during the philosophy faculty open day at which five faculty members gave an introductory talk, or an interdisciplinary conference at which only five from among the presenters of talks were philosophers, presenting a paper each. When we leave the scope underspecified on the level of syntactic structure, to be filled in by propositional modulation in accordance with post-Gricean contextualism, the pragmaticized version of compositionality gives us the Σ that we need – to be tried out in Section 4.1.

The proposition-like character of Σ is not a new idea. Prior suggests equating moments of time with 'a conjunction of all those propositions which would ordinarily be said to be true at that instant' or 'some proposition which would ordinarily be said to be true at that instant only, and so could serve as an index of it' (Prior 1968c: 123). For the purpose of the present argument we can extend this equation of instants with propositions to equating both instants and intervals on an equal footing – in view of post-Priorean developments in the semantics of time (see Bennett and Partee 1978; Kamp 1979; Dowty 1979; and, for example, Saurer 1984; Galton 1990; Pratt and Francez 2001; Kamp and Schiehlen 2002).[24] For Prior, propositions are therefore units about which temporality is predicated:

By a 'tense logic' I mean a calculus in which the variables p, q, r, etc. stand for 'propositions' which may be true or false at different times, and in which the usual two-valued truth-functions (...) are supplemented by the two forms Fp for 'It will be the case that p' and Pp for 'It has been the case that p'. (Prior 1968d: 145)

Subsequent discussions leave the problem of this unit of quantification unresolved, oscillating between proposition, events, and facts. While some equate events with facts (Taylor 1985), others separate 'real' events from 'unreal' facts (Asher 1993, 2000). DRT, offering arguably the best-developed dynamic semantic treatment of temporality in natural language, uses events as theoretical constructs, admitting that their status is left unclear:

From an ontological point of view (...) events form a notoriously problematic category, for which identity conditions and structural properties and relations are

---

[24] Kamp (1979: 394) gives an example of writing an article and the problem with an instant within the period of writing during which the author was asleep. The judgement as to whether being asleep belongs to the process of writing relies on a *conceptually prior* judgement as to whether a certain *interval* can be identified with the time of writing the article. However, from the perspective of the more recent developments in semantic theory, it seems that we need both instants and intervals in the semantics (see Kamp *et al.* forthcoming, and Srioutai 2006 for evidence from Thai). See also Moens and Steedman 1988 on *episodes* that lead to goals.

hard to pin down and have proved a never ending topic of debate. (Kamp *et al.* forthcoming: 75)[25]

In DRT, events and states are among the discourse referents of discourse representations: the universe of a model contains the categories of time, event, state, and individual. It is still unclear, however, whether all of these categories are necessary or rather a reduction is possible.

We can now move to the list of semantic categories that are likely candidates for assessing the type of eventuality as it is conceptualized by the addressee. We will make use of the widely acknowledged aspectual distinctions presented in Fig. 3.2.

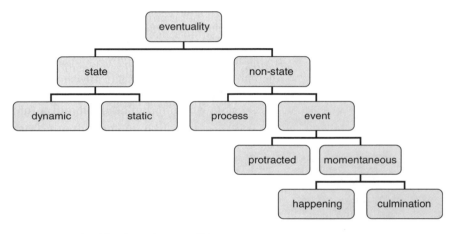

FIGURE 3.2 Classification of eventualities
Source: adapted from Bach (1986: 62)

An example of a construction referring to a dynamic state is 'sing'; static state 'like roses'; process 'run'; protracted event 'run to school'; happening 'notice'; and culmination 'reach the end'. This classification is essentially a version of the classical four-way distinction into activities, accomplishments, achievements, and states proposed by Vendler (1967), with the added improvement of more precise distinctions between states and actitivies and between accomplishments and achievements. While DRT makes use only of a binary distinction into state and event, it is often argued that the six-way distinction represented in the bottom-level boxes of Fig. 3.2 or some alternative finely-grained classification is the minimal necessary grid for semantic analyses

---

[25] See also Kamp and Reyle (1993: 505).

(see Bach 1986). Our semantic representation Σ is compatible with this finely-grained conceptual distinction. Events and states do not take the place of propositions here, neither are they reified to the status of actual happenings in time and space. They merely function as theoretical descriptive terms that provide the properties of verbs, verb phrases, or other indicators of situations. As Bach (1986: 68–9) correctly points out, questions of the type 'How many events took place in the last hour?' do not make sense: the real world is not composed out of events. Human conceptualization of the world, on the other hand, involves categories such as dynamic or static, culminated or not, protracted or punctual/momentaneous. We propose to retain the proposition-like unit Σ and make use of the categories in Fig. 3.2 as parts of a semantic description of what Σ represents. We will agree here with Bach (1981: 79) who says that human concept of time relies on our understanding of different types of eventualities. We also agree that these semantic categories to which eventualities belong are universal: all languages express states, events, or processes, be it in the lexicon, grammar, periphrastically, or through default pragmatic interpretations. In short, while we agree that semantic representations must make use of the semantic categories pertaining to types of eventualities, the operator of temporality/epistemic modality will be construed as an operator on propositions (our Σs) rather than states or events. There is further supporting evidence against the use of events in representing time that comes from models of natural language processing. Crouch and Pulman (1993), for example, allow quantification over events when they explain temporality in terms of plans in the so-called *plan query language*. This, however, translates on the level of logical form onto a language which uses intervals but not events. The term 'event', as they say, would run into the danger of confusing linguistically and non-linguistically motivated notions of event. For example, negation can convert an event into a process as in (22a) and (22b) and therefore the principle of eventuality conversion by grammatical means would have to be generalized into a linguistically motivated rule.

(22a)   Mary came to the party.
(22b)   Mary didn't come to the party.

Moreover, the notion itself creates a problem of delimiting the scope of quantifying over events vis-à-vis quantifying over nominals or the scope of tense operators (see Crouch and Pulman 1993: 272). Although verb phrase modifiers are not as easy to represent without the notion of event, the benefits of parsimony are greater, to mention only refraining from introducing an inherently unclear notion into semantic representation.[26]

There is an important question to address here, namely that of the interpretation of the logical form, or, in the case of our contextualist, truth-conditional-pragmatic framework, the interpretation of the pragmatics-rich Σ. To know the meaning of an utterance of a sentence is to know what the world would have to be like for the utterance to be true. If we disallow states and events from the semantic representation, can states of affairs function as truth-makers? Should we construe events as common-sense constituents of reality rather than as semantic units and assign to them the role of truth-makers? Schnieder (2006) develops a convincing argument that introducing events or facts as truth-makers is superfluous. For example, for the sentence 'Socrates is wise' to be true, one can argue that there has to be 'Socrates's wisdom' or 'the fact that Socrates is wise'. But this, Schnieder (2006: 41) argues, puts the horse before the cart: in order to understand Socrates's wisdom, or Brutus's killing of Caesar, one has to understand the structure of the proposition upon which this fact or event is constructed. In view of the fact that the structure of the uttered sentence is conceptually prior to events or facts, we are justified in opting for semantic representations where structured proposition is the entity undergoing such operations as an external assignment of temporal location.

Now, the class of characteristics of situation types that we adopt compels us to ask whether properties of situation *types* will be of any use for Σs or rather we proceed directly to properties of situation *tokens*. In view of admitting the semantic categories in Fig. 3.2, we will be able to make use of *telicity*. A situation type is telic when the verb phrase by which it is described represents it as tending towards natural completion.[27] By this definition, (23) is telic while (24) is atelic.

(23)   Lidia played a tango on the piano.
(24)   Lidia played the piano.

However, (25) is also telic.

(25)   Lidia was playing a tango on the piano.

---

[26] To compare, ter Meulen (1995) regards events as ineliminable building blocks for her semantic theory of aspect but she acknowledges the fact that her events are theoretical constructs, created on the basis of information given by tense, aspect, the lexicon, as well as pragmatic inference. She says, 'Since the world does not come prepackaged into events, our linguistic actions partition the continuously changing situation into discrete events' (1995: 120). Conceived of in this way, events seem to be performing a similar task to our Σ.

[27] See Declerck (2006: 60).

It is telic because the situation type is of a correct kind (tending towards completion). The fact that the actual situation token is not necessarily completed is accounted for by the category of *boundedness*. Declerck (2006: 77) compares the categories as follows. Telicity and atelicity pertain to the speaker's conceptualization of a situation type (or 'situation-template' in Declerck's terminology) as having or not having natural completion. Boundedness and non-boundedness, on the other hand, pertain to the actualization of a situation and the speaker's representation of a particular situation (situation token) as reaching a completion point. So, 'play a tango' is telic but it can be used in bounded and non-bounded constructions, as in (23) and (25) respectively. It is also possible for a situation to be bounded while the corresponding situation type is atelic as in (26).

(26)   Sixty-five pianists played in the International Chopin Contest.

It is bounded by the quantified noun phrase in the subject position but atelic due to the property of the clause of the situation type. As Cappelle and Declerck (2005) point out, conceptualization of a situation as bounded or non-bounded is not in a one-to-one correspondence with the properties of the real situation: the same situation token can be conceptualized as bounded or non-bounded. They observe that spatial boundaries can contribute to the understanding of an event as temporally bounded. For example, while (27a) is non-bounded, (27b) and (27c) are bounded: the addition of the definite article in (27b) provides spatial boundaries and at the same time the temporal boundaries of entering and emerging from the forest; the use of an adverbial particle 'through' in (27c) has a similar effect of expressing going in and coming out.

(27a)   You'll have to walk through thick forest.
(27b)   You'll have to walk through the thick forest.
(27c)   You'll have to walk through. (from Cappelle and Declerck 2005: 890)

In short, telicity is a property of verb phrases and pertains to situation types' inherent completion, while boundedness pertains to the addressee's conceptualization of a particular situation token as coming to an end. For completeness, Cappelle and Declerck also mention perfectivity which concerns the grammatical expression used when the situation is conceptualized as a whole, not extended in time. But since this is a grammatical means of expressing a property of a situation, in Σ it will be provided by a separate source.

Since meaning construction makes use of semantic properties of expression types as well as actual conceptualization of situation tokens, all these characteristics will prove essential in determining temporal location of utterances in a discourse. We will allow Σ to merge information from sentence structure, the semantics of aspectual categories, pragmatic principles for 'gluing' utterances in a discourse, as well as pragmatic inference and default interpretations construed in the post-Gricean way in Default Semantics, to be specified in Section 4.1. The need to view the semantics of temporal expressions as a merger of information coming from typologically different sources has been well acknowledged in the literature (see Dowty 1986: 41; ter Meulen 1995: 12), but in our Default-Semantic analysis it will be built into a comprehensive theory of utterance meaning and put into practical use (in Section 4.2). It appears to be an inescapable fact of utterance interpretation that eventualities require an immersion in context and in the interpreter's background knowledge and assumptions in order to faithfully render the situations of which they are formal equivalents. Bartsch (1995: 13) correctly observes that quantification over eventualities, which she calls 'basic situations', is only possible when these eventualities are embedded in the interlocutors' representations of them, that is in concepts that are formed when these eventualities are perceived, made parts of plans and goals, or made objects of intentional utterances. In other words, eventualities understood as pure, ontological, and objective situations do not figure in our intentional actions, including discourse. She moves on to proposing that eventualities are intensional entities. In formal models they are functions, with interpretations dependent on possible worlds and times as indices. One should recall that in formal semantics inspired by Montague (1960: 150), generic events are properties of time or properties of space-time or individual-time pairs. Specific events are then generic events with the added specification of time, or time and space, or time and individual (see, for example, Bartsch 1995: 19). So, for example, a generic event in (28) and the specific equivalent in (29) are of the same semantic type.

(28)   Skiing is fun.
(29)   This skiing is fun.[28]

However, as is well known from Davidson's (1969) seminal paper on the individuation of events discussed above, identifying space and time indices is not sufficient for the individuation of events. Instead, two events can only be deemed identical if they have the same causes and effects. Bartsch correctly

---

[28] Bartsch (1995: 19–20) analyses events as intensional objects in terms of individuals and *space-time regions* as basic types. So, we have (28′) and (29′) for (28) and (29) respectively:

(28′)   Fun ($^\wedge\lambda$r skiing (r))
(29′)   Fun ($^\wedge\lambda$r skiing (r) $\wedge$ r = r$_1$).

observes that this claim calls for intensional objects: one cannot introduce the concepts of cause and effect which are intrinsically intensional and at the same time attempt an extensional event semantics. The extensional equivalent of the Davidsonian event would have to be a concept of a situation whose space and time indexing is sufficient for its delineation. She says that the basic semantics of temporal expressions requires just extensional events with temporal specification. However, in sentences such as *John was dancing; it was really beautiful*, it will not suffice to say that the pronoun refers to an interval. We have to represent the meaning according to which it was the process of dancing that was beautiful. Eventualites require a semantics in which they are not merely space-time regions. The adjective 'beautiful' requires an object with the characteristics of a representation rather than those of an interval. Bartsch (1995: 26) concludes that basic situations have to include *conceptualization*. This is not far from our conclusion that the linguistic notion of event may, after all, be of limited use for semantics. Since it is intensional through being dependent on the agent's conceptualization, it is not intuitively an event, it is a representation of an event. Pragmatic inference, speaker's and addressee's assumptions about the situation, as well as salient scenarios will have to be recognized as contributors to this representation. It is evident now that the merged proposition of Default Semantics which I introduced above can satisfactorily fulfil such a role. In the following chapter I put into practice the proposal that eventuality as a linguistic construct is redundant and, instead, I reconstruct the scenarios conveyed in utterances by means of reconstructing the model speaker's representation as understood by the model addressee and arrived at through pragmatic composition. Merged proposition will then be given a semantic equivalent of a merger representation (Σ) standing for a fusion of meaning that comes from various sources: lexicon, sentence structure, and all other clues that can be subsumed under Bartsch's 'conceptualization' and which in the theory of Default Semantics adopted for this purpose are called *pragmatic inference* and *default assumptions*. So far I have referred to it by a rather enigmatic symbol Σ because all we needed at this stage of the argument was the assumption that the concept stands for a summation of information about meaning that comes from typologically different sources. It is time now to unpack Σ and discuss the contributing sources of meaning information, their interaction, the composition (and compositionality) of meaning so construed, and finally apply this concept to the semantic representation of time.

4

Time in Default Semantics

4.1 Primary meaning, merger representation, and pragmatic compositionality

As is well acknowledged, a satisfactory theory of discourse meaning should provide representations of discourse that have a status of mental representations, supported by a formal account of a compositional semantic structure. At the same time, as is evident from the discussion of temporality in Chapter 2 and of the semantic equivalent of a situation in Chapter 3, the theory has to provide a level of representation of meaning to which information from various sources would contribute, to mention only the lexicon, grammar, world knowledge including frequently encountered scenarios and predictable conversational behaviour, as well as context-driven pragmatic inference. We want to call this level of discourse representation a semantic representation, where semantics is understood in a broad way in agreement with the post-Gricean tradition, according to which the output of pragmatic processes contributes to the truth-conditional semantic representation of an utterance of the sentence (see, for example, Cole 1981; Sperber and Wilson 1986, 1995; Carston 1988, 2002; and Jaszczolt 1999 and 2002 for an overview). In Chapter 3 I proposed a proposition-like entity Σ which stands for linguistic equivalents of situations and whose temporal location has to be stated by means of an operator. This entity Σ is precisely such a level of representation of meaning on which information from the lexicon and structure of the uttered sentence merges with information from frequently encountered scenarios, predictable speaker's meanings, contextual inferences, and other chunks of information that have a default-like status, as well as with information from consciously performed inference triggered by the particular context in which the utterance was uttered or by putting together bits of world knowledge and the information retrieved from the sentence.[1] This merger should be conceived of in the

---

[1] It has to be pointed out that different post-Gricean accounts use different definitions of pragmatic inference, sometimes including automatic, unconscious enrichments of sentence meaning under this label. On differences between relevance-theoretic inference and Recanati's inference (who advocates automatic enrichment of the proposition expressed, called modulation) see Recanati 2004, but also the discussion in Carston 2007 and Recanati 2007c.

tradition of modularity and is not unlike, in its theoretical assumptions, the idea of massive modularity (Carruthers 2006): the human mind is composed of a great number of modules which are not entirely independent, unlike on the classical Fodorian account. Similarly, our sources of information about meaning that interact in building Σ are qualitatively different but semi-independent. In this essay my goal is to present a theory of utterance meaning with the focus on representing time and not the intricacies of processing, and therefore the issue of modularity will be tangential to the debate. But it has to be borne in mind that the theoretical underpinnings of this linguistic story lie precisely there. From this moment onwards I shall adopt a revised version of Default Semantics and the representations of time will be constructed in this approach. The enigmatic Σ will now be identified with the level of merger representation understood as a proposition-like, truth-conditionally evaluable unit to which information about meaning contributes and at which it interacts according to principles fixed by the intentional character of communication. I shall now explain this idea in more detail.

The sources of information on which a merger representation draws are listed in Fig. 4.1.

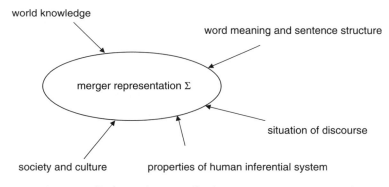

FIGURE 4.1 Sources of information contributing to a merger representation

The source 'word meaning and sentence structure' pertains to the processing of the sentence according to the principle of compositionality of sentence meaning attributed to Gottlob Frege. 'Situation of discourse' refers to that part of context that is provided by the situational embedding of the utterance, including the participants, location, time, co-text, and so forth. For example, in the context of a conversation about the skiing conditions in the Tatra Mountains at the moment of speaking, (1a) is likely to be enriched by the addressee as indicated in (1b). The symbol '$\rightarrow_\Sigma$' stands for 'results in a meaning merger' that is provided immediately after the symbol.

(1a)   It is snowing.
(1b) $\rightarrow_\Sigma$ It is snowing in the Tatra Mountains.

I also distinguish 'society and culture' as a separate source of meaning in that it is not specific to the situation but rather is shared across different scenarios in a linguistic and socio-cultural community. In this category we will place, for example, the enrichment of the meaning of 'Leonardo' in (2a) to 'Leonardo da Vinci' in (2b), triggered by shared cultural knowledge of the history of European painting.

(2a)   A painting by Leonardo was stolen from an art gallery in Cracow.
(2b) $\rightarrow_\Sigma$ A painting by Leonardo da Vinci was stolen from an art gallery in Cracow.

Next, 'world knowledge' pertains to knowledge of the laws governing the physical world, subsuming biological and physical natural sciences, which can be used in merging the utterance meaning as for example in (3a), where knowledge that water freezes below 0 degrees Celsius produces the resultative connection between the simple propositions and the merger meaning in (3b).

(3a)   The temperature fell to −15 degrees Celsius and we could go skating on the pond.
(3b) $\rightarrow_\Sigma$ The temperature fell to −15 degrees Celsius and as a result we could go skating on the pond.

Finally, 'properties of human inferential system' refer to the structure and operations of the human brain that are responsible for the way we interpret a certain subset of expressions which can obtain alternative interpretations but in practice default to one unique one unless there are reasons to believe that this interpretation is not the case. In this category we place for example the referential, as opposed to attributive, reading of definite descriptions. In (4a), 'the author of *The God Delusion*' is understood as a particular, intersubjectively identifiable person, Richard Dawkins.

(4a)   The author of *The God Delusion* was interviewed on BBC Radio 4 last week.
(4b) $\rightarrow_\Sigma$ Richard Dawkins was interviewed on BBC Radio 4 last week.

As I have been arguing in numerous places, in the past two decades or so, this default interpretation of definite descriptions, and by the same token the *de re*, as opposed to *de dicto*, interpretation of propositional attitude reports such as belief ascriptions, is attributable to the property of human mind/brain called intentionality, in virtue of which the mind targets a particular object of thought. Where alternatives are available, the most specific object is the default scenario in that the intentionality of the mental state is in its strongest form (see, for example, Jaszczolt 1999, 2000).

Now, in agreement with the principles of Default Semantics, all the sources of information are treated on a par. In other words, the output of each source can override the output of any other source. This is probably the most significant characteristic that differentiates Default Semantics from other post-Gricean contextualist frameworks. Relevance theory (e.g. Sperber and Wilson 1986, 1995) and Recanati's (e.g. 2002, 2004) truth-conditional pragmatics, for example, have the level of meaning that represents the modified (enriched, modulated, and so forth) logical form of the sentence, called by them an explicature or *what is said* respectively, which is delimited by principles worked out for this purpose, such as Carston's functional independence or Recanati's availability. Other thoughts generated by the uttered sentence, the ones that are not the development of the logical form of the uttered sentence as Sperber and Wilson (1986, 1995) put it, are called implicatures. The literature on this topic is vast (see e.g. Recanati 1989, 2001, 2002, 2004, 2007c; Carston 1988, 1998, 2007) and the topic need not be pursued at present. As I extensively argued in *Default Semantics* (Jaszczolt 2005), there is no obvious need for such a division into the aspects of meaning that add to the output of the meaning of the sentence and those that pertain to separate thoughts. The distinction is motivated solely by what we can call a *syntactic constraint*: the requirement that the primary object of study of the theory of meaning, and at the same time the primary object of a truth-conditional analysis, is directly related to the logical form of the sentence and does not depart from it in a way that changes it beyond recognition. Evidence from utterance processing points, however, in a different direction. People very often communicate their primary, most important, intended meanings through implicatures rather than the explicit content (explicature or *what is said*). According to the experiments conducted by Sysoeva (Sysoeva and Jaszczolt 2007), a vast majority of speakers, in the range of 60–80 per cent in total across the various carefully selected types of scenarios, identify the primary meaning with implicit content. As she found out, this is not a phenomenon that is restricted to English language: she obtained almost identical results for Russian language, where the scenarios were amended in such a way as to appear natural for Russian informants. Similar results were also obtained in analogous experiments performed with somewhat different experimental methods (Nicolle and Clark 1999; Pitts 2005). This evidence from processing is indeed compelling. We should reconsider the criteria for drawing the explicit/implicit distinction and, instead of relying on the logical form of the sentence, recognize the fact that the primary, main meaning that speakers communicate often does not pertain to the developed meaning of the sentence. As our experiments show, this is also the case for sentences that require completion in order to be truth-evaluable ('Tom is not good enough'), and ones that require merely further expansion in view of being obviously true or obviously false ('Everybody came to my party'). Such modified meaning may still not be the main intended meaning.

In view of this empirical evidence, Default Semantics regards the sources of information distinguished in Fig. 4.1 on a par rather than avowing word meaning and sentence structure a privileged position. In practice, this means that sentence (5a) is likely to produce the primary meaning as in (5c) or (5d) rather than (5b). And it is this primary meaning that we shall model in merger representations.

(5a)   I haven't eaten.
(5b)   The speaker hasn't eaten lunch yet.
(5c)   The speaker is hungry.
(5d)   The speaker wants to be invited to lunch.

The term *primary meaning* will from now on be used as a theoretical term for the main meaning as intended by the model speaker and recovered by the model addressee and will be the object that is modelled in merger representations Σ.

The benefits of this revised contextualist semantics for the representation of time are significant. At present, DRT, which, to repeat, arguably provides the most successful formal semantic, truth-conditional representation of discourse about time, is bound by the syntactic constraint and has difficulty with providing a systematic explanation of the time–tense mismatches as in (6) and (7), where the Simple Present tense form refers to future and past events respectively.

(6)   Tom goes to London tomorrow.
(7)   This is what happened in the last episode: Elizabeth Bennet receives a letter from home announcing Lydia's elopement with Mr Wickham. Mr Darcy visits her and sees her cry. He runs out of the room . . .

Although Kamp *et al.* (forthcoming: 70) acknowledge that 'the temporal information conveyed by a natural language sentence or discourse is the result of interaction between several kinds of elements, of which the tenses constitute only one', they proceed by beginning with the 'purely linguistic' (p. 80) interpretation of the sentence, allowing pragmatic contribution where underspecification occurs. Shifts from the norm have to be accounted for by rules specific for the tense or adverbial, such as their rule for the perspectival shift for *now* or ambiguity of the Simple Past. Since our objective is to model the psychologically real primary meaning, even when this primary meaning does not pertain to the sentence's logical form (either 'bare' or further developed), we can easily go further and, instead of complicating the rules for tenses, place the burden of the time–tense mismatches on other sources that make up Σ. In my previous analyses of time and tense, I criticized DRT for adopting the so-called feature TENSE discussed above in Section 2.3: the value of TENSE is *past* when the main verb is in the Simple Past, *pres* when it is in the Simple Present, and *fut* when there is the auxiliary *will* (Kamp and Reyle 1993: 512–13). I now think that feature TENSE should be preserved when it is understood as part of a more general mechanism of representing time in which its values can be overridden by information provided by other sources. In other words, rather than make tenses ambiguous, we should retain the earlier DR-theoretic feature TENSE as the default value of grammatical forms but add a principled, well-worked-out system for explaining how these values can be overridden.

Another difference as compared with my earlier analyses concerns Fig. 4.1. In my *Default Semantics* (Jaszczolt 2005), I identified the following sources of information about meaning that make up merger representations:

(i)   word meaning and sentence structure (WS)
(ii) conscious pragmatic inference (CPI)
(iii) social and cultural defaults (SCD)
(iv) cognitive defaults (CD)

The difference between these sources and the sources identified in Fig. 4.1 lies in the criteria by which they are individuated. In Fig. 4.1, I used the qualitative distinctions such as culture, society, physical laws, context, and co-text. In the list (i)–(iv) above, I used processing criteria. In other words, I was interested then in the type of processing that the source comes with and I combined the types of information with the types of processing to produce these categories. For example, the fact that some shared knowledge of the history of European painting may be so ingrained that it is activated automatically and subconsciously explains the separation of category (iii) from category (ii). For instance, the enrichment of 'Leonardo' to 'Leonardo da Vinci' can be assumed as automatic to an average educated representative of Western culture and is classified under (iii). On the other hand, the enrichment of 'Larry' to 'Larry Horn' in (8) is more likely to be the result of a conscious inferential process, even for post-Gricean pragmaticists.

(8)   Larry's book on negation is the best work ever written on this topic.

While the distinction seems in principle correct, the fact is that in the present state of empirical pragmatics we are not always able to say with certainty whether a particular case falls under the category of a conscious, effortful process and therefore (ii), or automatic, unconscious enrichment and therefore (iii). So, while I will retain the distinction introduced in Jaszczolt (2005), I will not have anything further to say about these two categories.[2] On the other hand, the category of cognitive defaults (CD) is straightforward and uncontroversial: mental architecture and operations of the brain make addressees default to the strongest 'aboutness', strongest reference to objects of discourse, and strongest intentionality.[3] Category (iv) of CD biuniquely corresponds to 'properties of human inferential system' in Fig. 4.1.

A further amendment as compared with my previous analyses concerns Stages I and II of Fig. 4.2.

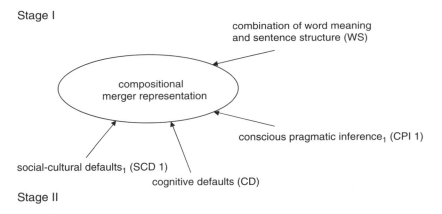

FIGURE 4.2 Utterance interpretation according to the *processing model* of the 2005 version of Default Semantics

Source: adapted from Jaszczolt 2005: 73

---

[2] Recanati (2007c: 53) makes a distinction here between *accidental* and *constitutive* availability to consciousness: primary pragmatic processes, which in Default Semantics have the processing equivalent in the sources that interact with WS to produce a merger representation Σ, may but need not be available to consciousness. By 'processing equivalent' I mean here an analogue as a source of information but not an analogue as far as the produced output is concerned: to repeat, while Recanati's theory obeys the syntactic constraint in defining what is said, Default Semantics is free from this constraint in defining the primary meaning.

[3] On intentionality see Jaszczolt 1999, Chapter 3.

The division of the process into Stage I and Stage II reflects the fact that in addition to the main, primary meaning that is modelled in the merger representation speakers also convey additional, 'secondary' meanings which we call implicatures. To repeat, the syntactic constraint is now abolished and the only criterion for distinguishing Stage I from Stage II is whether the proposition pertains to the primary intended meaning and thereby the strongest communicative intention or rather to subsidiary communicated senses. However, the term 'stages' is conducive to reading this diagram in terms of the temporal sequence of processing. Since there is evidence from the studies of discourse processing that processing of implicatures does not necessarily follow in time the processing of the explicit content/*what is said*, it pays off to be cautious and not imply chronological stages in our model. On the other hand, since our primary meanings given in merger representations are not bound by the syntactic constraint, it is very likely, and seems common sense, that primary meaning so construed is indeed normally processed first, unless an implicature sheds further light on it and the processing of this implicit meaning has to intervene. But we will leave this problem until it can be approached with a lesser degree of speculation.

We will preserve the tenet of Default Semantics that societal and cultural information can pertain to the construction of the primary meaning as well as to the construction of secondary meanings (called in the 2005 version 'implicatures'[4]). Similarly, context-driven inferences can produce the primary meaning and the secondary meanings. So, just as in the 2005 version there were SCD1, SCD2 and CPI1 and CPI2, so now, with reference to the amendments we made in Fig. 4.1, we shall distinguish contributions of stereotypes and presumptions about society and culture to (a) the primary meaning and (b) secondary meanings, as well as contributions of the situation of discourse to (c) the primary meaning and (d) secondary meanings. As qualitatively distinguished sources, however, they need not be further subdivided or annotated. Finally, in the 2005 version I did not allocate a separate node to world knowledge, subsuming some of the instances of its employment under SCD and some under CPI. This subsumption is correct when we are interested in the properties of the *processing* of utterance, for the reasons spelled out in detail in that book.[5] However, when we identify the *sources* in separation from the type of processing, physical laws warrant a separate category. The full model of sources of meaning in Default Semantics will now look as in Fig. 4.3.

---

[4] The term 'primary meaning' was used for the first time in this technical sense in Default Semantics in Sysoeva and Jaszczolt 2007.

[5] In Jaszczolt 2005, I devoted entire Chapter 2 to types of defaults and arguments for and delimiting default interpretations vis-à-vis conscious inference. I refer the reader to that source.

Primary meaning:

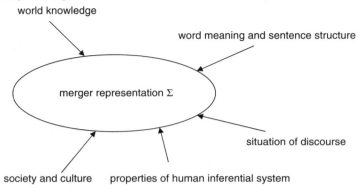

Secondary meanings:

- situation of discourse
- stereotypes and presumptions about society and culture
- world knowledge

FIGURE 4.3 Sources of meaning information contributing to primary and secondary meanings in the revised version of Default Semantics

As I indicated earlier in this section, the question of effortful processing vs. automatic utilization of knowledge of culture and society will not occupy us in what follows. However, for completeness, I present below a revised *processing model* of utterance interpretation in Default Semantics in Fig. 4.4. The indices 'pm' and 'sm' stand for 'pertaining to primary meaning' and 'pertaining to secondary meaning', respectively.

Primary meaning:

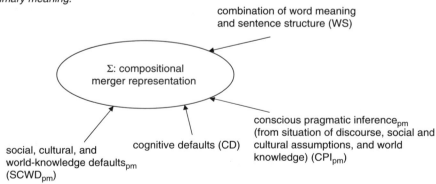

Secondary meanings:

- social, cultural, and world-knowledge defaults$_{sm}$ (SCWD$_{sm}$)
- conscious pragmatic inference$_{sm}$ (CPI$_{sm}$)

FIGURE 4.4 Utterance interpretation according to the *processing model* of the revised version of Default Semantics

It has to be pointed out that any model of utterance interpretation which, like Default Semantics or Levinson's (2000) presumptive meanings, retains the common intuition that the primary meaning is built *both* out of automatic, associative, unreflective components and conscious, inferential ones, has a significant advantage over restrictive and highly implausible accounts on which all such additions are inferential or all are associative. If, like Carston (e.g. 2002, 2007), one argues for inferential enrichments, some of those 'inferences' will have to be dubbed subconscious and spontaneous; if, like Recanati (e.g. 2004, 2007c), one opts for associative enrichments, one has to qualify this by saying that some of them may be open to retrospection and be conscious in this sense. In short, a common-sense 'inference and defaults' account of Default Semantics is clearly superior. It also reflects the state of the art in research on default reasoning.[6] Delimiting this object of study by adhering to or rejecting the syntactic constraint on the primary, intended meaning is another directly related question that I have just attended to above, proposing to free the primary meaning from the limitation of the logical form of the sentence – in accordance with empirical evidence and theoretical parsimony.

The final issue to address with respect to this model is the compositionality of Σ. This aspect of the theory has remained unchanged as compared with the 2005 version. In view of the notorious problems with the pursuit for compositional semantics of natural language, best exemplified in such intensional contexts as propositional attitude reports, modal expressions, and constructions with temporal adverbials, as well as in view of the fact that formal semantics that allows the contribution of pragmatic input to truth-conditional representation has by now proven to be very successful, I follow the approach on which compositionality belongs to the level of representation of *utterance* meaning rather than *sentence* meaning. This is what Recanati (2004: 138) calls the Pragmatic Composition view and an 'interactionist', 'Gestaltist' approach to compositionality (*ibid.*: 132). But, while for him this move called for the amendment of the label to truth-conditional *pragmatics*, we retain the truth-conditional *semantics* one, construed in the contextualist way. Composition of meaning is not dictated by the syntactic form of the uttered sentence but rather by the intended meaning of the speaker. He suggests that, although semantics of words is given by language and by context where necessary, as in the case of filling in indexical expressions, this does not suffice for the composition of meaning. According to his contextualist view, there are pragmatic processes which operate, so to speak, 'from above', without directives given by the syntactic representation, and

---

[6] See, for example, Thomason 1997. For an encyclopaedic overview of research on default reasoning and default interpretations see Jaszczolt 2006b.

these processes are necessary for the composition of meaning to be successful. In this sense, the semantic composition is also largely pragmatic. To repeat, in Default Semantics, this freedom from the syntactic form is taken one step further. Compositionality is predicated of merger representations – the Σs of primary meanings of utterances, as intended by model speakers and recovered by model addressees.[7] By locating compositionality on the level of the merger of information about meaning that comes from qualitatively different sources we can defend the object of study (the primary, intended meaning) and its formal representation from the superfluous and indeed harmful and misleading syntactic constraint (see also Sysoeva and Jaszczolt 2007). To repeat, the representation of the primary, most salient meaning in a discourse need not constitute a development of the logical form of the uttered sentence but may in some cases override it, as in example (5c) above. Like its parent theory DRT on which it is loosely modelled, Default Semantics regards formalization as subordinate to the overall objective of constructing representations of discourse that are cognitively real and reflect mental processing of natural language utterances (Hamm *et al.* 2006). It is also in agreement with Jackendoff (2002; Culicover and Jackendoff 2005), propounding that *conceptual semantics* is a superordinate objective: it makes use of formal methods but is not constrained by their limitations.

Pragmatic compositionality shares the overall orientation with the new developments in philosophy of language where the problem of substitutivity in intensional contexts is now more and more removed from the problem of substitution of coreferential expressions in sentences. For example, Pelczar (2004, 2007) proposes that the fact that a speaker may hold a certain belief about water, say, that it is in short supply, but fail to hold a belief that corresponds to 'H_2O is in short supply' should not be approached as a problem with the properties of the objects of belief but as a problem with the attitude of believing itself. In other words, rather than complicating the theory of the objects of thought à la Kaplan, Perry or Schiffer, he proposes that there is one single object of thought, referred to as 'water', 'H_2O', and some other contextually salient means, but belief relation itself is a context-

---

[7] The question as to 'whose meaning' a theory of discourse meaning should model is still an open one. Discussions frequently converge on the conflicting interpretations of Grice's Cooperatative Principle, allowing it a normative or intensional, speaker-oriented interpretation (see Saul 2002 and Davis 1998, 2007 respectively). Other post-Gricean approaches select the speaker's or the addressee's perspective (see Levinson 2000 and Sperber and Wilson 1995 respectively, with the proviso that Levinson's theory can also be read as normative). I argued in my 2005 essay that the normative perspective, in the sense of behavioural norms pertaining to rational communicative behaviour, is the correct perspective to adopt for modelling utterance meaning.

dependent, indexical predicate, whose content depends on the features of the context such as the topic of conversation, conceptual background of the interlocutors, or the discursive history (co-text). The problem with compositionality in belief reports is therefore solved by appeal to the representation of context which makes the belief itself, and the belief expression, indexical. Similarly, the representation of temporality requires such a contextual embedding but also going even further than indexing and treating context on a par with information from the logical form of the sentence. He calls this view *formal pragmatics* in that literal content is allowed to depend on contextual factors, including norms and maxims of conversation. As he adds, this construal need not violate the principle of compositionality: a compositional theory of meaning, expressions which enter into this composition of meaning, have themselves contextually determined contents (see Pelczar 2004: 71).[8] We go a little further. In liberating merger representations from the syntactic constraint, Default Semantics brings truth-conditional methods closer to cognitive, conceptual analyses, arguably to mutual benefit. Representation of time is now properly liberated from the constraints of tense, allowing for other sources of meaning to be treated on a par. The reason for this is that the concept of tense belongs to one particular source, namely WS (word meaning and sentence structure, and in particular to the 'sentence structure' component of it), rather than to the level of the merger of their outputs (Σ) where compositionality properly belongs.[9] I demonstrate in Section 4.2 below that this framework is particularly well suited for representing temporality. This applies not only to English but also to languages in which there is no formal indication of time on the sentence level. Equipped with our earlier answers to the questions as to what is internal time and what is real time, as well as how they are related to each other and to the concept of epistemic detachment, we can now proceed with the assumption that internal time is a form of epistemic modality in that it constitutes a degree of detachment from what would otherwise be 'timeless truth' and 'certainty'.

The main message from the above argument has to be that while compositionality is a necessary prerequisite for any theory of meaning and need not be questioned, principally because one has nothing better to hold on to instead (or, in other words, that non-compositional theory of meaning is, at

---

[8] See also Predelli 2005a, b on standard truth-conditional semantics being sufficiently 'contextualist'.

[9] I will not address here the debate between contextualism, to which Default Semantics belongs, and the view that free enrichment can be reduced to variables in the logical form. See e.g. Stanley 2000, 2002, 2005; Stanley and Szabó 2000; Martí 2006.

least to me, inconceivable), compositionality should not be seen as a methodological requirement on the syntax and semantic of *sentences*. Such a narrow view of compositionality has been proven to complicate formal methods in order to fit natural language into the mould of formal languages of deductive logic. Instead, we will agree with Jackendoff (2002: 293) that there is no 'strictly linguistic meaning' and that constructing mental representations of discourse is the fundamental objective of a theory of meaning. This view of compositionality permeates some recent accounts that give voice to the disillusionment with the strict methodological requirement of post-Montagovian theories. In 'Compositionality as an empirical problem', David Dowty (2007) suggests that compositionality is not a 'yes-no question' but rather a 'how-question' and belongs in the empirical domain of facts. The formulation of the proposed programme deserves to be quoted at length:

I propose that we let the term NATURAL LANGUAGE COMPOSITIONALITY refer to *whatever strategies and principles we discover that natural languages actually do employ to derive the meanings of sentences, on the basis of whatever aspects of syntax and whatever additional information (if any) research shows that they do in fact depend on*. Since we do not know what all those are, we do not at this point know what 'natural language compositionality' is really like; it is our goal to figure that out by linguistic investigation. Under this revised terminology, there can be no such things as 'counterexamples to compositionality', but there will surely be counterexamples to many particular hypotheses we contemplate as to the form that it takes. (Dowty 2007: 27)

I fully endorse this view, with the proviso that we go even further to compositionality of intentional meaning of utterances. While compositionality retains here the methodological character in that it is assumed as a goal to be discovered rather to be shown to be the case, the question becomes, what principles are responsible for the compositional, and hence calculable in the sense of 'predictable', character of the *entire system* of human communication. In other words, while non-compositional theory of meaning is not considered (*pace* Schiffer's 1991, 1994, 2003 compositional supervenience but non-compositional semantics), 'kicking compositionality up', so to speak, from the level of pure syntax to a multidimensional, merged, interactive, representation of discourse meaning is opened up as a viable option.[10]

The models in Figs 4.3 and 4.4 above summarize the main tenet of Default Semantics that the interaction of sentence structure with the results of pragmatic inference, knowledge of the world, beliefs, perception of the situation, etc. is to be construed as giving equal powers to all the contributing

---

[10] Not only need compositionality not be constrained to sentences, it need not even be constrained to approaches espousing truth conditions and reference. For a deflationist version of compositionality see Horwich 2005.

sources and that compositionality is to be sought at the level at which the output of these sources produces a conceptual/semantic representation of utterance meaning. At the present stage of empirical pragmatics, this is as far as we can go in proposing the merger. It is a task for future experimental projects to pave the way towards capturing this interaction of sources more formally as an algorithm for merging the output of the sources in processing information in discourse. But for what we intend to do in representing the modal characteristic of the concept of time, the above theory will suffice. The next and final task in this essay is to try to represent our findings from Chapters 1–3 in the framework of Default Semantics, that is construct merger representations (Σs) for utterances of sentences referring to the past, the present, and the future, trying to account for a wide spectrum of cases, including those where there is a tense–time mismatch, or the temporal location is left unspecified in the sentence. This is the task to which I now turn.

4.2 Merger representations for the future, present, and past

The analyses from Chapters 1–3 that will provide the foundation for our merger representations of temporality can be summarized as follows:

(I)   The concept of time supervenes on a more primitive concept of modality in the form of epistemic possibility, detachment from certainty.

(II) The concept of time (internal time) supervenes on the concept of real time (time of space-time of the universe).

(III) Real time supervenes on probability and hence is underlyingly modal. We also argued that

(IV) Time is not conceptualized as a flow but rather, like space, as a location. We further inferred that

(V)   The semantics of time should be constructed using the notion of epistemic possibility.
      Finally, in Chapter (3), we defended the view that

(VI) The unit to which the modal (*qua* temporal) specification pertains is a proposition-like unit, called in Default Semantics a merged proposition and analysed as a merger representation Σ.

To repeat, 'supervenience' is to be understood here in a loose way as a form of logical dependence where the differences on the level of temporality are explained by the differences on the level of modality. Whether the logical dependence also comes with metaphysical dependence is a question which indirectly acquired a positive answer in our earlier discussions but a thorough support of which will fall outside the scope of this essay. Since we also argued that time is inherently modal and are going to offer a modal semantics of temporal concepts, there is a strong argument here that supervenience should give rise to identity. But it would require a very different investigation to set clear principles distinguishing supervenience from identity. All that matters for our semantic analysis is that the theses that (i) the concept of time can be represented as epistemic detachment and (ii) real time can be represented as metaphysical detachment (possibilities of the universe) are well supported and can be reflected in a formal account of utterance meaning—to which I now turn. Some of the required formalism is already in place in the standard 2005 version of Default Semantics. I will now summarize it and point out the revisions that need to be introduced, mainly to do with (i) exorcising the concepts of state and event and (ii) revising the sources of information about meaning whose output makes up the Σ. To repeat, the main desideratum for merger representations Σ is for them to have the status of conceptual, cognitively real structures. They combine the formalism of truth-conditional approaches with the directive of conceptual adequacy of cognitive semantic approaches. Like, for example, conceptual semantics of Jackendoff (e.g. 2002; Culicover and Jackendoff 2005), Default Semantics draws on all sources of meaning accessible to an addressee. In this respect, we can compare the sources WS, SCWD, CD, and CPI identified in Fig. 4.4 above with the sources identified by Jackendoff (2002: 275) in his conceptualist semantics.[11] The latter integrates various aspects of cognition pertaining to 'linguistic semantics, (. . .) pragmatics, perceptual understanding, embodied cognition, reasoning and planning, social/cultural understanding, primate cognition, and evolutionary psychology'. We go further, however, with defining the object of merger representations. While Culicover and Jackendoff acknowledge that some dependencies such as anaphoric binding and quantifier scope are determined on the level of conceptual rather than syntactic structure (Culicover and Jackendoff 2005: 410), they, like all other semantic approaches, model the meaning of the structures. In other words, they are not in the business of modelling the main, primary intended meaning of the speaker when this main, primary meaning happens to have the status of what we would conventionally call an implicature. Default Semantics, on the other hand, is free from this syntactic constraint and the content of Σ is precisely such main, primary meaning, as intended by a model speaker and recovered by a model addressee, irrespective of its relation to the logical form of the uttered sentence. To repeat, as ample experiments demonstrate, main meanings that violate the syntactic constraint, i.e. the constraint that says that the represented explicit meaning has to be a development of the logical form

---

[11] For an overview of conceptual semantics see Culicover and Jackendoff 2005, Section 5.2.

of the uttered sentence (Sperber and Wilson 1986, 1995) and therefore correspond to what is standardly called an implicature, constitute between 60 and 80 per cent of all cases (Sysoeva and Jaszczolt 2007). Since similar results were obtained by using different methods (Pitts 2005; Nicolle and Clark 1999), the evidence can be considered to be strengthened through the method of triangulation and quite reliable. In short, Default Semantics, unlike other approaches, is in the business of modelling main meanings, even when they depart from the structure of the uttered sentence. Such main meanings acquire in our theory the status of primary meanings, and henceforth their place (but not characteristics) can be compared with that of an explicature of relevance theory (Sperber and Wilson, e.g. 1986, 1995) or *what is said* of Recanati (e.g. 1989). Default Semantics merely makes one more step in this post-Gricean tradition and rejects the syntactic constraint: the modelled primary meaning is whatever the main meaning is, full stop. To quote from *Simpler Syntax* again, 'syntactic structures may reflect to a greater or lesser degree the semantic structures they express' (Culicover and Jackendoff 2005: 527). We go a little further and say that the gradation that obtains here includes the case of no formal reflection at all.

To sum up, information from standard assumptions and from context is vital in delimiting the object that is to be represented in Σ. Again, this is hardly a novel proposal. Time–tense mismatch is one of the most common topics of research on temporality and many different recourses to contextual values have been made. To repeat, Langacker (2001: 268–9) argues for the omnipresence of the present tense with future and past reference by taking into account the 'viewing arrangements' of the event. In other words, it is not the actual event that is represented in the conceptual/semantic representation but rather the 'virtual event', event as it is represented by the speaker. Another good example of the importance of context is contrastive analysis of temporal phenomena. De Swart (2007), for example, argues for the importance of the discourse level in the contrastive study of the Perfect. She argues that the semantics of the Perfect in English, German, French, and Dutch makes use of the Reichenbachian structure of the event time, speech time, and reference time, orienting the situation with respect to the speech time, by which it creates a rhetorical structure of Elaboration (adopted from SDRT[12]) with the time of speech as topic. In French and German, the Perfect can enter into temporal relations with other times, hence it can be used in narration. In English and Dutch this is much more restricted. It is only looking at discourse structure that we can identify such cross-linguistic differences. In Default Semantics, we follow a similar route, representing the cognitive rather than

---

[12] See, for example, Asher and Lascarides 2003; Lascarides and Asher 1993.

the physical reality. Tense–time mismatches cease to be special cases because even syntactic form–semantic form mismatches in general are the standard and occur in a high proportion of cases as the experimental results suggest – a proportion that is further increased if we count mismatches produced by enriching the logical form of the sentence. Once we have taken the step to opt to make these primary intended meaning our represented objects, mismatches become the norm. They merely signal that in such cases it is not WS but rather some other source of information about meaning that takes preference in constructing Σ. We can now move to constructing merger representations for selected examples of English expressions with future-, present-, and past-time reference.

4.2.1 *Representing the future*

In Chapter 2, I proposed to order expressions of future time on a scale of the strength of commitment to the eventuality referred to in the utterance. Examples (18)–(21) from Section 2.1, repeated here as (9)–(12), can be placed on such a scale. The terms 'periphrastic future' and 'regular future' are used there in accordance with the standard use in expositions of the English grammar but we have to remember the ongoing historical process of 'remodalization' of *will* and the ongoing tendency to replace the regular expression of futurity with the *be going to* form.[13]

(9)   Peter goes to London tomorrow morning.   ('tenseless' future)
(10) Peter is going to London tomorrow   (futurative progressive)
      morning.
(11) Peter is going to go to London tomorrow   (periphrastic future)
      morning.
(12) Peter will go to London tomorrow morning.   (regular future)

The Simple Present is used in (9) as the so-called 'tenseless' future and signals a high degree of certainty founded on the existence of a reliable plan for Peter's going to London. When we discuss this expression in terms of real events, we have to say that the link with the present and past time, constituted by the fact that the trip to London was planned in the past and the plan exists now, gives this expression of a future event a high degree of probability and the expression is issued with a strong degree of epistemic commitment on the part of the speaker. When we discuss it in terms of the speaker's representations of events, i.e. virtual rather than real events in Langacker's (2001, 2006) terminology, we have to say that the perception of the event by the speaker

---

[13] See Section 2.2 and references discussed there: Fleischman (1982: 97–8, 135) and Eckardt (2006: 91–127).

pertains to the present moment and is strong at that moment, hence the present tense form. For the purpose of building a merger representation Σ, the choice between the 'objectivist' truth-conditional discourse and the 'subjectivist' cognitive-grammar discourse need not be made. To repeat, in the spirit of recent advances in the convergence of cognitive and formal truth-conditional approaches, we can do both; we can aim at a representation of the cognitive reality of a model speaker–model addressee interaction, at the same time using formal methods of truth-conditional semantics, understood in the contextualist way adopted in Default Semantics. In Chapters 1 and 2, we established the existence of a supervenience relation between real time as a property of the universe and the internal, psychological time as a constituent of human conceptualization of the world. Therefore, objectivism is preserved through the existence of this supervenience relation and there is no compromise involved in focusing on mental representations in constructing Σs. Next, in Chapter 3, we concluded that events and states are too problematic to serve as recipients of temporal qualifications in our Σs. We also concluded that the best unit of which we can predicate temporality is the representation in which information about meaning that comes from qualitatively different sources merges. Therefore, we will end up with merger representations Σ as recipients of temporal qualifications. These representations are embedded in representations pertaining to the whole sentence. In order to differentiate Σs that stand for linguistic equivalents for states and events from Σs pertaining to the entire utterance, we will henceforth index the first as Σ'. Indexing Σ as Σ', Σ'', etc. signals the levels of embedding of the merger representation.

In this essay I have introduced some significant changes in this Default-Semantic setup as compared with the 2005 version[14]: the object of which temporality is predicated is now Σ' rather than a state or an event; the sources of meaning information that contribute to the merger are slightly revised; and I have now distinguished the processing model of Default Semantics in Fig. 4.4 from the identification of sources of information in Fig. 4.3. What remained the same is the modal operator that represents the temporal location. For this purpose I am using the operator ACC, modelled on Grice's sentential operator of Acceptability.

In his relatively little-known posthumous and unfinished publication *Aspects of Reason*, Grice (2001) proposed a so-called Equivocality Thesis, saying that modals can be subsumed under one all-encompassing category: they are 'univocal across the practical/alethic divide' (*ibid.*: 90). For the purpose of a formal analysis he introduced an operator '*Acc*' meaning 'it is (rationally)

---

[14] See, for example, Jaszczolt 2003, 2005, 2006a; Jaszczolt and Srioutai forthcoming.

acceptable that'. This operator was to be applicable both to *alethic* and *practical* modalities as in (13) and (14) respectively.

(13)   Peter should be in London by now.
(14)   Peter should be more punctual if he wants to keep his job in the City.

In the formal analysis, Grice introduced further operators for alethic (⊢) and practical (!) modalities respectively and subsumed the practical and alethic 'must' and 'ought/should' under the general concept of acceptability, defining them as in (15) where *p* stands for a proposition.

(15) $Acc \vdash p$ 'it is acceptable that it is the case that *p*'
         $Acc\ !\ p$ 'it is acceptable that let it be that *p*'

It is diaphanous from examples (13) and (14) that alethic modality is not unlike epistemic modality, and practical modality is not unlike deontic. Since for our current purpose we need to discuss modalities that pertain to mental representations of reality, such as epistemic commitment, we will substitute the concept of the logical necessity and possibility with the concept of the epistemic possibility and necessity: Grice's argument will remain unaffected by this move.

The equivocality of *Acc*, and thereby the univocality of modals, can be summarized as follows. Reasons for belief (pertaining to alethic, epistemic, and dynamic modality) and reasons for action (pertaining to practical and deontic modality) are traceable to the same concept.[15] Grice went even further and attempted to derive practical modality from alethic by reasoning that if something *must* be the case in the deontic sense, it is so because it *must* be the case epistemically (*ibid.*: 90–1). He did not complete this argument, however, and we do not need this further reduction in the use we are going to make of *Acc*. Acceptability, meaning 'it is reasonable to think that', suffices as a formal equivalent of the concept of detachment from the state of affairs referred to in the utterance. In representing temporality, this acceptability is of the epistemic kind and we shall further add to it an index Δ that captures the relative degree of this acceptability/model speaker's commitment. Remembering that on our account, in view of the arguments developed in Chapter 3, we substitute Σ' for *p*, we end up with the semantic form in (16) for representing a temporal location of the state of affairs:

(16) $ACC_\Delta \vdash \Sigma'$

---

[15] On the unitary semantics of modals see also Papafragou 2000. She proposes an underspecified semantics for modals, supplemented with pragmatic inference that contributes to the truth-conditional content in agreement with the principles of contextualism. As in my Default Semantics, in Papafragou's account epistemic modality is the most fundamental type of modality. In Default Semantics this privileged status comes from the property of representing degrees of commitment to the eventuality, while in Papafragou's account it comes from the construal of epistemic modality as standing for the human ability to metarepresent.

where Σ' is further spelled out as a merger representation that pertains to the merged proposition – the semantic equivalent of states of affairs.[16] The formula reads as 'it is acceptable to the degree Δ that Σ' is true'. This is also a slight revision as compared with the previous version of the theory in that ACC now operates on merger representations for which truth conditions can be formulated, rather than states and events of whom we had to predicate existence. To repeat, in view of the facts that (i) states and events are ill-defined notions that come from an ontologically different bag, and (ii) we represent human concept of internal time and hence human conceptualizations of states of affairs (à la Langacker's (2001: 268–9) 'virtual occurrences of events') rather than 'raw', 'real' situations, this replacement of *s* and *e* by Σ' is an improvement – and, of course, a theoretical necessity. As in the 2005 version of Default Semantics, we will be using an amended and extended language of DRT (Kamp and Reyle 1993; van Eijck and Kamp 1997; Kamp *et al.* forthcoming) and our Σs are modelled on the DRSs of DRT, with the proviso that the syntactic constraint is lifted and our object of representation is more 'pragmaticky', so to speak: it is the main meaning as intended by the model speaker and recovered by the model addressee.

We are now ready to construct merger representations for the four types of expressing future-time reference exemplified in (9)–(12). I present them in the order of increasing epistemic commitment assessed above: *regular future* > *periphrastic future* > *futurative progressive* > *'tenseless' future* in Figs 4.5–4.8 respectively.

(12)   Peter will go to London tomorrow morning. (regular future)

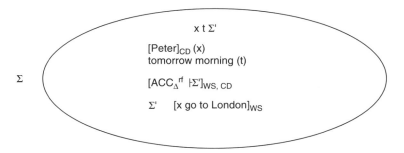

FIGURE 4.5 Σ for example (12), regular future

[16] Note that we amended the abbreviation for the acceptability operator from Grice's *Acc* to ACC in order to preserve the distinction between the theoretical assumptions such as that *Acc* applies to different types of modality: alethic and practical rather than epistemic and deontic and operates on a categorically different content: *p* rather than Σ'. Although Σ' is propositional, in virtue of the arguments put forward in Chapter 3, it is composed via pragmatic composition that is characteristic of merger representations.

The English *will* is regarded here as a species of modality and is subsumed under the category of acceptability ACC of the epistemic kind $\vdash$: $ACC_\Delta{}^{rf}\vdash \Sigma'$. Next, acceptability, which is to be read as 'it is reasonable to think that', 'it is rationally plausible that', allows for degrees. An eventuality, whose formal linguistic equivalent[17] in the merger representation Σ is Σ', can be more, or less, acceptable, just as the speaker can be committed to its truth to varying degrees. This degree is marked by the subscript Δ, indexed for a value that pertains to the particular type of expression of the future-time location, such as *rf* (regular future), *pf* (periphrastic future), *fp* (futurative progressive), and *tf* ('tenseless' future). It has to be noted that we are not considering here the form *shall*. Were we to include it in our analysis, the index on Δ in Fig. 4.5 would have to be *rf will* rather than bare *rf* in order to indicate the lexical source of the regular future. Finally, the subscripts WS and CD indicate the particular source of information that contributes to the merger representation of the meaning of the utterance as identified in Fig. 4.4 for the revised version of Default Semantics. The CD subscript on the proper name 'Peter' signals the default referential interpretation, in that proper names, as directly referential expressions, are normally used to refer to an identifiable individual or object.[18] The WS and CD indices on ACC signal that the content of ACC Σ' is given by the lexicon + grammar (the WS source) and further specified by the normal, default use of *will* (by the CD source).

Merger representations constructed here are partial in that they do not present the detailed composition of meaning. They do not show how the output of the WS source is composed, neither do they show how the mechanism of the interaction of the WS, CD, and CPI_{pm} sources works. This is partly due to the fact that the state of our knowledge of discourse processing is far from satisfactory. Apart from some evidence concerning the incremental nature of processing, the use of the principle of economy and hence optimal informativeness at the minimal cost as put into maxims, principles, and heuristics in Gricean pragmatics,[19] experimental pragmatics of discourse processing is still in its infancy and is largely confined to testing automatic vs. inferential processing while these terms are themselves ill-defined. On the other hand, a formal model of discourse can always be developed as a hypothesis that is to be tested experimentally at a later stage. The important component is, however, to balance the evidence and theorizing and ensure that the formal model rests on sufficiently sound assumptions about processing.[20]

---

[17] Again, in the sense of a proposition composed according to the principles of pragmatic compositionality.

[18] See also Chapters 4 and 5 of Jaszczolt 2005.

[19] By Grice, Levinson, Horn, and Sperber and Wilson in their respective accounts. The literature on this topic is vast: see Jaszczolt 2002, Chapters 10–11 for an overview.

[20] See Jaszczolt 2008 on the need for moderate psychologism in the theory of meaning.

We are still some way away from the stage at which the algorithm for the interaction of the sources that make up Σ can be completed.

Other, non-future uses of *will* are discussed in Section 4.2.2 below. Next, just as future *will* can be subsumed under *Acc*, so can the remaining three types of expressions with future-time reference. Merger representations for utterances that employ them are given in Figs 4.6–4.8.

(11)   Peter is going to go to London tomorrow morning. (periphrastic future)

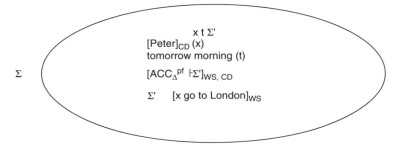

FIGURE 4.6 Σ for example (11), periphrastic future

(10)   Peter is going to London tomorrow morning. (futurative progressive)

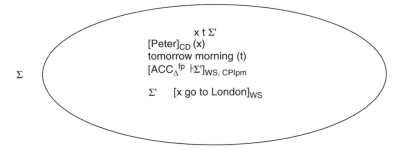

FIGURE 4.7 Σ for example (10), futurative progressive

In Fig. 4.7, the CPI_{pm} source is responsible for the future-time reference of a form which by default refers to the present moment. The same mechanism of triggering a departure from the default in the process of pragmatic composition is at work in the case of 'tenseless' future in Fig. 4.8.

(9)   Peter goes to London tomorrow morning. ('tenseless' future)

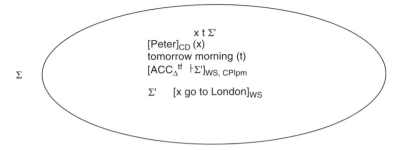

FIGURE 4.8 Σ for example (9), 'tenseless' future

The scale of epistemic commitment can be continued by adding modal verbs as in (17)–(19), repeated from (48), (50), and (51) in Chapter 2.

(17)   Peter must be going to London tomorrow morning.   (epistemic necessity future/inferential evidentiality)

(18)   Peter may go to London tomorrow morning.   (epistemic possibility future)

(19)   Peter might go to London tomorrow morning.   (epistemic possibility future)

Other forms are also possible when they interact with other sources of meaning of Σ to produce future-time reference. The composition of the merger representation proceeds in exactly the same way and is relatively unproblematic in that modal verbs are given exactly the same semantic treatment as other forms that are used for temporal location: ACC comes with the degree of strength of epistemic attachment.[21] For example, (18) has the value of Δ assigned by the modal verb *may*. Again, as in the case of *will*, there are salient values for expressions and values that depart from them as a result of the interaction with other sources of meaning. In the case of modal verbs, these values are compositional already on the level of grammar, without resorting to pragmatic compositionality: modal verb followed by an action verb obtains a future-time reading as in (20), and this value is obtained through the source WS: *may* plus *go* results in the future-time reference in virtue of the juxtaposition of these two lexical items.

---

[21] See also Asher and McCready 2007 for a compositional semantics of *would* and *might* that uses discourse context and discourse update – updating the set of epistemic possibilities as discourse progresses.

(20)   Peter may go to London.

May accompanied by a stative verb defaults to the present-time interpretation as in (21). However, this interpretation, although salient, is easy to override by the output of other sources of Σ. The dialogue in (22) is one such example, and the addition of a future-oriented adverbial in (23) is another.

(21)   Peter may be in London.

(22)   A: Could you both come and see me on Sunday?
       B: I am not sure, Peter may be in London.

(23)   Peter may be in London next Sunday.

Similarly, *may* followed by a progressive aspect form obtains a present-time interpretation in virtue of CD as in (24). That this interpretation is the effect of CD rather than WS is evident from example (25).

(24)   Peter may be preparing his talk.
(25)   Peter may be preparing his talk tomorrow.

Merger representations for utterances with *may* are constructed as follows. (18), repeated below, makes use of the CD source for the meaning of *may* and produces a proposition with future-time reference as in Fig. 4.9. The index on Δ is *epf may*, for the epistemic possibility future use of *may*. Note that since *epf* is also realized by other modal verbs, the specification of the lexical source (*may*) is necessary.

(18)   Peter may go to London tomorrow morning.

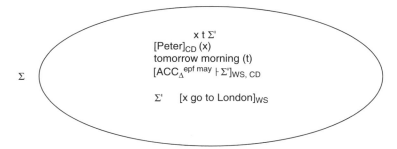

$$x \, t \, \Sigma'$$
$$[\text{Peter}]_{CD} (x)$$
$$\text{tomorrow morning (t)}$$
$$[\text{ACC}_\Delta^{\text{epf may}} \vdash \Sigma']_{WS, \, CD}$$

$$\Sigma' \quad [x \text{ go to London}]_{WS}$$

Σ

FIGURE 4.9 Σ for example (18), future *may*

It has to be pointed out that temporal reference can be quite easily handled in the above examples because it is unambiguously indicated by a temporal adverbial such as 'tomorrow morning' or 'now'. If an utterance of the sentence does not contain an unambiguous lexical indication of temporality of that kind, according to Default Semantics, the specification of temporal reference proceeds in the following way. The merger representation combines information about meaning that comes from various sources, including pragmatic inference and salient, default interpretations. Since the default reading of *will* is undeniably future-time reference, and is, in addition, future in virtue of WS when followed by an action verb, (26) obtains a merger representation as in Fig. 4.10, where the *rf* value of Δ comes from the default reading of *will*.

(26)   Peter will go to London.

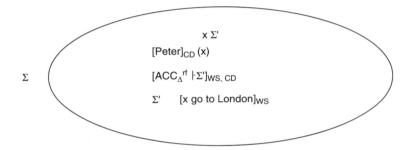

FIGURE 4.10 Σ for example (26): regular future

Analogously, the utterance of the sentence 'Peter is in London' will trigger the regular present reading as a cognitive default associated with the grammatical form of the Simple Present tense, as discussed in Section 4.2.2. However, since the merger representation Σ is a result of interaction of information coming from sources which work on an equal footing, it also happens that information processed in a particular context, that is information owed to the source CPI_{pm}, may take precedence over the temporal default of the grammatical expression although no overt adverbial is present in the utterance. For example, (27) may obtain a dispositional necessity, and hence not a future, reading, when the context triggers pragmatic inference to that effect.

(27)   Tom will go all the way to London on his bike.

A dispositional necessity reading may also be triggered by the very content of the sentence itself. The most salient reading of (28) is precisely that of dispositional necessity. It is rather unlikely that the speaker is predicting a future chain of events of this kind.

(28)   Tom will take off his dirty clothes, leave them on the floor, and then leave them there for days without noticing.

In short, the mechanism by which Σ is created allows for a variety of combinations of the output of information from the contributing sources: WS, CD, CPI$_{pm}$, and SCWD$_{pm}$ as depicted in Fig. 4.4.

We are now in a position to make general, summing-up remarks on the ways of expressing future-time reference in English by means of the forms discussed in this section. The types of expressions that are used to refer to future eventualities can be ordered with respect to the degree of commitment to the truth of the proposition on the part of the speaker, or, in other words, the degree of epistemic commitment. In the 2005 version of Default Semantics I presented two principles for relative ordering of some of the common expressions, namely regular future (*rf*), futurative progressive (*fp*) and 'tenseless' future (*tf*). We will now add periphrastic future (*pf*) as exemplified in (11), as well as other overtly modal expressions with future-time reference such as epistemic necessity future (*enf*) exemplified in (17) above, and epistemic possibility future (*epf*), exemplified in (18) and (19). The final two categories are of a slightly different status though than the remaining four. They are generic labels for expressions that use various modal verbs employed to convey epistemic necessity or possibility. *Enf* can be expressed by (17) repeated below, as well as by (29), repeated from (49) in Chapter 2, where *must*, *should*, and *ought to* are all functioning as verbs of epistemic modality.

(17)   Peter must be going to London tomorrow morning.
       (epistemic necessity future/inferential evidentiality)

(29)   Peter ought to/should be going to London tomorrow morning.
       (epistemic necessity future/inferential evidentiality)

Analogously, *epf* can be realized by employing modal verbs *may* or *might* as in (18) and (19) respectively (repeated below).

(18)   Peter may go to London tomorrow   (epistemic possibility future)
       morning.
(19)   Peter might go to London tomorrow   (epistemic possibility future)
       morning.

The *will/shall* alternation notwithstanding, the remaining categories of *rf*, *fp*, *tf*, and *pf* are all uniform types delimited by a particular grammatical construction. During the construction of the scales of semantic properties this difference has to be borne in mind and an extended area of the scale has to be allocated to the categories in order to leave room for the variation within a category.

The first obvious principle for classification is the degree of epistemic commitment to the proposition on the part of the speaker. We have already established that 'tenseless' future comes with the strongest commitment, founded on the existence of a reliable plan: unless something unexpected happens, p is going to be the case. Next comes futurative progressive which is also conditioned by planned action. Regular future is strongly modal and indicates less commitment than the now standard periphrastic construction. Hence, we obtain the cline in (30).

(30) $tf > fp > pf > rf$

Expressions with modal verbs in the categories of epistemic necessity and epistemic possibility follow with considerably weaker commitment and we obtain the cline in (31).

(31) $tf > fp > pf > rf > enf > epf$

Fig. 4.11 presents the scale of epistemic commitment for the forms in (31). The '1' end of the scale stands for the strongest commitment to the truth of the proposition and the '0' end for the weakest.

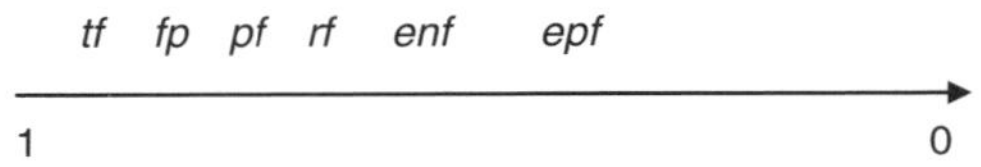

FIGURE   4.11 Degree of epistemic commitment for expressions with future-time reference

Modal adverbs such as 'certainly', 'possibly' and epistemic attitude expressions such as 'I think' (the latter used in the full clausal way or as a semantically bleached discourse marker) also contribute to the degree of modal detachment but, as I pointed out in Section 2.5.2, I will not be concerned with them in that they are not directly relevant for the discussion of the concept of time. It has to be remembered, however, that, to repeat, their contribution to the process of composing utterance meaning is not rigidly fixed by their semantic content but rather pertains to their rhetorical function (Simon-Vandenbergen and Aijmer 2007): they interact with other markers of modality and decrease or increase the degree of certainty, also sometimes acting along some other semantic dimensions such as the evidential ('clearly', 'evidently') and the mirative ('surely', 'indeed'[22]). As I pointed out in Section 2.5.2, the presence of modal adverbs of certainty may decrease rather than

---

[22] But see Simon-Vandenbergen and Aijmer (2007: 37) on the emotive emphasis of 'indeed'.

increase certainty, in accordance with the Gricean heuristic that marked expressions signal marked situations (e.g. Levinson 2000). In other words, the pragmatic effect of additional assurances is that the threshold of certainty assumed at the beginning of the conversational exchange becomes lowered: 'Surely, it is Friday today' signals that there was an uncertainty on the part of the speaker or the addressee concerning the day of the week they were in that had to be resolved. These adverbs may contribute slightly different content when interacting with different temporal orientations expressed in utterances. For example, 'surely' in 'Surely, it's Friday today' differs in its semantic contribution from 'surely' in 'Surely, I will do it'. But this interaction of modal adverbs with temporal orientation is a topic for a corpus-based empirical investigation, separate form the current philosophical-pragmatic enquiry.

Coming back to the scales of modality, expressions with future-time reference can also be ordered according to other criteria. One obvious principle for ordering is the speaker's informative intention. As I argued in the previous version of my analysis of futurity in Default Semantics (e.g. Jaszczolt 2005), this principle yields exactly the same results as far as the relative ordering is concerned as the principle of the degree of commitment. On the other hand, when we use the degree of modality as a criterion, the scale becomes reversed: the 'more modal' the construction, so to speak, the more detached the utterance from certainty. The scale of degrees of modality is given in Fig. 4.12.

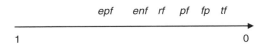

FIGURE 4.12 Degree of modal detachment for selected expressions with future-time reference

The scales do not offer exact values for the forms but rather suggest a relative ordering with approximate values from 0 to 1 for the reasons I explain in the following paragraph. It also has to be pointed out that, since on our construal epistemic commitment is scalar, the labels *enf* and *epf*, for epistemic necessity and epistemic possibility future respectively, are rather misleading. The semantic difference on the dimension of the degree of possibility and commitment between (17) and (18), that is between stating that Peter must, or may, in the epistemic sense, be going to London tomorrow, is a difference of degree rather than quality of commitment. Therefore, the labels 'necessity' and 'possibility' are to be understood as referring to the type of modal verb used in these constructions rather than as semantic labels signalling the kind of commitment. As can be seen from the axes in Figs 4.11 and 4.12, *enf* and *epf* are only areas on the larger scale and epistemic necessity does not by any means signal a qualitatively different commitment approximating 1 as the label 'necessity' may suggest.

Two pertinent questions arise at this point: [1] how are the placements of the categories on the axis determined, on the basis of what evidence, and [2] why should we stop at approximate values and qualitative rather than quantitative distinctions. A disclaimer is in order here. Merger representations of Default Semantics have numerous advantages over other extant contextual semantic analyses of utterances and discourses. Perhaps the main advantage is that they model the primary meaning which, to repeat, is free from the syntactic constraint that characterizes explicatures (developments of the logical form of the sentence, Sperber and Wilson 1986, 1995) and *what is said* (automatic enrichments of the sentence, Recanati 1989, 2004). They also go further than these other contextualist construals in that they offer a degree of formalization for these primary meanings. However, this formalization, while a big step forward in post-Gricean pragmatics, is substantially inferior to the formal accounts of discourse in dynamic semantics, such as DRT. It is inferior precisely because its object is too 'pragmaticky' to yield to formalization easily. An algorithm for the interaction of WS, CPI_{pm}, CD, and $SCWD_{pm}$ is still a task for the future. For example, the values of Δ are assigned by the concepts associated with lexical items or grammatical forms (e.g. $\Delta^{epf\ may}$, Δ^{rf}) and, while it seems the correct way to proceed[23] because this assignment is executed through WS, CD, or CPI_{pm} and therefore accounts both for context-free and context-dependent values, this is not the ultimate explanation as far as computational implementation of Σs is concerned. What is required next is adding more quantitative detail to the qualitative scales on which I put expressions for the past, present, and future. At the moment we are able to locate them relative to one another on the cline of degree of epistemic commitment as we did for the expressions of the future above: from 'tenseless' future, through futurative progressive, periphrastic *be going to*, regular future *will*, to expressions with modal verbs such as *may* and *might*. The exact placement on such a scale is, however, not available. In other words, we cannot compare these forms in relative quantitative terms. For example, if we stipulated that the commitment associated with 'tenseless' future is 1, we

---

[23] The judgement that it is the correct way to proceed is based on the assumption that lexical items and grammatical forms have core meanings from which mappings can be executed to new concepts constructed *ad hoc* in the context. An alternative view would be late-Wittgensteinian stance of meaning as use, negating the existence of core meanings. See Recanati 2004, 2005 for meaning eliminativism and Carston 2002, Chapter 5, for *ad hoc* concepts and concept shift.

would not be able to associate, say, 0.9 with futurative progressive, 0.8 with *be going to* of periphrastic future, or, say, 0.75 with regular future *will*, and so on. In the 2005 version of Default Semantics I suggested that this can be achieved after a substantial, corpus-based study and after a careful laying out of the criteria by which the numbers are to be assigned. It seems to me at present that such further reduction of qualitative scales to numerical scales for epistemic commitment may not be necessary if the assumption that words and grammatical constructions indeed have their core, salient meanings is correct. In other words, if there are salient concepts associated with them, then an appeal to these concepts and processing them through the WS or DC sources is as far as we need to go, even in a computationally implementable theory. If, however, late Wittgenstein and so-called meaning eliminativists are correct,[24] not only would we have to dispose with the lexicon- and grammar-based indices on Δ but also amend the sources of Σ so as to account for the output of the current WS in an alternative way. The disclaimer is therefore this: the model of discourse interpretation offered in Default Semantics works on the assumption that there are salient, core concepts. This is more than a theoretical assumption, though, and more than a conviction or stipulation based on intuition. There has been substantial evidence in experimental linguistics demonstrating that salient meanings are activated even in contexts which do not support them. They are activated to different degrees but nevertheless they *are* present. Giora (2003), for example, discusses the results of her numerous experiments corroborating this tenet:

I show that privileged meanings, meanings foremost on our mind, affect comprehension and production primarily, regardless of context or literality. Specifically, I show that access of salient meanings is hard to prevent, even when context is highly supportive of the less or nonsalient meaning, irrespective of whether they are literal or nonliteral. (Giora 2003: 103)

These meanings are salient because they are conventional, frequent, prototypical, and familiar. They are the standard *coded* meanings (see *ibid.*: 10). Salient meanings are always accessed, even when the context does not support them. While context can weaken them, it cannot pre-empt them (see, for example, *ibid.*: 59). In other words, lexical access is modular: context cannot penetrate it, it can only weaken its effects. She calls this view a graded salience hypothesis. According to graded salience, coded meaning is always accessed but subsequently the contextual effect on coded meaning of low salience may be so strong as to override this meaning very early on in processing. In fact,

---

[24] See fn 23.

the contextual processing and lexical decoding may run in parallel, creating the impression of direct access of the non-coded meaning.[25] This tends to be the case in figurative language and in utterances where the item with non-standard interpretation is placed towards the end of the sentence. In the latter case the incremental processing of the sentence up to the point where the item in question is encountered produces strong contextual effects and facilitates the retrieval of the non-coded meaning. *Nota bene*, the literality is not the definitional property of such salient meanings. Meanings are salient because they are frequent, familiar, and accessible to memory. Their literality is the product of language use and language history. What it means for the model of utterance processing offered by Default Semantics is that (a) the WS source is justified and (b) the lexically or grammatically derived index on Δ is also justified: if words and structures have salient, core meanings, then (a) there is a component of Σ provided by words and grammatical constructions, and at the same time (b) there is a value of epistemic commitment Δ that can be associated with these core meanings of words and structures such as *will, may,* or *be going to,* provided in some cases by WS and in others by CD. While Default Semantics can in principle be revised should meaning eliminativism be proved correct, extant evidence such as Giora's experiments suggests that core meanings are the best empirically supported foundation for the construction of meaning.[26]

4.2.2 *Representing the present*

Present-time reference can be represented analogously, using the scale of strength of epistemic commitment. An utterance of sentence (32) makes use of the Simple Present tense form, which is the standard way of conveying the *now* and which we can call *regular present*. It can be juxtaposed and contrasted with other types of constructions such as the one in (33), which is a version of (13).

(32)   Peter is in London now.   (regular present)
(33)   Peter will be in London now.   (epistemic necessity present/inferential evidentiality)

Analogously to our analysis of the future-time reference, we assign to some expressions, this time to the Simple Present tense form, a cognitive-default interpretation. The value of the degree of epistemic commitment Δ is assigned as that pertaining to regular present (abbreviated here as *rn*, for 'regular *now*')

---

[25] Cf.: 'To disconfirm the graded salience hypothesis, it would be necessary to show that contextual information can exclusively activate less salient information, as maintained by the direct, selective access model' Giora (2003: 40–1).

[26] Many thanks to Istvan Kecskes for drawing my attention to Rachel Giora's experimental findings on lexical access and to her graded salience hypothesis.

and the source of information is indicated as WS, CD in that it is word meaning together with the salient, cognitive-default reading of 'is' that produces the present-time reference. Utterance of sentence (32) obtains a merger representation as in Fig. 4.13.

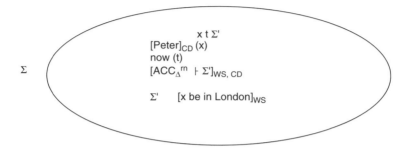

FIGURE 4.13 Σ for example (32), regular present

Utterance without an overt temporal adverbial, such as (32′), also triggers a regular present interpretation by means of CD as in Fig. 4.14.

(32′)   Peter is in London.

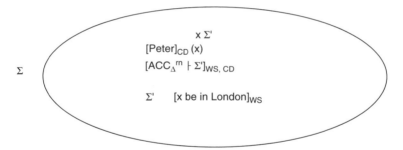

FIGURE 4.14 Σ for example (32′), regular present

The evidential, epistemic necessity present use of *will* in (33) is represented in Fig. 4.15. The value of Δ is arrived at in the process of interaction of the output of the sources WS and CPI_{pm} because *will* has here a non-standard temporal reference to the present rather than the future. This modal value is represented as an *enn will* (for epistemic necessity *now*) index on Δ: $\Delta^{enn\ will}$.[27]

---

[27] In the 2005 version of Default Semantics I indicated the source (*rf*) rather than the product (*enn*) as the index on Δ, allowing for the compositional (in the sense of pragmatic compositionality) derivation of the epistemic necessity reading of *will*. In order to standardize with the representation of other forms, this has now been altered to *enn*.

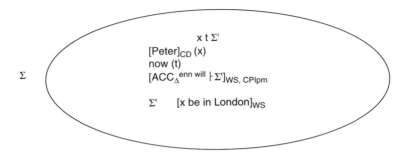

FIGURE 4.15 Σ for example (33), epistemic necessity present with *will*

CPI$_{pm}$ is responsible for turning *will* into epistemic necessity (evidential) *will*. This pragmatic inference is enabled by the set value for *t* that comes from the adverb 'now'. This representation of the *enn* use of *will* as a result of pragmatic inference is also independently supported by Giora's (2003) findings concerning graded salience of word retrieval discussed in Section 4.2.1. Applying her evidence to the area of temporal expressions, we accept that even in contexts in which futurity is not intended, the default, future sense is activated to some degree and then overridden by the contextually salient sense as in (33). I discussed the non-future uses of *will* in detail in Chapter 6 of Jaszczolt 2005 and will not repeat the analysis here. The gist of the argument, *pace* some notational revisions, carries forward to the current revised version. It should only be pointed out that in addition to providing an argument for a modal treatment of *will* in general, these uses also testify to the plausibility of using the scale of modal commitment: Peter's being in London now can be expressed not only by (33) but also by a straightforward regular present form in (32) ('Peter is in London now') or various modal expressions with weaker degree of commitment. These types of expressions can be further embedded in the cline of present-time reference which is undeniably modal but at the same time constitutes a clear continuation of the gradation of certainty from (32) and (33), such as (34), which is another form of epistemic necessity present, and (35)–(36) which exemplify epistemic possibility present.

(34) Peter must be in London now.   (epistemic necessity present/
                                      inferential evidentiality)
(35) Peter may be in London now.   (epistemic possibility present)
(36) Peter might be in London now.   (epistemic possibility present)

The scale of epistemic commitment to the truth of the proposition on the part of the speaker can be constructed analogously to that for the future presented in Fig. 4.11. We will use abbreviations *enn* for epistemic necessity present (epistemic necessity *now*), as above, and introduce *epn* for epistemic possibility present (epistemic possibility *now*). As in the case of the scale for the future, the labels have to be taken as generic categories to be realized by a variety of expressions (e.g. *will, must* for *enn* and *may, might* for *epn*). Further, the disclaimer used for the labels for the future-time reference also carries forward: there is no clear boundary between epistemic necessity and epistemic possibility but instead there is a scale of epistemic commitment and the categories *enn* and *epn* are used in order to conveniently label the types of expressions that are used for the purpose of making this temporal reference. The relative ordering of the types is straightforward and intuitively available and is presented in Fig. 4.16.

FIGURE 4.16 Degree of epistemic commitment for expressions with present-time reference

Next, *will* of dispositional necessity also has present-time reference, as in (37).

(37)   Peter will often prepare his lectures on the train on his way to London. (dispositional necessity present)

Again, assuming the coded meaning hypothesis in accordance with Giora's (2003) evidence discussed in Section 4.2.1, the construction of the merger representation for (37) proceeds analogously to that for epistemic necessity *will* in (33), using the core meanings arrived at through WS, as well as contextual meanings arrived at through CPI$_{pm}$ and triggered by the adverb 'often'. The merger representation for (37) is given in Fig. 4.17, with the *dnn will* index on Δ standing for the dispositional necessity present use of *will*. Like before, this is a partial representation in which those aspects of the structure which are not relevant for the current discussion are not spelled out in detail.

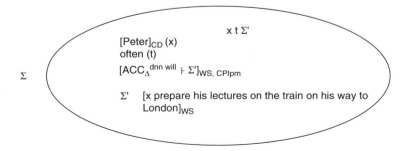

FIGURE 4.17 Σ for example (37), dispositional necessity present with *will*

Just as epistemic necessity present is realized by a variety of expressions, so the category of dispositional necessity present can be rendered by various constructions. (37) is only one way of expressing the iterative aspect. Hence the index *dnn* is accompanied by the specification of the lexical source, *will*.

To sum up, present tense forms acquire the default present interpretation through WS and CD. They don't acquire it through WS alone because other, non-default uses of the Present, with the future- and past-time reference, are also possible and hence it would not be adequate to ascribe the future reading to WS alone. Modal verbs *may* and *might* produce default (CD) as well as CPI_{pm}-triggered readings, arrived at in their interaction with the aspectual type of expression that follows, the adverbial, and the role the context has to play. *Will* produces present-time reference by means of CPI_{pm}, triggered by the present-time or iterative adverbial, or by the context of utterance.

It has to be remembered that merger representations (Σs) represent the internal time, that is the *concept of time* rather than real time. Although, as I argued in Chapters 1 and 2, internal time supervenes on real time and they both supervene on relevant modalities, of probability and epistemic possibility respectively, the *now* of merger representations is the *now* of the language user: on the model assumed in Default Semantics, it is the *now* of the model speaker–model addressee interaction, or the temporal location intended by the model speaker and recovered by the model addressee. Therefore, shifts of deictic centre from the time of producing the utterance to the time of its receipt as in (38) count not as future-time reference but as present-time reference: it is the *now* intended by the speaker/writer, and received, in the future, by the addressee.

(38)   That is all I have to say in this chapter. You know all about the present now.

On the other hand, the present tense forms used for past eventualities will count as representations of the past eventualities with a degree of commitment altered by the use of the past of narration. They will be non-standard, non-regular expressions with past-time reference, obtained from the present-tense grammatical forms through context-triggered CPI_{pm}. Representing past-time reference is the topic to which I now turn.

4.2.3 *Representing the past*

I argued in Section 2.4 that the concept of the past is inherently modal. My argument was founded on the principle of supervenience of the conceptual on the metaphysical, as well as the temporal on the modal (probability). Other ways of defending the modal character of the past have also been attempted in the literature, such as Ludlow's (1999) view that past-tense morphology consists of evidential markers. In view of the arguments collected in Chapters 1 and 2, we shall now attempt a Default-Semantic analysis of past-time reference and construct merger representations for utterances of sentences about the past. Analogously to the situation encountered for the future and the present, we can discern various ways of referring to the past which pertain to various degrees of epistemic commitment on the part of the speaker, as demonstrated in examples (39)–(42).

(39) Peter went to London yesterday.   (regular past)
(40) Peter would have gone to London by then.   (epistemic necessity past/
                                                   inferential evidentiality)
(41) Peter may have gone to London yesterday.   (epistemic possibility
                                                   past)
(42) This is what happened yesterday. Peter goes to London, meets Sue at King's Cross Station, suggests going for a cup of coffee...(past of narration).

The Simple Past tense form is the standard way of referring to past eventualities and we can call it *regular past* and assign the index *rp* to indicate the degree of epistemic commitment Δ in the merger representation Σ. Δ^{rp} is the outcome of the operation of the WS source of meaning information because it is the direct result of the processing of the grammatical, past-tense form of the verb *go*. Fig. 4.18 is the merger representation for the utterance of sentence (39).

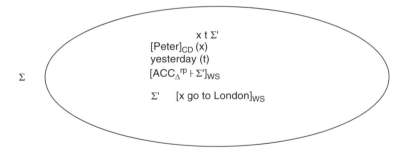

Σ

$$x\ t\ \Sigma'$$
$$[\text{Peter}]_{CD}(x)$$
$$\text{yesterday}(t)$$
$$[ACC_\Delta{}^{rp} \vdash \Sigma']_{WS}$$

$$\Sigma' \quad [x\ \text{go to London}]_{WS}$$

FIGURE 4.18 Σ for example (39), regular past

Examples (39)–(42) can be easily ordered on a scale of decreasing epistemic commitment, analogous to my ordering of future-time-referring forms in Section 4.2.1 and present-time-referring forms in Section 4.2.2. But since the semantic values of the expression types are slightly different, I will discuss them in more detail. The past of narration (*pn*) in (42) serves the purpose of making the events more vivid to the addressee. It creates the illusion of witnessing the situations or being a participant. The degree of commitment is high and similar to that ascribed to regular past. The differentiation between them seems to be not on the scale of commitment but on the scale of communicative intention or effectiveness in engaging the audience and therefore we will assume that *pn* and *rp* occupy approximately the same area on the scale. Utterance of sentence (40) comes with epistemic commitment that derives from inference from other facts, judgement from indirect evidence. Although it is not as strong as regular past, it is called epistemic *necessity* past (*enp*) precisely due to the reliability of this inference from facts. This form of referring to past eventualities can be placed further from the 1 end of the scale and towards the 0 end. Next, the epistemic possibility *may + Past Participle* in (41) is considerably weaker in the degree of commitment to the proposition on the part of the speaker. The scale of epistemic commitment for (39)–(42) is given in Fig. 4.19.

FIGURE 4.19 Degree of epistemic commitment for selected expressions with past-time reference

The values of *rp*, *pn*, *enp*, and *epp* are not indicated precisely on the axis because, as I pointed out in Section 4.2.1, numerical values can only be assigned as a result of a detailed corpus-based study of the use of the relevant forms. The criterion for assigning numerical values would also have to be carefully worked out. However, as I also contended in that section, this further pursuit is not needed as long as we are justified in adopting the assumption that words and grammatical forms have their core, salient meanings. And, to repeat, as I argued there with the help of evidence from Giora's experiments and her graded salience hypothesis, we are justified in making this assumption, *pace* late Wittgenstein and contemporary meaning eliminativists, and are able to rest with assigning *rp*, *pn*, *enp*, and *epp* as values to Δ in Σ precisely because the relevant grammatical forms do have their core meanings.

The scale in Fig. 4.19 is far from being complete. It merely presents the principle of ordering four examples of common ways of referring to the past. Epistemic necessity past and epistemic possibility past should be viewed as generic terms which subsume sets of various constructions, each coming with a different degree of commitment. For example, (43) belongs to *enp* and (44) to *epp*.

(43) Peter must have gone to London yesterday.
(44) Peter might have gone to London yesterday.

The scale is also only one of several possible construals for ordering the types of past-time-referring expressions. In addition to the degree of epistemic commitment, we can employ the degree of informative intention on the part of the speaker. Analogously to the case of the future and the present, the scale of informative intention will equal the one in Fig. 4.19 as far as the relative ordering of the expression types is concerned: the stronger the commitment to the truth of what the speaker is saying, the stronger the informative intention. Again, as in Fig. 4.19, while the absolute numerical values are not available and are beside the point for this argument, the relative ordering in the form of the cline *rp, pn* > *enp* > *epp* is the same. As before, the category of degree of modality will reverse the ordering: the stronger the modality the weaker the commitment to the truth and the weaker the informative intention. We will therefore obtain *epp* > *enp* > *rp, pn*.

Merger representations for the remaining past-time-referring forms can now be constructed according to the principles laid out for the future and the present. We will construct them here for the sake of completeness and clarity. An utterance of sentence (40), repeated below, obtains a merger representation as in Fig. 4.20.

(40) Peter would have gone to London by then.
      (epistemic necessity past/inferential evidentiality)

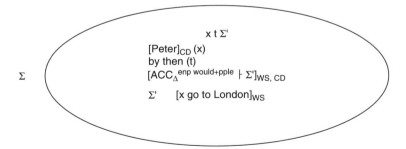

FIGURE 4.20 Σ for example (40), epistemic necessity past with *would + Past Participle*

Similar to the analysis of present-time-referring *may*, the value of Δ is here assigned by the construction *would + Past Participle* (indicated as

$\Delta^{\text{enp would + pple}}$). The reading of this construction can be obtained as a result of the application of WS and CD. One could pause and ask at this point, why CD, if the *would + Past Participle* construction also exhibits the counterfactual conditional reading. This is not the place to delve into the semantic properties of epistemic necessity reading of *would + Past Participle* as opposed to the counterfactual conditional. Suffice it to say that the latter is marked either by the presence of the antecedent of the conditional (the *if*-clause), the uniquely disambiguiating context, or by an intonation pattern (flat intonation) that signals the *irrealis*. Finally, the deictic expression 'by then' in the discourse condition 'by then (t)' is resolved by contextual filling in, in the process of pragmatic composition of Σ' and in accordance with the contextualist view of the truth-conditional content of the utterance.

Next, an utterance of sentence (41), repeated below, is represented in Fig. 4.21. The value for Δ is arrived at here directly through the WS source.

(41)   Peter may have gone to London yesterday. (epistemic possibility past)

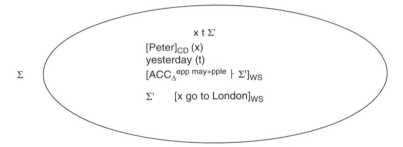

FIGURE 4.21 Σ for example (41), epistemic possibility past with *may + Past Participle*

Merger representations for forms with modal verbs *must* and *might* in epistemic necessity past in (43) and epistemic possibility past in (44), repeated below, are analogous and will not be constructed here. The value of Δ is arrived at though WS in (43), analogous to (41), and through WS and CD in (44), analogous to (40).

(43)   Peter must have gone to London yesterday.

(44)   Peter might have gone to London yesterday.

Finally, an utterance of the relevant sentence from the discourse in (42) given in (45) below has the merger representation as in Fig. 4.22. The value of *t* as 'yesterday' is carried forward from the initial sentence: 'This is what happened yesterday....'. We must remember that merger representations represent entire discourses and hence utterances of sentences that compose to form a discourse unit are presented in one Σ. The *pn* value of Δ is arrived at through conscious pragmatic inference (CPI_{pm}) which interacts with the output of the processing of the sentence structure (WS) to produce past of narration as the primary, compositional meaning (*pm*) of this utterance.

(45) ... Peter goes to London ... (past of narration)

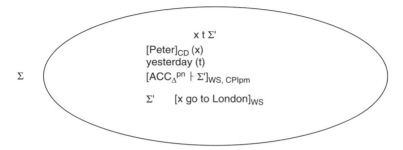

$$x\ t\ \Sigma'$$
$$[Peter]_{CD}\ (x)$$
$$yesterday\ (t)$$
$$[ACC_\Delta^{pn} \vdash \Sigma']_{WS,\ CPIpm}$$
$$\Sigma' \quad [x\ go\ to\ London]_{WS}$$

FIGURE 4.22 Σ for example (45), past of narration

To repeat, this presentation does not aspire to a typology of expressions with past-time reference. Default Semantics provides a framework for representing internal time and the examples discussed above demonstrate how this mechanism can be implemented. We did not, for example, elaborate on the contribution of aspectual distinctions, such as progressive-nonprogressive, to the representation of temporality. Typology of English temporal expressions is not our aim also for another important reason. The devices used for building merger representations are applicable to various languages, including those where temporal reference is largely left to pragmatic inference due to the fact that both aspect and tense markers are optional and temporal adverbials are not present when the temporal reference is contextually salient. Thai is a perfect example of such a language and temporality in Thai cannot be analysed by means of providing a typology of relevant expressions: speakers have relative freedom to draw on a wide array of constructions and the constructions themselves are very flexible as far as temporal reference with which they are employed is concerned. Merger representations for the past, present, and future in Thai were shown to corroborate the view of temporality as modal detachment operating on a pragmatics-rich unit Σ' defended here (see Srioutai 2004, 2006). In short, an important aspiration of this analysis of temporality in the framework of Default Semantics is its universal applicability, subject to small modifications such as the language under scrutiny may necessitate, but within the confines of the recognized sources of information for pragmatic compositionality.

4.3 Summing up

I have presented in this chapter contextual semantic representations of utterances with future-, present-, and past-time reference, making use of the principles of Default Semantics in its revised version. The merger representations constructed here demonstrate that the arguments discussed in Chapters 1–3 for the modal basis of all temporality are sound and defensible in that the thesis that *temporal location* is construed as *modal detachment* can be succinctly stated in the form of semantic, and at the same time, mental, representations. To repeat, this modal basis of temporality is a two-pronged thesis: real time supervenes on probability, and internal time supervenes on epistemic detachment. The latter was construed here as a graded category and represented by means of a modal operator on merger representations ACC, adapted from Grice's sentential operator *Acc*, of the epistemic type ($\vdash$). The degree of this detachment, represented as an index on Δ, was derived from the lexical basis through the standard sources of information about meaning identified in Default Semantics: WS, CD, and CPI_{pm}. Tense is a deictic category and it is no surprise that formal accounts of temporality have to incorporate information from context through CPI_{pm}.[28] But the way this contextual information interacts with the information from the logical form of the sentence is conceived of differently in different approaches. What I proposed in this chapter is a radical contextualist account, more radical than other post-Gricean accounts in that it disposes of the syntactic constraint and models the primary meaning, as intended by the model speaker and recovered by the model addressee, in whatever form this content happens to assume: close to the sentence structure, going beyond it some way, or even overriding it altogether.

[28] See also, for example, Saurer 1984.

Conclusion: 'Looking forward' into the future

I have put forward in this essay a hypothesis that the human concept of time can be traced to the more basic concept of graded possibility (or epistemic modality) upon which it supervenes. I supported this thesis by theoretical arguments as well as evidence from the grammatical and lexical means of expressing time. First, I juxtaposed the concept of time with real time of space-time and argued that they are related via the relation of a form of supervenience. The concept of time is not independent from time in the world, albeit its properties appear to depart from those of real time mainly due to the importance of finiteness of human existence for any conceptualization. Next, I briefly discussed real time and suggested that it is founded on a more basic property, namely that of probability. Further, I moved to the main topic of this essay, the properties of the human conceptualization of time, as evidenced in linguistic expression of natural language. In the example of English, and occasionally some typologically different languages, I argued that temporality is underlyingly detachment from certainty, and hence is essentially modal in the sense of epistemic commitment/possibility. So, just as the concept of time supervenes on real time, so both real and conceptual time supervene on forms of modality. On the basis of evidence and argumentation presented here, I was able to offer this view as a possible theory of the human conceptualization of temporality and as a viable hypothesis to be tested by empirical linguists and psychologists. I also pointed out that the question as to whether modal semantics for temporal expressions justifies replacing the relation of supervenience by that of identity is an open topic for a different (philosophical) investigation. Taking a stance on this issue would not contribute to the current argument.

The semantic representations of temporal expressions proposed in Chapter 4 give further support to the thesis of the underlying modality of the concept of time in that they offer a modal semantics for temporal expressions in English, also making recourses to the applicability of the used framework of

Default Semantics to other languages. This modal semantics is constructed with the help of a suitably indexed operator of acceptability, operating on a proposition-like content called merged proposition, put together according to the principles of pragmatic compositionality of information about utterance meaning that comes from qualitatively different sources. But this proposal also opens up a plethora of further research questions, the most important of which is perhaps how the view of pragmatic compositionality is to be developed into an algorithm for merging information about meaning that comes from such diversified sources. This is a topic for another time, at present with a high degree of modal detachment.

References

Abusch, D. (1988). 'Sequence of tense, intensionality and scope'. In: H. Borer (ed.). *Proceedings of the Seventh West Coast Conference on Formal Linguistics*. Stanford, CA: CSLI Publications. 1–14.

Aikhenvald, A. Y. (2004). *Evidentiality*. Oxford: Oxford University Press.

Allan, K. (2001). *Natural Language Semantics*. Oxford: Blackwell.

Ambjørn, J., J. Jurkiewicz and R. Loll. (2008). 'The self-organizing quantum universe'. *Scientific American*, July 2008: 24–31.

Aristotle. 1928. *De Interpretatione*. Transl. by E. M. Edghill. In: *The Works of Aristotle*. Vol. 1. Oxford: Clarendon Press. 16a–23b.

Asher, N. (1993). *Reference to Abstract Objects in Discourse*. Dordrecht: Kluwer.

—— . (2000). 'Events, facts, propositions, and evolutive anaphora'. In: J. Higginbotham, F. Pianesi and A. C. Varzi (eds). *Speaking of Events*. Oxford: Oxford University Press. 123–50.

—— . and A. Lascarides (2003). *Logics of Conversation*. Cambridge: Cambridge University Press.

—— . and E. McCready (2007). '*Were, would, might* and a compositional account of counterfactuals'. *Journal of Semantics* 24: 93–129.

Atlas, J. D. (1977). 'Negation, ambiguity, and presupposition'. *Linguistics and Philosophy* 1:321–36.

—— . (1979). 'How linguistics matters to philosophy: Presupposition, truth, and meaning'. In: D. Dinneen and C. K. Oh (eds). *Syntax and Semantics 11: Presupposition*. New York: Academic Press. 265–81.

—— . (1989). *Philosophy without Ambiguity: A Logico-Linguistic Essay*. Oxford: Clarendon Press.

—— . (2006). 'How insensitive can you be? Meanings, propositions, context, and semantical underdeterminacy'. Paper presented at the *J. Atlas: Distinguished Scholar Workshop*, University of Cambridge, May 2006.

van der Auwera, J. and V. A. Plungian (1998). 'Modality's semantic map'. *Linguistic Typology* 2. 79–124.

Bach, E. (1981). 'On time, tense, and aspect: An essay in English metaphysics'. In: P. Cole (ed.). *Radical Pragmatics*. New York: Academic Press. 63–81.

—— . (1986). 'The algebra of events'. *Linguistics and Philosophy* 9: 5–16. Reprinted in: I. Mani, J. Pustejovsky, and R. Gaizauskas (eds). 2005. *The Language of Time: A Reader*. Oxford: Oxford University Press. 61–9.

Bach, K. (2004). 'Minding the gap'. In: C. Bianchi (ed.). *The Semantics/Pragmatics Distinction*. Stanford: CSLI Publications. 27–43.

—— . (2006). 'The excluded middle: Semantic minimalism without minimal propositions'. *Philosophy and Phenomenological Research* 73: 435–42.

Balaguer, M. (2005). 'Indexical propositions and *de re* belief ascriptions'. *Synthese* 146: 325–55.

Bartsch, R. (1995). *Situations, Tense, and Aspect: Dynamic Discourse Ontology and the Semantic Flexibility of Temporal System in German and English*. Berlin: Mouton de Gruyter.

Beaver, D. I. (1997). 'Presupposition'. In: J. van Benthem and A. ter Meulen (eds). *Handbook of Logic and Language*. Amsterdam: Elsevier. 939–1008.

Bell, D. (1990). *Husserl*. London: Routledge.

Bennett, M. and B. Partee (1978). *Toward the Logic of Tense and Aspect in English*. Bloomington: Indiana University Linguistics Club.

Binnick, R. I. (1991). *Time and the Verb: A Guide to Tense and Aspect*. Oxford: Oxford University Press.

Borg, E. (2004). *Minimal Semantics*. Oxford: Oxford University Press.

Brisard, F. (2002). 'The English present'. In: F. Brisard (ed.). *Grounding: The Epistemic Footing of Deixis and Reference*. Berlin: Mouton de Gruyter. 251–97.

——— . (2006). 'Conceptual viewpoints: Elements of a Cognitive-Grammar account of English past-nonpast tense'. Paper presented at *Chronos 7*, Antwerp.

Brogaard, B. (2006). 'Tensed relations'. *Analysis* 66: 194–202.

Brown, P. and S. C. Levinson (1987). *Politeness: Some Universals in Language Usage*. Cambridge: Cambridge University Press.

Bybee, J., R. Perkins, and W. Pagliuca (1994). *The Evolution of Grammar: Tense, Aspect, and Modality in the Languages of the World*. Chicago: University of Chicago Press.

Cappelen, H. and E. Lepore (2005). *Insensitive Semantics: a Defense of Semantic Minimalism and Speech Act Pluralism*. Oxford: Blackwell.

Cappelle, B. and R. Declerck (2005). 'Spatial and temporal boundedness in English motion events'. *Journal of Pragmatics* 37: 889–917.

Cappelli, G. (2007). *'I reckon I know how Leonardo da Vinci must have felt . . .': Epistemicity, Evidentiality and English Verbs of Cognitive Attitude*. Pari: Pari Publishing.

Carruthers, P. (2006). *The Architecture of the Mind: Massive Modularity and the Flexibility of Thought*. Oxford: Clarendon Press.

Carston, R. (1988). 'Implicature, explicature, and truth-theoretic semantics'. In: R. M. Kempson (ed.). *Mental Representations: The Interface Between Language and Reality*. Cambridge: Cambridge University Press. 155–81.

——— . (1998). 'Postscript (1995) to Carston 1988'. In: A. Kasher (ed.). *Pragmatics: Critical Concepts*. Vol. 4. London: Routledge. 464–79.

——— . (2002). *Thoughts and Utterances: The Pragmatics of Explicit Communication*. Oxford: Blackwell.

——— . (2007). 'How many pragmatic systems are there?'. In: M. J. Frápolli (ed.). *Saying, Meaning and Referring: Essays on François Recanati's Philosophy of Language*. Basingstoke: Palgrave Macmillan. 18–48.

Casasanto, D. and L. Boroditsky. (2008). 'Time in the mind: Using space to think about time'. *Cognition* 106: 579–93.

Chisholm, R. M. (1970). 'Events and propositions'. *Noûs* 4: 15–24.

Chomsky, N. (2004). 'Beyond explanatory adequacy'. In: A. Belletti (ed.). *Structures and Beyond: The Cartography of Syntactic Structures*. Vol. 3. New York: Oxford University Press. 104–31.

Cole, P. (ed.). (1981). *Radical Pragmatics*. New York: Academic Press.

Comrie, B. (1985). *Tense*. Cambridge: Cambridge University Press.

Condoravdi, C. (2002). 'Temporal interpretation of modals: Modals for the present and for the past'. In: D. Beaver *et al.* (eds). *The Construction of Meaning*. Stanford: CSLI Publications. 59–88.

Cram, D. (2007). 'Shelf life and time horizons in the historiography of linguistics'. *Historiographia Linguistica* 34: 189–212.

Crouch, R. S. and S. G. Pulman (1993). 'Time and modality in a natural language interface to a planning system'. *Artificial Intelligence* 63: 265–304. Reprined in: F. C. N. Pereira and B. J. Grosz (eds). 1994. *Natural Language Processing*. Cambridge, MA: MIT Press. 265–304.

Culicover, P. W. and R. Jackendoff (2005). *Simpler Syntax*. Oxford: Oxford University Press.

Dahl, Ö. (1985). *Tense and Aspect Systems*. Oxford: Blackwell.

Davidson, D. (1967). 'The logical form of action sentences'. In: N. Rescher (ed.). *The Logic of Decision and Action*. Pittsburgh: University of Pittsburgh Press. Reprinted in: D. Davidson. 1980. *Essays on Actions and Events*. Oxford: Clarendon Press. 105–22.

——. (1969). 'The individuation of events'. In: N. Rescher (ed.). *Essays in Honor of Carl G. Hempel*. Dordrecht: D. Reidel. Reprinted in: D. Davidson. 1980. *Essays on Actions and Events*. Oxford: Clarendon Press. 163–80.

——. (1970). 'Events as particulars'. *Noûs* 4: 25–32. Reprinted in: D. Davidson. 1980. *Essays on Actions and Events*. Oxford: Clarendon Press. 181–7.

Davies, A. Morpurgo (1983). 'Mycenaean and Greek prepositions: *o-pi, e-pi* etc.'. In: A. Heubeck and G. Neumann (eds). *Res Mycenaeae: Akten des VII. Internationalen Mykenologischen Colloquiums in Nürnmerg vom 6.–10. April 1981*. Göttingen: Vandenhoeck and Ruprecht. 287–310.

Davis, W. A. (1998). *Implicature: Intention, Convention, and Principle in the Failure of Gricean Theory*. Cambridge: Cambridge University Press.

——. (2007). 'How normative is implicature'. *Journal of Pragmatics* 39: 1655–72.

Declerck, R. (2006). *The Grammar of the English Verb Phrase. Vol. 1: The Grammar of the English Tense System. A Comprehensive Analysis*. Berlin: Mouton de Gruyter.

Dekker, P. (2000). 'Coreference and representationalism'. In K. von Heusinger and U. Egli (eds). *Reference and Anaphoric Relations*. Dordrecht: Kluwer. 287–310.

Diller, A. (1996). 'Thai and Lao Writing.' In: Peter T. Daniels and William Bright (eds). *The World's Writing Systems*. New York: Oxford University Press. 457–66.

Dowty, D. R. (1979). *Word Meaning and Montague Grammar: The Semantics of Verbs and Times in Generative Semantics and in Montague's PTQ*. Dordrecht: D. Reidel.

——. (1982). 'Tenses, time adverbs, and compositional semantic theory'. *Linguistics and Philosophy* 5: 23–55.

——. (1986). 'The effects of aspectual class on the temporal structure of discourse: Semantics or pragmatics?'. *Linguistics and Philosophy* 9: 37–61. Reprinted in: I. Mani, J. Pustejovsky, and R. Gaizauskas (eds). 2005. *The Language of Time: A Reader*. Oxford: Oxford University Press. 333–51.

Dowty, D. R. (2007). 'Compositionality as an empirical problem'. In: C. Barker and P. Jacobson (eds). *Direct Compositionality*. Oxford: Oxford University Press. 23–101.

Dummett, M. (1969). 'The reality of the past'. *Proceedings of the Aristotelian Society* 69: 239–58. Reprinted in: M. Dummett. 1978. *Truth and Other Enigmas*. London: Duckworth. 358–74.

—— . (2004). *Truth and the Past*. New York: Columbia University Press.

—— . (2006). *Thought and Reality*. Oxford: Clarendon Press.

Eckardt, R. (2006). *Meaning Change in Grammaticalization: An Enquiry into Semantic Reanalysis*. Oxford: Oxford University Press.

van Eijck, J. and H. Kamp (1997). 'Representing discourse in context'. In: J. van Benthem and A. ter Meulen (eds). *Handbook of Logic and Language*. Amsterdam: Elsevier Science. 179–237.

Enç, M. (1987). 'Anchoring conditions for tense'. *Linguistic Inquiry* 18: 633–57.

—— . (1996). 'Tense and modality'. In: S. Lappin (ed.). *The Handbook of Contemporary Semantic Theory*. Oxford: Blackwell. 345–58.

Evans, V. (2003). *The Structure of Time: Language, Meaning and Temporal Cognition*. Amsterdam: J. Benjamins.

—— . (2005). 'The meaning of *time*: Polysemy, the lexicon and conceptual structure'. *Journal of Linguistics* 41: 33–75.

Farkas, K. (2008). 'Time, tense, truth'. *Synthese* 160: 269–84.

Fernández, J. (2008). 'Memory, past and self'. *Synthese* 160: 103–21.

Fine, K. (2005). 'Tense and reality'. In: K. Fine. *Modality and Tense: Philosophical Papers*. Oxford: Clarendon Press. 261–320.

Fleischman, S. (1982). *The Future in Thought and Language: Diachronic Evidence from Romance*. Cambridge: Cambridge University Press.

Foer, J. (2007). 'Remember this'. *National Geographic*, November 2007: 32–55.

Galton, A. (1990). 'A critical examination of Allen's theory of action and time'. *Artificial Intelligence* 42: 159–88. Reprinted in: I. Mani, J. Pustejovsky, and R. Gaizauskas (eds). 2005. *The Language of Time: A Reader*. Oxford: Oxford University Press. 277–99.

Gennari, S. P. (2003). 'Tense meanings and temporal interpretation'. *Journal of Semantics* 20: 35–71.

Geurts, B. (1999). *Presuppositions and Pronouns*. Oxford: Elsevier Science.

Giora, R. (2003). *On Our Mind: Salience, Context, and Figurative Language*. Oxford: Oxford University Press.

Givón, T. (2005). *Context as other Minds: The Pragmatics of Sociality, Cognition and Communication*. Amsterdam: J. Benjamins.

Grice, H. P. (1975). 'Logic and conversation'. In: P. Cole and J. L. Morgan (eds). *Syntax and Semantics*. Vol. 3. New York: Academic Press. Reprinted in: H. P. Grice. 1989. *Studies in the Way of Words*. Cambridge, MA: Harvard University Press. 22–40.

—— . (1978). 'Further notes on logic and conversation'. In: P. Cole (ed.). *Syntax and Semantics*. Vol. 9. New York: Academic Press. Reprinted in: H. P. Grice. 1989. *Studies in the Way of Words*. Cambridge, MA: Harvard University Press. 41–57.

—— . (2001). *Aspects of Reason*. Ed. by R. Warner. Oxford: Clarendon Press.

Groenendijk, J. and M. Stokhof (1991). 'Dynamic Predicate Logic'. *Linguistics and Philosophy* 14: 39–100.

Gumperz, J. J. and S. C. Levinson (eds) (1996). *Rethinking Linguistic Relativity.* Cambridge: Cambridge University Press.

Guttenplan, S. (1994). 'Memory'. In: S. Guttenplan (ed.). *A Companion to the Philosophy of Mind.* Oxford: Blackwell. 433–41.

de Haan, F. (2006). 'Typological approaches to modality'. In: W. Frawley (ed.). *The Expression of Modality.* Berlin: Mouton de Gruyter. 27–69.

Hamblin, C. L. (1972). 'Instants and intervals'. In: J. T. Fraser, F. C. Haber, and G. H. Müller (eds). *The Study of Time.* Vol. 1. Berlin: Springer-Verlag. 324–31.

Hamm, F., H. Kamp, and M. van Lambalgen (2006). 'There is no opposition between Formal and Cognitive Semantics'. *Theoretical Linguistics* 32: 1–40.

Hawking, S. W. (1988). *A Brief History of Time: From the Big Bang to Black Holes.* London: Bantam Press.

——— . (2001). *The Universe in a Nutshell.* London: Bantam Press.

Heidegger, M. (1953). *Sein und Zeit.* Tübingen: Max Niemeyer. Transl. by J. Stambaugh as *Being and Time.* 1996. Albany: State University of New York Press.

Higginbotham, J. (1985). 'On semantics'. *Linguistic Inquiry* 16: 547–93.

——— . (1995). 'Tensed thoughts'. *Mind and Language* 10: 226–49. Reprinted in: W. Künne, A. Newen, and M. Anduschus (eds). 1997. *Direct Reference, Indexicality, and Propositional Attitudes.* Stanford, CA: CSLI Publications. 21–48.

——— . (2000). 'On events in linguistic semantics'. In: J. Higginbotham, F. Pianesi, and A. C. Varzi (eds). *Speaking of Events.* Oxford: Oxford University Press. 49–79.

Horn, L. R. (2004). 'Implicature'. In: L. R. Horn and G. Ward (eds). *The Handbook of Pragmatics.* Oxford: Blackwell. 3–28.

——— . (2006). 'The border wars: A neo-Gricean perspective'. In: K. von Heusinger and K. Turner (eds). *Where Semantics Meets Pragmatics: The Michigan Papers.* Oxford: Elsevier. 21–48.

Hornstein, N. (1990). *As Time Goes By: Tense and Universal Grammar.* Cambridge, MA: MIT Press.

Horwich, P. (1987). *Asymmetries in Time: Problems in the Philosophy of Science.* Cambridge, MA: MIT Press.

——— . (2005). *Reflections on Meaning.* Oxford: Clarendon Press.

Husserl, E. (1900–01). *Logische Untersuchungen.* Vol. 2. Halle: Max Niemeyer. Reprinted in 1984 after the second edition (1913–21). The Hague: Martinus Nijhoff. *Husserliana* 19/1. Transl. by J. N. Findlay as *Logical Investigations.* 1970. London: Routledge and Kegan Paul.

——— . (1928). *Vorlesungen zur Phänomenologie des inneren Zeitbewusstseins. Jahrbuch für Philosophie und phänomenologische Forschung* IX. Halle: Max Niemeyer. Transl. by J. B. Brough as *Lectures on the Phenomenology of the Consciousness of Internal Time* in: *On the Phenomenology of the Consciousness of Internal Time* (1893–1917). Part A. 1991. Dordrecht: Kluwer.

——— . (1939). *Erfahrung und Urteil. Untersuchungen zur Genealogie der Logik.* Prague: Academia Verlagsbuchhandlung. Transl. by J. S. Churchill and K. Ameriks as

Experience and Judgment. Investigations in a Genealogy of Logic. 1973. London: Routledge and Kegan Paul.

Husserl, E. (1950). *Cartesianische Meditationen.* In: *Cartesianische Meditationen und Pariser Vorträge.* The Hague: Martinus Nijhoff. 41–201. Transl. by D. Cairns as *Cartesian Meditations. An Introduction to Phenomenology.* 1960. The Hague: Martinus Nijhoff.

Jackendoff, R. (2002). *Foundations of Language: Brain, Meaning, Grammar, Evolution.* Oxford: Oxford University Press.

James, W. (1890). *The Principles of Psychology.* London: Macmillan. Reprinted in 1952. Chicago: Encyclopaedia Britannica Inc.

Jaszczolt, K. M. (1996). 'Reported speech, vehicles of thought, and the horizon'. *Lingua e Stile* 31: 113–33.

—— . (1999). *Discourse, Beliefs, and Intentions: Semantic Defaults and Propositional Attitude Ascription.* Oxford: Elsevier Science.

—— . (2000). 'Belief reports and pragmatic theory: the state of the art'. Introduction to: K. M. Jaszczolt (ed.). *The Pragmatics of Propositional Attitude Reports.* Oxford: Elsevier Science. 1–12.

—— . (2002). *Semantics and Pragmatics: Meaning in Language and Discourse.* London: Longman.

—— . (2003). 'The modality of the future: A Default-Semantics account'. In: P. Dekker and R. van Rooy (eds). *Proceedings from the 14th Amsterdam Colloquium,* ILLC, University of Amsterdam. 43–8.

—— . (2005). *Default Semantics: Foundations of a Compositional Theory of Acts of Communication.* Oxford: Oxford University Press.

—— . (2006a). 'Futurity in Default Semantics'. In: K. von Heusinger and K. Turner (eds). *Where Semantics Meets Pragmatics: The Michigan Papers.* Oxford: Elsevier. 471–92.

—— . (2006b). 'Defaults in semantics and pragmatics'. In: E. N. Zalta (ed.). *Stanford Encyclopedia of Philosophy.* http://plato.stanford.edu/contents.html.

—— . (2007). 'On being post-Gricean'. In: R. A. Nilsen, N. A. A. Amfo, and K. Borthen (eds). *Interpreting Utterances: Pragmatics and Its Interfaces. Essays in Honour of Thorstein Fretheim.* Oslo: Novus. 21–38.

—— . (2008). 'Psychological explanations in Gricean pragmatics and Frege's legacy'. In: I. Kecskes and J. Mey (eds). *Intentions, Common Ground, and the Egocentric Speaker-Hearer.* Berlin: Mouton de Gruyter. 9–45.

—— . (forthcoming). 'Semantics and pragmatics: The boundary issue'. In: K. von Heusinger, P. Portner, and C. Maienborn (eds). *Semantics: An International Handbook of Natural Language Meaning.* Berlin: Mouton de Gruyter.

—— . and J. Srioutai (forthcoming). 'Communicating about the past through modality in English and Thai'. In: F. Brisard and T. Mortelmans (eds). *Cognitive Approaches to Tense, Aspect and Modality.* Amsterdam: J. Benjamins.

Kamp, H. (1979). 'Events, instants and temporal reference'. In: R. Bäuerle, U. Egli, and A. von Stechow (eds). *Semantics from Different Points of View.* Berlin: Springer-Verlag. 376–417.

——— . (1981). 'A theory of truth and semantic representation'. In: J. Groenendijk, T. M. V. Janssen, and M. Stokhof (eds). *Formal Methods in the Study of Language*, Mathematical Centre Tract 135, Amsterdam, 277–322. Reprinted in: J. Groenendijk, T. M. V. Janssen, and M. Stokhof (eds). 1984. *Truth, Interpretation and Information. Selected Papers from the Third Amsterdam Colloquium*. Dordrecht: FORIS. 1–41.

——— . (2001). 'Presupposition computation and presupposition justification: One aspect of the interpretation of multi-sentence discourse'. In: M. Bras and L. Vieu (eds). *Semantic and Pragmatic Issues in Discourse and Dialogue: Experimenting with Current Dynamic Theories*. Oxford: Elsevier. 57–84.

——— . (2007). 'Discourse linking as (simultaneous) constraint solving'. Paper presented at the meeting of the *Linguistics Association of Great Britain*, King's College London, August 2007.

——— , J. van Genabith, and U. Reyle (forthcoming). 'Discourse Representation Theory'. In: D. M. Gabbay and F. Guenthner (eds). *Handbook of Philosophical Logic*. Second edition.

——— . and U. Reyle (1993). *From Discourse to Logic: Introduction to Modeltheoretic Semantics of Natural Language, Formal Logic and Discourse Representation Theory*. Dordrecht: Kluwer.

——— . and M. Schiehlen (2002). 'Temporal location in natural languages'. In: H. Kamp and U. Reyle (eds). *How We Say WHEN It Happens: Contributions to the Theory of Temporal Reference in Natural Language*. Tübingen: Max Niemeyer. 181–232.

Kaplan, D. (1989). 'Demonstratives: An essay on the semantics, logic, metaphysics, and epistemology of demonstratives and other indexicals'. In J. Almog, J. Perry, and H. Wettstein (eds). *Themes from Kaplan*. New York: Oxford University Press. 481–563.

Kaufmann, S., C. Condoravdi, and V. Harizanov (2006). 'Formal approaches to modality'. In: W. Frawley (ed.). *The Expression of Modality*. Berlin: Mouton de Gruyter. 71–106.

Kelly, S. D. (2005). 'Temporal awareness'. In: D. W. Smith and A. L. Thomasson (eds). *Phenomenology and Philosophy of Mind*. Oxford: Clarendon Press. 222–34.

Kempson, R. M. (1977). *Semantic Theory*. Cambridge: Cambridge University Press.

Kim, J. (1973). 'Causation, nomic subsumption and the concept of event'. *Journal of Philosophy* 70: 217–36. Reprinted in: J. Kim. 1993. *Supervenience and Mind: Selected Philosophical Essays*. Cambridge: Cambridge University Press. 3–21.

——— . (1976). 'Events as property exemplifications'. In: M. Brand and D. Walton (eds). *Action Theory*. Dordrecht: D. Reidel. 159–77. Reprinted in: J. Kim. 1993. *Supervenience and Mind: Selected Philosophical Essays*. Cambridge: Cambridge University Press. 33–52.

——— . (1987). ' "Strong" and "global" supervenience revisited'. *Philosophy and Phenomenological Research* 48: 315–26. Reprinted in: J. Kim. 1993. *Supervenience and Mind: Selected Philosophical Essays*. Cambridge: Cambridge University Press. 79–91.

Künne, W. (2003). *Conceptions of Truth*. Oxford: Clarendon Press.

Kuhn, S. T. and P. Portner (2002). 'Tense and time'. In: D. Gabbay and F. Guenthner (eds). *Handbook of Philosophical Logic*. Vol. 7. Dordrecht: Kluwer. 277–346.

Ladusaw, W. (1977). 'Some problems with tense in PTQ'. *Texas Linguistic Forum* 6: 89–102.

Lakoff, G. (1987). *Women, Fire, and Dangerous Things: What Categories Reveal about the Mind.* Chicago: University of Chicago Press.

——. and M. Johnson (1980). *Metaphors We Live By.* Chicago: University of Chicago Press.

——. and —— (1999). *Philosophy in the Flesh: The Embodied Mind and Its Challenge to Western Thought.* New York: Basic Books.

——. and M. Turner (1989). *More than Cool Reason: A Field Guide to Poetic Metaphor.* Chicago: University of Chicago Press.

van Lambalgen, M. and F. Hamm (2005). *The Proper Treatment of Events.* Oxford: Blackwell.

Landman, F. (2000). *Events and Plurality: The Jerusalem Lectures.* Dordrecht: Kluwer.

Langacker, R. (1987). *Foundations of Cognitive Grammar. Vol. 1: Theoretical Prerequisites.* Stanford: Stanford University Press.

——. (1991). *Foundations of Cognitive Grammar. Vol. 2: Descriptive Application.* Stanford: Stanford University Press.

——. (1999). *Grammar and Conceptualization.* Berlin: Mouton de Gruyter.

——. (2001). 'The English present tense'. *English Language and Linguistics* 5: 251–72.

——. (2006). 'The English present: Temporal coincidence vs. epistemic immediacy'. Paper presented at *Chronos 7*, Antwerp. Forthcoming in: F. Brisard and T. Mortelmans (eds). *Cognitive Approaches to Tense, Aspect and Modality.* Amsterdam: J. Benjamins.

Lascarides, A. and N. Asher (1993). 'Temporal interpretation, discourse relations, and commonsense entailment' *Linguistics and Philosophy* 16: 437–93. Reprinted in: I. Mani, J. Pustejovsky, and R. Gaizauskas (eds). 2005. *The Language of Time: A Reader.* Oxford: Oxford University Press. 353–95.

Leech, G. (1983). *Principles of Pragmatics.* London: Longman.

Leith, M. and J. Cunningham (2001). 'Aspect and Interval Logic'. *Linguistics and Philosophy* 24: 331–81.

Levinson, S. C. (2000). *Presumptive Meanings: The Theory of Generalized Conversational Implicature.* Cambridge, MA: MIT Press.

——. (2003). *Space in Language and Cognition: Explorations in Cognitive Diversity.* Cambridge: Cambridge University Press.

——. *et al.* (2002). 'Returning the tables: Language affects spatial reasoning'. *Cognition* 84: 155–88.

——, Meira, S., and The Language and Cognition Group (2003). ' "Natural concepts" in the spatial topological domain – adpositional meanings in crosslinguistic perspective: An exercise in semantic typology'. *Language* 79: 485–516.

Ludlow, P. (1999). *Semantics, Tense, and Time: An Essay in the Metaphysics of Natural Language.* Cambridge, MA: MIT Press.

——. (2006). 'Tense'. In: E. Lepore and B. C. Smith (eds). *The Oxford Handbook of Philosophy of Language.* Oxford: Clarendon Press. 689–715.

Łukasiewicz, J. (1961). 'O determinizmie'. In: J. Słupecki (ed.). *Jan Łukasiewicz. Z zagadnień logiki i filozofii. Pisma wybrane.* Warszawa: Państwowe Wydawnictwo

Naukowe. Transl. by Z. Jordan as 'On determinism' in: L. Borkowski (ed.). 1970. *Jan Łukasiewicz: Selected Works*. Amsterdam: North-Holland. 110–28.

Lyons, J. (1977). *Semantics*. 2 volumes. Cambridge: Cambridge University Press.

McCready, E. and N. Ogata. (2007). 'Evidentiality, modality and probability'. *Linguistics and Philosophy* 30: 147–206.

McLaughlin, B. and K. Bennett. (2005). 'Supervenience'. In: E. N. Zalta (ed.). *Stanford Encyclopedia of Philosophy*. http://plato.stanford.edu/contents.html

McTaggart, J. E. (1908). 'The unreality of time'. *Mind* 17. Reprinted in: J. E. McTaggart. 1934. *Philosophical Studies*. London: E. Arnold. 110–31.

Maienborn, C. (2005). 'On the limits of the Davidsonian approach'. *Theoretical Linguistics* 31: 275–316.

Manni, H. M. (2007). 'Tense in Mocoví: The temporal property of DP'. In: A. R. Deal (ed.). *Proceedings of SULA 4: Semantics of Under-Represented Languages in the Americas*. *University of Massachusetts Occasional Papers* 35. Amherst, MA: Graduate Linguistics Student Association. 129–40.

Martí, L. (2006). 'Unarticulated constituents revisited'. *Linguistics and Philosophy* 29: 135–66.

Matthewson, L. (2006). 'Temporal semantics in a superficially tenseless language'. *Linguistics and Philosophy* 29: 673–713.

Mellor, D. H. (1993). 'The unreality of tense'. In: R. Le Poidevin and M. MacBeath (eds). *The Philosophy of Time*. Oxford: Oxford University Press. 47–59.

—— . (1998). *Real Time II*. London: Routledge.

ter Meulen, A. G. B. (1995). *Representing Time in Natural Language: The Dynamic Interpretation of Tense and Aspect*. Cambridge, MA: MIT Press.

Meyer, U. (2002). 'Prior and the platonist'. *Analysis* 62: 211–16.

Mitchell, D. (2004). *Cloud Atlas*. London: Hodder and Stoughton.

Moens, M. and M. Steedman (1988). 'Temporal ontology and temporal reference'. *Computational Linguistics* 14: 15–28. Reprinted in: I. Mani, J. Pustejovsky, and R. Gaizauskas (eds). 2005. *The Language of Time: A Reader*. Oxford: Oxford University Press. 93–114.

Moltmann, F. (2006). 'Presuppositions and quantifier domains'. *Synthese* 149: 179–224.

Montague, R. (1960). 'On the nature of certain philosophical entities'. *The Monist* 53: 159–94. Reprined in: R. Thomason (ed.). 1974. *Formal Philosophy: Selected Papers of Richard Montague*. New Haven: Yale University Press. 148–87.

Montminy, M. (2006). 'Semantic content, truth conditions and context'. Review article of Cappelen and Lepore 2005. *Linguistics and Philosophy* 29: 1–26.

Mozersky, J. M. (2001). 'Smith on times and tokens'. *Synthese* 129: 405–11.

Nicolle, S. and B. Clark. (1999). 'Experimental pragmatics and what is said: A response to Gibbs and Moise'. *Cognition* 69: 337–54.

Nuyts, J. (2001). *Epistemic Modality, Language, and Conceptualization: A Cognitive-Pragmatic Perspective*. Amsterdam: J. Benjamins.

—— . (2006). 'Modality: Overview and linguistic issues'. In: W. Frawley (ed.). *The Expression of Modality*. Berlin: Mouton de Gruyter. 1–26.

Oaklander, L. N. and V. A. White. (2007). 'B-time: a reply to Tallant'. *Analysis* 67: 332–40.

Ogihara, T. (1996). *Tense, Attitudes, and Scope.* Dordrecht: Kluwer.

Øhrstrøm, P. and P. F. V. Hasle (1995). *Temporal Logic: From Ancient Ideas to Artificial Intelligence.* Dordrecht: Kluwer.

Palmer, F. R. (1979). *Modality and the English Modals.* London: Longman.

—— . (1986). *Mood and Modality.* Cambridge: Cambridge University Press.

—— . (2001). *Mood and Modality.* Cambridge: Cambridge University Press. Second edition.

Papafragou, A. (2000). *Modality: Issues in the Semantics-Pragmatics Interface.* Amsterdam: Elsevier Science.

Parsons, J. (2002). 'A-theory for B-theorists'. *The Philosophical Quarterly* 52: 1–20.

—— . (2003). 'A-theory for tense logicians'. *Analysis* 63: 4–6.

Parsons, T. (1990). *Events in the Semantics of English: A Study in Subatomic Semantics.* Cambridge, MA: MIT Press.

Partee, B. H. (1973). 'Some structural analogies between tenses and pronouns in English'. *Journal of Philosophy* 70: 601–9. Reprinted in: B. Partee. 2004. *Compositionality in Formal Semantics.* Oxford: Blackwell. 50–8.

—— . (1984). 'Compositionality'. In: F. Landman and F. Veltman (eds). *Varieties of Formal Semantics.* Dordrecht: Foris. Reprinted in: B. H. Partee (ed.). 2004. *Compositionality in Formal Semantics: Selected Papers by Barbara H. Partee.* Oxford: Blackwell. 153–81.

Patterson, D. (2003). 'What is a correspondence theory of truth?'. *Synthese* 137: 421–44.

Pederson, E. *et al.* (1998). 'Semantic typology and spatial conceptualization'. *Language* 74: 557–89.

Pelczar, M. W. (2004). 'The indispensability of *Farbung*'. *Synthese* 138: 49–77.

—— . (2007). 'Forms and objects of thought'. *Linguistics and Philosophy* 30: 97–122.

Penrose, R. (1989). *The Emperor's New Mind: Concerning Computers, Minds, and the Laws of Physics.* Oxford: Oxford University Press.

Perry, J. (2001). *Reference and Reflexivity.* Stanford, CA: CSLI Publications.

Pianesi, F. and A. C. Varzi (2000). 'Events and event talk: An introduction'. In: J. Higginbotham, F. Pianesi, and A. C. Varzi (eds). *Speaking of Events.* Oxford: Oxford University Press. 3–47.

Pietroski, P. M. ((2005). *Events and Semantic Architecture.* Oxford: Oxford University Press.

Pitts, A. (2005). 'Assessing the evidence for intuitions about *what is said*'. Ms, University of Cambridge.

Le Poidevin, R. (2007). *The Images of Time: An Essay on Temporal Representation.* Oxford: Oxford University Press.

Portner, P. (2003). 'The (temporal) semantics and (modal) pragmatics of the perfect'. *Linguistics and Philosophy* 26: 459–510.

Pratt, I. and N. Francez (2001). 'Temporal prepositions and temporal generalized quantifiers'. *Linguistics and Philosophy* 24: 187–222.

Predelli, S. (2005a). *Contexts: Meaning, Truth, and the Use of Language.* Oxford: Clarendon Press.

——— . (2005b). 'Painted leaves, context, and semantic analysis'. *Linguistics and Philosophy* 28: 351–74.

——— . (2006). 'The problem with token-reflexivity'. *Synthese* 148: 5–29.

Prior, A. N. (1957). *Time and Modality*. Oxford: Clarendon Press.

——— . (1959). 'Thank goodness that's over'. *Philosophy* 34: 12–17. Reprinted in A. N. Prior. 1976. *Papers in Logic and Ethics*. London: Duckworth. 78–84.

——— . (1967). *Past, Present and Future*. Oxford: Clarendon Press.

——— . (1968a). *Papers on Time and Tense*. Oxford: Clarendon Press.

——— . (1968b). 'Now'. *Noûs* 2: 101–19.

——— . (1968c). 'Tense logic and the logic of earlier and later'. In: *Papers on Time and Tense*. Oxford: Clarendon Press. 116–34.

——— . (1968d). 'Tense logic for non-permanent existents'. In: *Papers on Time and Tense*. Oxford: Clarendon Press. 145–60.

——— . (2003). *Papers on Time and Tense: New Edition*. Oxford: Oxford University Press.

Quine, W. V. O. (1960). *Word and Object*. Cambridge, MA: MIT Press.

Ramchand, G. and P. Svenonius (forthcoming). 'Mapping a parochial lexicon onto universal semantics'. In: M. T. Biberauer (ed.). *Limits of Syntactic Variation*. Amsterdam: J. Benjamins.

Ramsey, F. (1927). 'Facts and propositions'. *Aristotelian Society Supplementary Volume* VII: 153–70.

Recanati, F. (1989). 'The pragmatics of what is said'. *Mind and Language* 4: 295–329. Reprinted in: S. Davis (ed.). 1991. *Pragmatics: A Reader*. Oxford: Oxford University Press. 97–120.

——— . (1993). *Direct Reference: From Language to Thought*. Oxford: Blackwell.

——— . (2001). 'What is said'. *Synthese* 128: 75–91.

——— . (2002). 'Unarticulated constituents'. *Linguistics and Philosophy* 25: 299–345.

——— . (2004). *Literal Meaning*. Cambridge: Cambridge University Press.

——— . (2005). 'Literalism and contextualism: Some varieties'. In: G. Preyer and G. Peter (eds). *Contextualism in Philosophy: Knowledge, Meaning, and Truth*. Oxford: Clarendon Press. 171–96.

——— . (2007a). *Perspectival Thought: A Plea for (Moderate) Relativism*. Oxford: Oxford University Press.

——— . (2007b). 'It is raining (somewhere)'. *Linguistics and Philosophy* 30: 123–46.

——— . (2007c). Reply to Carston 2007. In: M. J. Frápolli (ed.). *Saying, Meaning and Referring: Essays on François Recanati's Philosophy of Language*. Basingstoke: Palgrave Macmillan. 49–54.

Reichenbach, H. (1948). *Elements of Symbolic Logic*. New York: Macmillan.

Rothstein, S. (2004). *Structuring Events: A Study in the Semantics of Lexical Aspect*. Oxford: Blackwell.

Sattig, T. (2006). *The Language and Reality of Time*. Oxford: Clarendon Press.

Saul, J. M. (2002). 'What is said and psychological reality; Grice's project and relevance theorists' criticisms'. *Linguistics and Philosophy* 25: 347–72.

Saul, J. M. (2007). *Simple Sentences, Substitution, and Intuitions.* Oxford: Oxford University Press.

Saurer, W. (1984). *A Formal Semantics of Tense, Aspect and Aktionsarten.* Bloomington: Indiana University Linguistics Club.

Schein, B. (2002). 'Events and the semantic content of thematic relations'. In: G. Preyer and G. Peter (eds). *Logical Form and Language.* Oxford: Clarendon Press. 263–344.

Schiffer, S. (1991). 'Does Mentalese have a compositional semantics?'. In: B. Loewer and G. Rey (eds). *Meaning in Mind: Fodor and his Critics.* Oxford: Blackwell. 181–99.

——— . (1994). 'A paradox of meaning'. *Noûs* 28: 279–324.

——— . (2003). *The Things We Mean.* Oxford: Clarendon Press.

Schnieder, B. (2006). 'Truth-making without truth-makers'. *Synthese* 152: 21–46.

Schopenhauer, A. (1819). *Die Welt als Wille und Vorstellung.* Leipzig. Transl. by E. F. J. Payne as *The World as Will and Representation.* 2 vols. 1969. New York: Dover Publications.

Simon-Vandenbergen, A.-M. and K. Aijmer (2007). *The Semantic Field of Modal Certainty: A Corpus-Based Study of English Adverbs.* Berlin: Mouton de Gruyter.

Smessaert, H. and A. G. B. ter Meulen (2004). 'Temporal reasoning with aspectual adverbs'. *Linguistics and Philosophy* 27: 209–61.

Smith, Q. (1993). *Language and Time.* Oxford: Oxford University Press.

Sperber, D. and D. Wilson (1986). *Relevance: Communication and Cognition.* Oxford: Blackwell.

——— . and ——— (1995). *Relevance: Communication and Cognition.* Oxford: Blackwell. Second edition.

Srioutai, J. (2004). 'The Thai *cɪa*: A marker of tense or modality?' In: E. Daskalaki *et al.* (eds). *Second CamLing Proceedings.* University of Cambridge. 273–80.

——— . (2006). *Time Conceptualization in Thai with Special Reference to Dɪay1II, Kh3oe: y, K1aml3ang, Y3u:I and Cɪa.* PhD Thesis. University of Cambridge.

Stanley, J. (2000). 'Context and logical form'. *Linguistics and Philosophy* 23: 391–434.

——— . (2002). 'Making it articulated'. *Mind and Language* 17: 149–68.

——— . (2005). 'Semantics in context'. In: G. Preyer and G. Peter (eds). *Contextualism in Philosophy: Knowledge, Meaning, and Truth.* Oxford: Clarendon Press. 221–53.

——— . and Z. G. Szabó (2000). 'On quantifier domain restriction'. *Mind and Language* 15: 219–61.

Steedman, M. (1997). 'Temporality'. In: J. van Benthem and A. ter Meulen (eds). *Handbook of Logic and Language.* Amsterdam: Elsevier Science. 895–938.

de Swart, H. (2007). 'A cross-linguistic discourse analysis of the Perfect'. *Journal of Pragmatics* 39: 2273–307.

Sysoeva, A. and K. Jaszczolt (2007). 'Composing utterance meaning: An interface between pragmatics and psychology'. Paper presented at the *10th International Pragmatics Conference*, Göteborg, July 2007.

Tallant, J. (2007). 'What is B-time?'. *Analysis* 67: 147–56.

Taylor, B. (1985). *Modes of Occurrence: Verbs, Adverbs and Events.* Oxford: Blackwell.

Thomason, R. H. (1997). 'Nonmonotonicity in linguistics'. In: J. van Benthem and A. ter Meulen (eds). *Handbook of Logic and Language.* Oxford: Elsevier Science. 777–831.

—— . (2002). 'Combinations of tense and modality'. In: D. Gabbay and F. Guenthner (eds). *Handbook of Philosophical Logic.* Vol. 7. Dordrecht: Kluwer. 205–34.

Thornton, A. (1987). *Maori Oral Literature As Seen by a Classicist.* Dunedin: University of Otago Press.

Tonhauser, J. (2007). 'Nominal tense? The meaning of Guaraní nominal temporal markers'. *Language* 83: 831–69.

Traugott, E. C. (2006). 'Historical aspects of modality'. In: W. Frawley (ed.). *The Expression of Modality.* Berlin: Mouton de Gruyter. 107–39.

—— . and R. B. Dasher (2002). *Regularity in Semantic Change.* Cambridge: Cambridge University Press.

Tynan, J. and E. Delgado Lavín (1997). 'Mood, tense and the interpretation of conditionals'. In: A. Athanasiadou and R. Dirven (eds). *On Conditionals Again.* Amsterdam: J. Benjamins. 115–42.

Ultan, R. (1972). 'The nature of future tenses'. *Working Papers on Language Universals* 8. Reprinted in: J. H. Greenberg (ed.). 1978. *Universals of Human Language.* Vol. 3, *Word Structure.* Stanford, CA: Stanford University Press. 83–123.

Ungerer, F. and H.-J. Schmid (1996). *An Introduction to Cognitive Linguistics.* London: Longman.

Vallesi, A., M. A. Binns and T. Shallice. (2008). 'An effect of spatial-temporal association of response codes: Understanding the cognitive representations of time'. *Cognition* 107: 501–27.

Vendler, Z. (1967). *Linguistics in Philosophy.* Ithaca, NY: Cornell University Press.

Wekker, H. C. (1976). *The Expression of Future Time in Contemporary British English.* Amsterdam: North-Holland.

Werth, P. (1997). 'Remote worlds: The conceptual representation of linguistic *would*'. In: J. Nuyts and E. Pederson (eds). *Language and Conceptualization.* Cambridge: Cambridge University Press. 84–115.

Young, J. (1997). *Heidegger, Philosophy, Nazism.* Cambridge: Cambridge University Press.

Zeevat, H. (1989). 'A compositional approach to Discourse Representation Theory'. *Linguistics and Philosophy* 12: 95–131.

Index

Page numbers followed by *fn* denote references in the footnote. Page numbers followed by (fig.) denote references within one or more figures on that page. References to names: Where two names are cited in the same reference, they are listed as 'Surname, Initial and Initial, Surname'.

Example   Kamp, H. 62, 117*fn*
            and U. Reyle 16, 27, 71, 85–6, 129

Where the two names are listed in the same format, i.e. 'Surname, Initial and Surname, Initial', these denote two separate references which are related in the text.

Example   James, William 10–11
            and Husserl, Edmund 11